AN
INNOCENT
IN
*N*EWFOUNDLAND

ALSO BY DAVID W. McFADDEN

POETRY

Intense Pleasure, 1972
A Knight in Dried Plums, 1975
The Poet's Progress, 1977
On the Road Again, 1978
My Body Was Eaten by Dogs, 1981
The Art of Darkness, 1984
Gypsy Guitar, 1987
Anonymity Suite, 1992
The Death of Greg Curnoe, 1995
There'll Be Another, 1995
Five Star Planet, 2002
Cow Swims Lake Ontario, 2003

FICTION

The Great Canadian Sonnet, 1975, 2002
Animal Spirits, 1983
Canadian Sunset, 1986

NON-FICTION

A Trip Around Lake Erie, 1981
A Trip Around Lake Huron, 1981
A Trip Around Lake Ontario, 1988
An Innocent in Ireland, 1995
Great Lakes Suite, 1997
An Innocent in Scotland, 1999

AN
INNOCENT
IN
$\mathcal{N}$EWFOUNDLAND

Even More Curious Rambles and Singular Encounters

DAVID W. McFADDEN

M&S

National Library of Canada Cataloguing in Publication

McFadden, David, 1940-
An innocent in Newfoundland : even more rambles and singular encounters/
David W. McFadden.

Includes index.
ISBN 0-7710-5535-8

1. McFadden, David, 1940- – Journeys – Newfoundland and Labrador.
2. Newfoundland and Labrador – Description and travel.
I. Title.

FC2167.6.M32 2003   917.1804'4   C2002-905988-7
F1122.M32 2003

We acknowledge the financial support of the Government of Canada through the Book Publishing Industry Development Program and that of the Government of Ontario through the Ontario Media Development Corporation's Ontario Book Initiative. We further acknowledge the support of the Canada Council for the Arts and the Ontario Arts Council for our publishing program.

Published simultaneously in the United States of America by
McClelland & Stewart Ltd., P.O. Box 1030, Plattsburgh, New York 12901
Library of Congress Control Number: 2002116591

Typeset in Goudy by M&S, Toronto
Map by Visutronx
Printed and bound in Canada

McClelland & Stewart Ltd.
The Canadian Publishers
481 University Avenue
Toronto, Ontario
M5G 2E9
www.mcclelland.com

1   2   3   4   5   07   06   05   04   03

For the poets of Newfoundland, including

Sir Cavendish Boyle (1849–1916)
"We love thee, we love thee,
We love thee, frozen land"

and

Al Pittman (1940–2001)
"In virtue we are very rich.
In rapture very poor."

CONTENTS

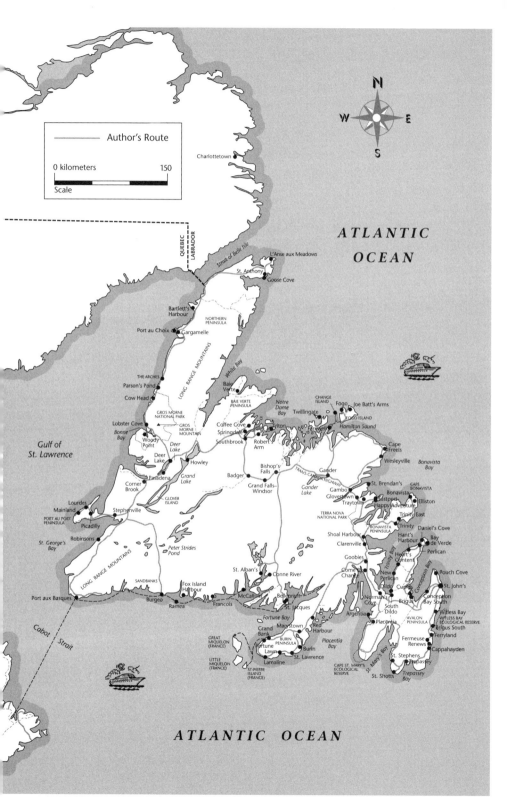

Author's Route

0 kilometers 150

Scale

N
W E
S

ATLANTIC
OCEAN

ATLANTIC OCEAN

Charlottetown

QUEBEC
LABRADOR

Strait of Belle Isle

L'Anse aux Meadows
St. Anthony
Goose Cove

Bartlett's
Harbour

NORTHERN
PENINSULA

Port au Choix
Gargamelle

LONG RANGE MOUNTAINS

White Bay

THE ARCHES
Parson's Pond
Cow Head

Baie
Verte

BAIE VERTE
PENINSULA

CHANGE
ISLAND

Fogo
Joe Batt's Arms

GROS MORNE
NATIONAL PARK

GROS
MORNE
MOUNTAIN

Notre
Dame
Bay

Twillingate

FOGO ISLAND

Lobster Cove

Coffee Cove

Triton

Fortune

Hamilton Sound

Bonne
Bay

Springdale

Woody
Point

Southbrook

Robert's
Arm

Cape
Freels

Deer
Lake

Howley

Wesleyville

Bonavista
Bay

Gulf of
St. Lawrence

Deer Lake

Bishop's
Falls

Gander

Pasadena

Corner
Brook

Grand
Lake

Badger

Grand Falls–
Windsor

Gander
Lake

Gambo
Glovertown

St. Brendan's

CAPE
BONAVISTA

TRANS-CANADA HIGHWAY

Traytown

Bonavista
Eastport
Happy Adventure

Elliston

GLOVER
ISLAND

Lourdes
Mainland

Stephenville

TERRA NOVA
NATIONAL PARK

Trinity East

PORT AU PORT
PENINSULA

Shoal Harbour

BONAVISTA
PENINSULA

Trinity

Daniel's Cove

Picadilly

Clarenville

Hant's
Harbour

Bay
de Verde

St. George's
Bay

Robinsons

Peter Strides
Pond

Goobies

Heart's
Content

Perlican

LONG RANGE MOUNTAINS

St. Alban's

Conne River

Come by
Chance

New
Perlican

Pouch Cove

SANDBANKS

Fox Island
Harbour

McCallum

Dildo

Cupids

St. John's

Port aux Basques

Burgeo

Ramea

Francois

St. Jacques

Belleoram

Norman's
Cove

South
Dildo

Brigus

Concepcion
Bay South

Conception Bay

Fortune Bay

Argentia

Witless Bay

Grand
Bank

Maystown

Red
Harbour

Placentia

AVALON
PENINSULA

WITLESS BAY
ECOLOGICAL RESERVE

GREAT
MIQUELON
(FRANCE)

BURIN
PENINSULA

Burin

Placentia
Bay

Brigus South

Ferryland

LITTLE
MIQUELON
(FRANCE)

Fortune
Lawn

St. Lawrence

Fermeuse
Renews

Cappahayden

Cabot

Strait

Lamaline

ST-PIERRE
ISLAND
(FRANCE)

CAPE ST. MARY'S
ECOLOGICAL
RESERVE

St. Stephens

St. Mary's Bay

Trepassey

St. Shotts

Trepassey
Bay

KOUNTRY KORNERS

North Sydney • *Gulf of St. Lawrence* • *Port aux Basques* • *Robinsons*

Tuesday, May 15. The ferry across the Gulf of St. Lawrence to Port aux Basques leaves at nine. It's a surreal dawn, with a fleet of four Lay's Dorito potato-chip trucks waiting to get put aboard. We have three hours to wait. I'm chatting with a fellow in the next car. "Those trucks are empty," he says. "We can't get any free samples."

"Why are they going to Newfoundland empty? Is there a potato-chip plant over there?"

"No way!" he says. "Look. No plates. Somebody bought them, see? I don't know who. Maybe the newspaper. They could do a good job of delivering the news all around Newfoundland with a fleet of trucks like that."

Also at dockside: a small man sitting on a big motorcycle, and several stubby little tractor-trailer cabs without the trailer – all with engines running. My car's turned off, but it seems as if it's running, because it's shaking along with all the surrounding engines. In fact so am I, but if I get out of the car, the noise and fumes will be worse.

The ferry's moored at the dock a mere two hundred yards away, but we can't get aboard. We have to wait for the shuttle bus at 8:30 – for "safety reasons."

There are two ferries docked – the *Caribou*, with its engines off, and the *Smallwood*, with black smoke belching from its smokestack. As I start getting steamed about all the unnecessary soot in the air, the smoke from the *Smallwood* thins out and wafts away. The truck drivers start turning their engines off. And I hear one driver yelling over to another: "Don't be good, Peter. You *gotta* be bad."

Nova Scotia has different slogans for car plates – "Canada's Ocean Playground" – and for trucks – "Open for Business." But Newfoundland and Labrador have just one, and it's a subtler one – "A Sense of Difference," a line worthy to be used when signing tourist-home guest books.

I managed only the briefest snooze on the new *Caribou*, named after its predecessor that was torpedoed by a German U-boat at 3:10 a.m. on October 14, 1942, with the loss of 137 lives, including those of Captain Ben Tavenor and his two teenage sons. I can offer no impressions of my first sight of Newfoundland, as impressions don't make much of an impression on weary souls. In retrospect, I shouldn't have been driving. After doing some shopping in the old seven-hilled former fishing village of Port aux Basques, I had to ask directions on three occasions before finding my way out of that miniature maze. I needed a full night's sleep, but only in a quiet place in the country.

Another hour and I found the perfect spot, called Kountry Korners, near the town of Robinsons, on the shore of St. George's Bay, about forty miles northeast of Port aux Basques, way off the main road. There was a filling station, a garage, a convenience store, a large dining room, a large barroom, a large cook, a poolroom, a convenience store, and a dozen rooms upstairs, along with an indoor sauna and hot tub. Why indoors? They said they had plans to build an outdoor set-up as well for heartier folk like me.

I staggered to my room and was assailed by the strongest smell of solvents. A workman noticed me sniffing and offered an unsolicited apology for the fumes. It was some work they were doing on the hot tub.

So I tore off my clothes and threw myself in bed. The clock said 5:00 p.m. I closed my eyes. I opened them. The clock said 2:00 a.m. I closed them. I opened them. Clock said 2:00 p.m.

AN ENTIRE PROVINCE
OF FUN LOVERS

Robinsons • Corner Brook

Wednesday, May 16. "Sleep well?" asked the desk clerk, without a hint of sarcasm. I'd missed out on supper, breakfast, and lunch. I was the only overnight guest, and the "girl" had arrived at eight specially to cook my breakfast. She had knitted a whole pair of baby booties before finally leaving. I felt terrible and asked for the girl's wages to be added to my bill. But the boss wouldn't hear of it. "You're human. We're all human. We all make mistakes."

In the parking lot, a broken case of lager was lying in a pool of foam beside a Labatt's beer truck. A wiry little guy was wheeling a stack of empty cartons to the truck. I held the door open for him.

"Dropped a case, did you?"

"I never dropped a case in my life," he said.

"What's that one there then?"

He looked.

"Oh, I forgot about that one."

"They won't fire you for that, will they?"

4

"No, I'll just tell them I got thirsty."

Back inside, the desk clerk was telling me "they're refittin' the hot tub." I insisted I'd had twenty hours of amazing dreams because of all the fumes. She was too smart to believe that, so I fishingly asked if they ever had hot-tub and sauna parties for the neighbours.

"Is that the image they have in Ontario about Newfoundlanders – party party party all the time, an entire province of fun lovers?"

"Afraid so."

"We couldn't have lasted this long if we were like that."

"Right."

"What part of Ontario are you from?"

"You probably never heard of it."

"Try us."

"Toronto?"

"Heh! I know more people there than I do in Corner Brook and Stephenville combined."

Across St. George's Bay, snow fields shine from the distant high hills of the Port au Port Peninsula. At Arlene's Place, where coffee beckoned, Arlene was eager to know how I liked her new sign out front. She had finally replaced the previous sign, Eva's Place, last September 16, although Eva had died, or gone to Toronto (honestly, I can't remember which), long before then.

Arlene said this spring had already been good for tourism. There had been lots of older tourists, and they said they like to do their tours early, because they are so old they can't stand the summer heat.

"Maybe it's the summer rates they don't like."

"We has the same prices all year round," she said, her voice vibrant with virtue.

I told her it's true, the older you get the more appealing becomes the off-season for exploring the world. "Best of all / Are spring and fall," I extemporized rhymingly.

"You're a poet," she said.

"Do you find much time to read poetry these days?"
"To be truthful, no. But I shore wish I could write it."

In Corner Brook I've gone into Mad Man Murphy's to have my electronic notebook tested. Though the store doesn't have the glitz one
may be accustomed to in larger centres, it's nevertheless well-stocked
with technological marvels. A gentleman about fifty, with a little
moustache, stands behind the counter. His look embodies sweetness
and sanity, virtues for which Newfoundland is undeservedly not
renowned. Did I have the honour of addressing Mr. Mad Man? He
squeaked out a deadpan "Yes."

He pronounced my notebook in good shape and showed me how
to use it properly. He suggested that, if I were to be "using it to
record vital information" in "remote areas of the province," I might
wish to "take along" a second such machine "as backup." I flashed
him a look of admiration for his cunning sales pitch. He pursed his
lips innocently.

A pair of newlyweds, early twenties, sleek and chic, were stroking
a JVC World's Smallest Digital Camcorder and purring with excitement. Who wouldn't want to have one of those, and maybe another
as backup?

"That's a good camera you've got there," said Mad Man.

"Oh, I know," said the male half of the bargain. "I've looked it up
on the Internet already. And I know exactly which camera I want.
And here it is. And I'm just looking at it. And this is it. And I'm
pretty sure I'm going to buy it." The girl's lips and eyes were moist
and shining. Her youthful radiance was going to be endlessly immor-
talized as it became less and less youthful.

Mad Man seemed to be preparing his pitch for selling them an
extra one to use as backup if they were at Veradero Beach and it
broke. He seemed to be thinking: "No, that'd be no good, it wouldn't
do to have them question the reliability of the product. Ah! I know!

So they could take shots of each other taking shots of each other down through the years. Yes, that's it. I'll go with that."

Mad my eye!

My pals the poet Victor Coleman and the printer Stan Bevington have been trying for years to get me to check out Newfoundland. "It's your kind of place," they implore. "You'll love it. You cannot *not* go to Newfoundland. It would be wrong of you. It's like going back to the thirties."

"But what if I decide to stay there?"

"We'd come and visit you."

But alas, there's not much trace of the thirties left in Corner Brook, with the exception of the pulp mill. This is a cutting-edge town. The people are bright as tomorrow. And there are so many attractive well-dressed women, as if I'd erred and landed in Milan, Italy, or Hamilton, Ontario. Yet here they are working at Alley Oop's Pizza Express, Greco's Pizza across the street, or the Padarnic Lodge, Breaker's Dance Bar, the Dental Arts Clinic, Tim Hortons, the Humber Community Development Corporation, the Franklin Gallery, the Western Environmental Centre, Signature Designs, West Coast Chiropractic – or even the Corner Brook Pulp and Paper Mill, which today is smoking as vigorously as it has for the past seventy-six years (with a workforce of 1,300). But it's clean smoke, puffy and white as a cherub's chubby cheeks. Also the pulpish smell around town is minimal, because of the new filters and buffers. Yes, the mill is trying to clean up its act after serious fines ten years ago for polluting the river and killing ten million fish.

What drives me around the bend is the Second World War British bombing-raid foghorn of a mill whistle that tells the workers when to start and when to stop. It would be hard to live here with that horn so loud you can hear it all the way across the Bay of Islands, and with a good wind all the way to the Squires Memorial at Big Falls.

It's highly conducive to panic attacks. For a moment even a casual visitor feels as if he's late for work – or about to be torpedoed.

The stoplights are down all over Corner Brook today, but motorists are handling the situation with dignity and grace. Nobody is bothered at all, for there are no cops around to misdirect the traffic, screw everything up, and get everybody all steamed. The cops know everything will be fine as long as they stay undercover and take the phone off the hook till things get back to normal. Motorists are waving each other on with great Christian charity. Perhaps they are striving to live up to Newfoundland's official motto – "Seek Ye First the Kingdom of God."

One sneaky motorist decided to zip up the wrong way on a one-way street, to save time, and he knew the cops would be nowhere around anyway. But he drew a loud civilian chorus of honking horns and was forced to make a red-faced U-turn.

Bridget Jones's Diary and *Blow* are playing in the local cinema. The shrewd desk clerk at the Hotel Corner Brook says the good Christians around town will be agonizing over whether to see the latter flick, which is alleged to glorify drug abuse. Apparently it's not the seeing of the movie that matters so much as having people know you saw it. We wouldn't want the word to get around. But we wouldn't want to miss *Blow* either. Surely it's our Christian duty to see it, at a private screening preferably, in order to be able to warn others away from it with stern Methodist authority.

It's always best to get a second opinion on a Mad Man's pronouncements, so I went into the glitzier Sony Store just up the street. The two bright young sales clerks have been studying the retail stereo business with great avidity and are on their way up. One was from Corner Brook originally, and one had recently moved here from London, Ontario. "I gave up trying to get him to speak with a Newfie accent," said the former of the latter, "so I decided to speak with his Ontario accent." He then shyly admitted that, though born in Corner Brook, he'd spent five years "studying English" in Toronto.

The London fellow said he moved here after his parents retired to Newfoundland. "There's good parts and bad parts to living here," he said. "Up there in Toronto and London and stuff like that you can shop around more often and stuff like that, and you can go out and see sporting events and stuff like that. But for a nice, quiet, laid-back easy life you can't beat it here. Two cinemas – which could be better. Good clubs – if you're into clubs. There's always stuff to do."

The famous Broadway Fire of April 8, 1953, with ground zero on Broadway Avenue, wiped out most of the Corner Brook business section. The fire must have been particularly depressing, because post-war business had been just starting to pick up. The fire department had been strictly volunteer since it started way back in the thirties, when Corner Brook was little more than a construction camp. But after the Broadway Fire, all the volunteers got put on salary!

Almost overnight, another business section on the other side of town began to sprout up. So when the burned-out section got rebuilt, lucky shoppers found themselves with the choice of two thriving areas to shop in. Recently, a third business section has been added, a shopping mall ideal for motorists from all over western Newfoundland. The mall, far from small, is nestled in the valley between the two business sections like a new diamond between two old rubies. Since the mall is at the side of the brook (after which Corner Brook would have been named) and near the mill, it's known far and wide as the Millbrook Mall.

The mall doesn't seem to be drawing much business from the older business areas. It has a twin-cinema complex, a small but well-stocked second-hand bookstore, and a nice public washroom – if you don't mind someone showing up and starting to bang two garbage cans together right outside your cubicle.

"Hey, please pipe down out there."

"Scared the shit out of you, did I?" said the witty culprit.

When I was leaving he looked at me, saw that I was from away, and maybe even a shopper, and became apologetic. "Sorry about that," he said.

SMILING APHRODITE

Pasadena • Deer Lake • Burnt Berry

Thursday, May 17. A pair of married couples are looking at pictures on the wall of a coffee shop, in the town of Pasadena, on Deer Lake, which on the map seems to be shaped like a low-slung cabin cruiser speeding sleekly along in a southwesterly direction. The four are Americans, from what I can hear of their conversation. And so they are probably from Pasadena, California. How would I know? Because people from that Pasadena – particularly poets and painters, apparently – have been visiting this Pasadena ever since 1955, when it decided to name itself after the California city, for a reason too boring to recount here.

Most of the art on the wall appears to be framed photos of icebergs, and the Californians are most appreciative. One of the women says, "The characteristics of their melting is just so elegant," while the other three smile in appreciation.

Meanwhile, on the front page of today's paper, a boat full of fishermen out of Stephenville was supposed to have been back three days ago. Family members were worried sick. But a multi-thousand-dollar search-and-rescue operation had been launched, and the guys were quickly found last night partying in a strip joint over on the south shore of Quebec.

The community on the northeastern end of Deer Lake, older and larger than Pasadena on the southwestern tip, didn't have to go to California for its name. Who wouldn't love to live in, or even just visit, a town with a pretty name like Deer Lake? In the spring of 1894, a meeting had been called to give a name to the fledgling community. A lot of floor-pacing ensued, then someone glanced out the window and was greeted with the magnificent sight of a vast herd of caribou crossing the frozen lake. Not knowing they were caribou, he said, "How about Deer Lake?" Everybody went for it. That's the story anyway.

A hundred years later, David Vecsey, who writes for *Sports Illustrated*, was interviewing Darren Langdon, then designated team enforcer for the New York Rangers, and wanted to know what Darren and his buddies did on Saturday nights during high-school days back in Deer Lake.

Darren, called "Newfie" by his teammates (he's now with the Carolina Hurricanes), is known for his "colourful" way of speaking English, his rugged good looks (six-foot-one, 205 pounds), his terrific sense of humour, and for spending most of his time in the penalty box. "What do we do on Saturday nights? What are you talking, sixteen, seventeen? What do you think we do? Same as anywhere else – we go to the movies."

Farther east on the Trans-Canada Highway, I'm sitting on a bridge, taking another break from my dash to St. John's to deliver this little car to its rightful owner. A talking raven lands on a rock in the middle of Crooked Feeder Creek, just for the thrill of having the rushing water, newly released from the penitentiary of winter, stream around her.

"I'm not a raven, you nitwit," quoth the bird. "I'm a crow."

This highway is almost a pleasure to drive, with well-designed passing lanes on the many hills and generous left-turn lanes that remove a lot of the terror from long-distance motoring. It cuts an artistically shaped grey rainbow scar across the island from Port aux Basques to St. John's, with branch roads connecting the various outports, Beothuk boneyards, Micmac middens, old shipyards, dry docks, coal mines and lumber camps, old churches that are still an inspiration, and probably a few undiscovered Viking settlements. It was opened in 1966 and replaced the magnificent train known around the world as the "Newfie Bullet." The train is now gone, and the narrow-gauge tracks have been ripped up – even though they were intended to last forever.

The forest, intermittently, sometimes for ten miles at a time, crowds so close to both shoulders it makes the road seem like a long, narrow casket – and it's easy for a moose, a caribou, or a bear to be leaping around in the forest and, suddenly, through no fault of its own, to find itself landing on all fours in the middle of the highway with a high-speed transport truck bearing down on it. But whenever you get behind the wheel in Newfoundland, there's always someone there to say, as naturally as a fare-thee-well, "Watch out for de moose and de caribou both," or words to that effect. "Don't go over the speed limit or you could be run down by a moose." Et cetera. It's generally agreed that this communal, voluntary, and pleasant reminder system cuts down on inter-species collisions.

When the forest gives way to the barrens, as it does from time to time, the narrow shoulders present another problem. For many long sections, guardrails have yet to be installed, and it would be easy for a sleepy motorist to go zooming off the elevated roadway to crash-land in the bog (as the barrens are called in the summer and fall), or the swamp (as they're called during the torrents of spring), or the tundra (as they're called in the winter). The wrecks are sometimes left there for scavengers to pick over. There's nothing more naked than a wrecked car that has been stripped bare of anything of value – unless it's the exoskeleton of a lobster after a big meal.

Every half-klick or so, the shoulder has had a recent half-moon extension of crushed stone and clay added on, a flat-top mound extending over the bog or into the forest for just a few feet. The purpose seemed baffling, but after some heavy thinking I realized that these are little platforms for guardrails to be added later, and which will further save lives.

Across Deer Lake, high mountains rise steeply and are forested all the way. There's no snow on the mountains but there are large chunks of ice here and there along the beach. Then suddenly there's an A-frame log cabin peeking out through the trees a hundred feet almost straight up from the shore. It's the only sign of human life in many miles of primeval shoreline.

Farther east from Deer Lake, the mountains on the right fizzle out, the lake vanishes, and the mountains on the left become less lofty and more "birchy" – a Newfoundland term describing an area where the birch have made territorial gains on the spruce in the never-ending, slow-motion war of the trees. Deciduous and coniferous are at it like Neanderthals and Cro-Magnons, staring at each other across a bridgeless river, as the Trans-Canada Highway threads its quiet way through utter wilderness. There's not even a column of smoke on the horizon, or a power line, or the scar of an old railroad. Nor is there a castle, a cathedral spire, an ancient bridge, or hill fort.

A faintly green, transparent aura surrounds each naked little birch. It seems as if we're somewhere north of Baffin Island, but actually we're smack on the forty-ninth parallel, the same long line that marks the boundary between Canada and the United States all the way from Lake Superior to the Pacific Ocean. We're on the same latitude as the English Channel, but there's no Gulf Stream to give the growing season a head start. In the depths of summer, icy blasts are never far away.

When the road becomes elevated above the treetops, you can see the forest stretching away in the distance, amid snowy hillocks and thick sunlit mist – and then you see it gradually rising, till it suddenly becomes a steep, high-peaked mountain, with the forest ever so smoothly covering over any mark in the landscape that may indicate where the mountain actually begins to rise. And ever so gradually signs of commercial life begin to appear here and there along the road. Signs advertising motels, guest homes, whale-watching, iceberg viewing, boat cruises, Beothuk museums . . .

One sign near a turnoff says Welcome to Scenic Green Bay, and under it some understandably disaffected local poet has scrawled:

Formerly Seasick Green Bay.
The Tourist Board Insisted We Change It.
And no, we're not the Home of no Packers, no way.

Communities have unusual signs announcing their presence. Some are like business cards, sometimes as big as the side of a bus, and often with the town's motto on the side. The populations are never mentioned. Some things we just don't like to talk about. On a warm day, the population of some of these towns will be lower than the temperature, and we're talking Celsius. And every year they're a little lower.

As for the Green Bay sign, the official name of the town is actually Baie Verte. And the local poet is probably correct when he says the tourist board "insisted we change it," probably on the grounds that most tourists find Green Bay easier to say. Port aux Basques is easy to say, so it stays. Baie Verte is harder to say clearly (it tends to come out "beaver"), so it goes. Meanwhile, the list of larger Canadian communities outside Quebec with French names has dwindled alarmingly (though Sault Ste. Marie is easier to say than Saint Mary's Rapids, and Qu'Appelle is more dignified than "Who Calls?" so they persist).

Newfoundland is a feast for the eyes, the air so clear the eyes become clear, and everywhere you look there's something looking back. For instance, there's a highway souvenir shop, and on the front lawn someone has erected a twenty-foot pyramid construction of wood and plaster, painted white with overlaid washes of green, blue, and a pale yellow. It's an iceberg, but one that will burn before it will melt, and without the strange inner light of actual icebergs, those other northern lights. No one would mistake this piece of Lawn Art for a real iceberg, except maybe from down the road a mile, or if it got blown into the sea and was floating by on the horizon. The artist did a terrific job with the materials on hand, but if you touch this iceberg, your hand might come away covered in white chalk rather than tingling wet and cold. Also the peak is too steeple-like, the iceberg looks too much like a church, and perhaps to the craftsman, church and iceberg, both redolent of ancient purities, are symbolically united.

If you dream of an iceberg, says the psychiatrist of a friend of mine, it's just the spirit of lost innocence peeking in at your tormented soul. Yet this homemade iceberg is more like a real iceberg than this book is like a real Newfoundland. It's not every day you spot originality on the Trans-Canada Highway. Any further bright and beautiful creations of such originality – as this homemade iceberg can be seen to be – no matter how commercially motivated, will be duly reported in these pages. Many of us have seen duller and uglier works, whether original or not, in some of the world's great galleries.

Night has fallen, and here's an inviting sight at the side of the northernmost section of the Trans-Canada Highway, in the Springdale–Southbrook area. It's a large, rough-hewn sign saying Burnt Berry Lodge, but there are no pumps, no bright lights, no convenience store – just the lonesome lodge, with a dining room, a large barroom, and an intimately short bar. There's an office, a front desk, and clean rooms for tourists and whoever else may be interested. Along a short wall in the barroom are several slot machines. The players seem heavily hypnotized, emotionally deadened to the pain of the money being lost. They will not awaken until they win the jackpot – and then only for a fleeting moment.

Brenda, the blond bartender, spoke of last winter being so long and cold that everybody she knew saw every video in the Stop and Shop three times. Even those people playing the slots? Well, maybe not them. But she claimed people all the way up to Lushes Bight can recite every line of dialogue in such movies as *Meatballs III* and *Beyond the Valley of the Dolls*. And they recite said lines with passable New York or Hollywood accents.

Yet when U.S. movies – such as *The Shipping News* – are filmed in the Newfoundland outports, the locals tend to get more excited about the regional stars, such as Gordon Pinsent, than renowned Hollywood stars such as Kevin Spacey, who is never seen in public unless surrounded by professional bodyguards, and therefore is not highly regarded locally.

"Really?"

"I only tells you what dey tells me. I wasn't dere myself," says Brenda.

To my left at the bar there's an initially quiet and brooding transcontinental truck driver. When he finally gets talking, it's about his job, and how the only way truckers can make money is by fudging their reports. He despises the regulations regarding the number of hours one can drive in one day-night cycle. Deregulation is his desire – and driving day and night with the help of handfuls of Dexedrine, the trucker's breakfast. He has heard that United States Air Force pilots get all the Dexedrine they want free, and he has to pay unsavoury dealers top dollar. It wasn't fair. Schlepping strawberries from Florida to Newfoundland was just as important as whatever it is the U.S. Air Force pilots do.

On my right are three shaggy Newfoundland males, all well over six feet, taking turns delivering philosophical narratives spiced with delirious flights of scatological hyperbole. Brenda the bartender is ultra-petite, with blond curls to her shoulders, a long thin nose, and a long thin mouth set in a permanent half-smile of contentment.

She's perched rigidly on a behind-the-bar stool. She seems comfortable with her spine perfectly erect for long stretches at a time. She smiles exactly the same pleasant smile non-stop, whether talking or listening, like a comforting Donald Duck night light, and with cute laugh lines around her eyes.

She mostly listens, but when she speaks it's about the Stop and Shop video store, or how wonderful her husband is, and how happy she'll be when he gets home. He's a logger, he's six-feet-seven, and he treats her like royalty. A precognitive flash tells me I'll meet him. Not tonight, but when I do I'll get a different impression of him, for when a woman talks about how wonderful her husband is, she's likely lying. No man's a hero to his wife.

These three drunks are speaking in such a vulgar manner they'd get cut off and tossed out of any bar in any city. But nothing they say is vulgar enough to remove the happy smile from Brenda the bartender's pretty face.

The three of them have me diagnosed in a flash and are quick to offer words of advice. They want me to know I'll be better off when I take up moose hunting, rabbit shooting, caribou corralling, freshwater fishing, living off the land, growing my own marijuana, brewing my own brandy, renting movies from the Stop and Shop, and having intimate relations with every woman within forty miles of my cabin. Yes, they want me to settle down in Newfoundland. Life's too short to waste it in Toronto.

One of the three is emaciated and unsteady on his feet. He keeps mumbling through his Velasquez moustache; then he decides to drive home. Nobody blinks. Brenda keeps smiling like a hand puppet in a box. It's not my place to express alarm, I've scarcely arrived. This central-north area of Newfoundland, like the Glengarry region of Scotland, or the Coboconk area of Ontario, doesn't get excited about driving when you're shit-faced. There's so little traffic, so few cops, and so much highway. The guy staggers out to his car. He's never too sloshed to drive home.

An hour later he's back, a little steadier, as if he's grabbed a sandwich from the fridge. He announces he didn't want to go home after all. He wants more to drink and a room to spend the night. When he got home his wife wasn't there, so he didn't want to stay alone. That was his excuse.

> *"They say that faint heart never won fair lady; and it is amazing to me how fair ladies are won, so faint are often men's hearts!"*
> – Anthony Trollope, *The Warden* (1855)

One of the three, a heavy-set fellow with a bushy full beard, has taken as his theme for the evening the need of men to be tough with fair ladies. "You gotta be tough wif women, you gotta be really tough." And when he got tired of repeating that over and over he would say, "Newfoundland women are okay, but the Mainland women – oh me, oh my!" and "French-Canadian women are the best, they know exactly what to do, they just run you ragged," over and over, with occasional Philip Glass-like variations. He also has a fondness for Chinese women and tells us a smutty old joke which purports to explain why.

Brenda beams her steady-but-genuine smile and pours another round of Screech and Cola. There are rumours that the sophisticated set in St. John's refers to this drink as a "Newfoundland Libre," but around here it's just Screech and Cola.

The bushy-bearded Bertrand Russell is off on another riff, with numerous variations, each moving a bit farther from the original, and he wants us to know that he doesn't like all women. There are certain kinds of women he definitely cares not a hoot for. For instance, he does not like women from Corner Brook or the women from Grand Falls–Windsor – they are the worst of all Newfoundland women. But wherever the women are from, you gotta be tough, you can't be gentle wif 'em. It has probably registered how polite and respectful I'm being to Brenda behind the bar, and he kindly wishes to point out the errors of my ways.

Meanwhile the emaciated man with the absent wife feels the lesson's intended for him. "I knows yer right fer shore," he says. "I's been gentle for two years now, and I hasn't got laid once. From now on I's fer bein' tough again."

The third fellow has an excellent set of protruding front teeth, with a receding jaw. I'd love to have a photo of him at the front of a boat facing into the wind. He seems to be the most sober and reasonable of the three, but this has nothing to do, in my mind, with the fact that he's originally from Ontario. When he was a young fellow in Sault Ste. Marie, he met a beautiful woman from Newfoundland. They married. For their honeymoon they went to Newfoundland and stayed with her parents for two weeks.

When he got back to Ontario, he was unable to stop thinking about Newfoundland. It had got under his skin. So he and his bride sold up, moved back, and settled here permanently. Unfortunately the lady couldn't stop thinking about Sault Ste. Marie, and the marriage didn't last. She went back alone. But he still loves it here, and maybe even more now that he's by himself. They thought they were marrying each other, but they were marrying each other's province. This is known as fate.

"It's a hunter's and fisherman's paradise," he says with great authority and conviction. "Endless hunting, endless fishing, it's just wonderful. Endless drinking, too, and everybody grows marijuana around here, and everybody's just as happy as can be."

That conversation dries up and the truck driver on my left, who it turns out is from Halifax, wants to get the word out that a trucker makes less money today than fifteen years ago. Every working stiff does, I object. You're right, he says, but I mean *considerably* less money.

Then he bombards me with stats and figures that purport to prove his contention that the unions have been hung out to dry, and that the entire system is intricately set up to make the drivers poor and the owners rich. He seems like an intelligent fellow, but he's so focused on his own field he's forgotten the same thing's happening all over, not just in the trucking business.

I don't think for a moment this guy's a professional grouch or a chronic complainer; it's more that he has something to get off his chest tonight. But he tires of the subject, as do we, and starts joining in on the vulgar chit-chat about women, with Brenda smiling all the way through it and not saying a thing. Her look never changed, even when the trucker began speaking graphically about the different women you get in different states of the United States and provinces of Canada, and which of his vast repertoire of pickup methods works best in which geographical and ethnic area.

To be truthful, the chit-chat isn't as vulgar as it may seem. There's a pleasant absence of hypocrisy in the tone. They are who they are, every fibre of their character shows through, and they're definitely not snobs. Every detail of every conceivable sort of one-night fling is being described to my blushing ears. They instinctively sense that as a city boy I have to be mindful of my behaviour at all times, and so I'm innocent of country manners where Smiling Aphrodite (sitting on her barstool) rules the roost.

The trucker says this is what he does every night of his working life: He looks for small, intimate Burnt Berry-type places all over the continent. When he finds one he pulls in, goes into the bar for a few drinks, chats up the bartender, and checks out the women in general. Then he heads back to his truck, often with a woman, for a few hours of whatever, in the spacious cot you may not know these truckers have back there, with stereo, television, medicine chest, shower, telescope, chess board, an entire set of Shakespeare, Internet connection, various electronic instruments to induce sleep states, or hypnotic states, and so on.

But even when I was a kid growing up in a dirty old town in southern Ontario, and this kind of talk was more common, I can't remember ever being in a place where the guys were being so unapologetically outspoken about their sex lives – and in the presence of a smiling and happily married lady Buddha.

NINE DAYS OF FOG

Rocky Brook • Badger • Grand Falls • Gambo • Glovertown
Charlottetown • Avalon Peninsula • St. John's

Friday, May 18. With a topped-up tank and a highway all to myself, I'm passing through dense birch forests, each tree having decided to wait one more day before daring to unfold its lovely little leaves.

It's easy in Newfoundland to make a building wheelchair-accessible, and nobody has to shame you into doing it, it's just the right thing to do. On the Mainland, you cave in only after intense lobbying, and it's a huge, expensive headache, involving architects, lawyers, broken marriages. But in Newfoundland, you just nail down a few planks and the wheelchair and motorized-scooter crowd will soon be wheeling right into your place of worship, credit union, bingo hall, dance hall, convenience store, bowling alley, motel, or slot-machine bar.

Early this morning, somebody ran into the caution sign on a simple wooden post on the median of the Trans-Canada Highway, marking the spot where it begins to widen for a short multi-lane stretch. Now the two-man highway crew bores a new hole with a simple auger, refits the post, and puts the sign back up. Something to fill an otherwise idle hour.

Whether it's a wheelchair ramp or a road sign, the unofficial motto of Newfoundland seems to be Keep It Simple.

Bushy-bearded Bertrand last night was wearing a black leather cap and jacket, and a New York Yankee sweatshirt, and his lecture on how to impress women was followed by tall tales about his four years in Toronto, climbing the ladder at Hi-Tech Global Communications or some such corporate nonentity. He was the boss of bosses. He told the bosses who to hire and who to fire, they gave him a "solid-gold" credit card with his own name on it ("Ooh boy, I'd love like de devil t'have one of dose," interjected the lovelorn and emaciated fellow), and when I asked why he had returned to the land of his birth, he said, "Who could stay away from Newfoundland long?"

I thought he was a terrible storyteller, and Brenda agreed. He tells all these stories so often people are beginning to think he's actually been off the island, she whispered, but to the best of her knowledge he's never even been to St. John's.

Brenda just sat there, pleased to be surrounded by large hairy mammals miles from the nearest village. She saw them as innocents; so I did too. She didn't look a day over forty, but she said she had two grandchildren, and she had a son working up in Inuvik on the Arctic Ocean – a strange coincidence, because I happened to be wearing an old sweat-stained peach-coloured Inuvik *Drum* baseball cap. But she didn't get the coincidence, because she hadn't noticed what it said on the cap. Even as she was pretending to squint to make it out, I dropped a subtle hint about what it said. I think maybe her reading was a little rusty, so I just changed the subject.

But then again it may have been her eyesight. She was a grandma twice over, and she wasn't wearing specs. For all I know she's president of the Robert's Arm–Pilley's Island Reading Club, and they're right now breezing through the *Areopagitica* of John Milton.

"Ah, freshwater fishing, saltwater fishing, we got everything." That's what they were saying last night. And coming from these shaggy drunks it had the ring of pristine and uncriticizable sincerity. Go shoot a caribou, shoot a moose, have enough meat for the whole village, I hear them saying, as I pass the village of Rocky Brook and approach the town of Badger, with its white-fenced Anglican cemetery and a pure-white goat with snow-white horns keeping the blades of grass and towering dandelions down to a respectable height.

"There's something the matter with a man who wouldn't rather live in Newfoundland" – that was last night's recurring theme. Maybe the fellows were trying to convince themselves rather than me. But I was full of positive reinforcement and said it looks like a pretty easy place for a man to keep his head above water and always have something to eat, and you don't have to worry about who's diddling your pension plan . . . or who's diddling your wife.

"Ye still has t'worry about dat," they all shouted in unison.

I'm a mile past a billboard suggesting YEAR ROUND TOURIST ADVEN-TURES, when a man-sized model of a leaping salmon announces the approach of Grand Falls. A little guy in a red jumpsuit is putting a new roof on a rundown house. The house itself looks ready for a grand fall, but it's got a new roof. The salmon is well executed; it's a multicoloured, handsome Nijinsky, svelte and proud, leaping into the air, the colours running as deep as in yesterday's front-yard iceberg at least. It'd make the eyes pop out of a real salmon, or maybe even a real Nijinsky! But I prefer the iceberg.

The Salmonid Interpretation Centre is billed as "the largest salmon enhancement project in the world." And if you're into salmon enhancement, then you'll be into habitat restoration, fundraising, stream monitoring, community education, editing and writing the annual *Fish Tales Newsletter*, and probably transplanting excess salmon roe from a well-stocked stream to a barren stream.

The owner of the car I'm driving, Ann Shigeishi, is a prosthetic-device fitter by trade, and has just taken a new job in St. John's after a long stint working in a hospital in Barrie, Ontario. The strange thing about the car, and one that would set it apart from any other white 1995 Honda Civic on the road, I'd suspect, is that, instead of a gear-shift knob, it has a baby's foot – with the sole pointing up, flesh-coloured and flexible, a sort of rubbery plastic. I can wiggle its five little toes, stroke the perfect contours of the foot, and tickle it to keep it amused on long stretches between filling stations. It's just like massaging a three-year-old child's bare foot all the way along the Trans-Canada Highway from Toronto to St. John's. It looks as if it was part of a prosthetic device, and the poor kid outgrew it, it was going to be replaced, and so Ann got a bright idea and salvaged it for her gear shift. And the fit was perfect.

I try to drive the car carefully, because the last thing Ann wants right now, after such a major relocation, is to have to buy a new one. It has 130,000 klicks on it. The glove compartment keeps falling on the floor. The battery keeps fading out, requiring occasional boosts. There's a new radio-tape player, but it has little power, and the only way you can turn it off is to pull it straight out of the dashboard and put it in the glove compartment, which will then fall on the floor.

But the baby's foot, no matter how many times it's shifted, stays put.

Last night's truck driver was saying he has no ambition to own his own rig. The amount he would make on his investment wouldn't pay his cocaine bill. The way it is now, if he's driving along and he runs into a moose on the road and it knocks out his headlights, fan, radiator, distributor, and maybe even ruins the engine, why he just phones up the boss and says, "You've got a problem." And he walks away from it. But he says it'll never happen, because he won't drive at night in Newfoundland. He said Newfoundland was the worst place in North America for moose. I maintained British Columbia was much worse.

He said I'd been misinformed, because in Newfoundland some nights you can't go five miles without seeing a moose. I said in British Columbia, on the same Trans-Canada Highway, you often can't go five feet – and nobody told me, I saw it many times with my own misinformed eyes. Herds come out of the forest to soak up the heat from the road by night, or to sun themselves by day. You have to push them out of the way and/or wind your way in and out between them. He didn't like me talking like that in front of Brenda, because he'd just been boasting to her that he'd driven in all ten provinces and fifty states. I said that, by tomorrow, I'll have driven every inch of the Trans-Canada Highway. We were competitive little monkeys. Brenda was beaming. He was eyeing her, she was eyeing me, and I was eyeing my watch.

But he did acknowledge that perhaps he had not driven in the interior of British Columbia during moose season. It's actually elk season, but I didn't say anything.

I mentioned having seen a moulting caribou the other day, and the bare patches of hide were black. He said it wasn't really moulting. Rather, what I was seeing was a caribou in the final stages of some horrible disease they get from licking the road for salt. They inadvertently pick up all the chemicals laid down by the rubber tires in whose honour the roads were built. I did not argue, but later I was officially told that they were just moulting and this trucker had a vivid imagination.

Also I heard Brenda telling the trucker that she had the greatest husband in the world, but he was spending the night with his girlfriend. Maybe she was joking, but I decided to excuse myself, and let these two not-so-young folks – the others had left by now – see if they might be better off in my absence.

St. John's may not turn out to be my favourite part of Newfoundland, but how will I develop an authentic feel for the body parts of the island until I've visited its heart? The radio informs me that St. John's and the surrounding Avalon Peninsula are in the eighth day of dense fog, and the temperature is hovering a few degrees above freezing. But I do hope to get down there before the fog lifts, for it will be fun to see St. John's for the first time in a peasouper so dense you can't see it. It would even be nice to sit in the window of a Duckworth Street restaurant, in the middle of dense fog, and order pea soup.

Perhaps fun is not the right word, because this is a serious fog, with six hundred Newfoundlanders stuck in the Halifax airport waiting to get home, and another six hundred in St. John's airport waiting to fly out to Halifax. And every day the numbers increase.

St. John's is famous for fog, but it's unusual for it to be so heavy so long, and it's been decades since the airport has been down for more than just an hour or two now and then. One local news flash said that business at fogless Gander airport has picked up.

When I'm an old geezer, I'll be able to say things like "Fog? Don't tell me about fog. I was in St. John's when they had the worst fog of the first three millennia. You young people don't know what fog is. In fact, I have some of that fog in quart jars up in the attic. Who wants to come up and help me find them?"

Suddenly, while I was thinking about the fog in St. John's, and excited because in a few hours I'd be getting my first glimpse of the Avalon Peninsula, the bushy-bearded philosopher from last night flashed into my mind again. Brenda claimed he was a terrible liar, but at one point he sobered up and wanted to talk about books. With no one else paying any attention, he offered me a glimpse of his heart, and very shyly told me that he had just finished reading *The Colony of Unrequited Dreams*, a novel set in Newfoundland and written by Wayne Johnston. I too had read it and enjoyed it, but it was hard to get him to talk about it, beyond saying he'd read it. It wouldn't have seemed right for me to start firing questions at him like a school-teacher, and in fact there was something in his eye that told me he'd found it hard going. He was proud to have read it all the way through, and was quietly excited about it, but he really didn't have much to say about it. He also said he was a couple of chapters into *Cat's Eye* by Margaret Atwood and seemed relieved to find it a bit less challenging. He was proud and pleased to be talking about books, even in such a limited fashion, and without saying much he gave me the impression he'd only started reading recently, and these were the first serious full-length adult novels he'd cracked.

Generalists often note that Newfoundlanders are shy when it comes to talking about things that are close to their hearts. Such shyness seems to me a very special virtue, a quality that demands respect.

But it's time to forget about last night. I'll be returning to Burnt Berry at least once more before I head home, if only because it's so central. And here's Joey's Lookout, overlooking the town of Gambo, where Newfoundland's most famous prime minister – and Canada's most recent father of Confederation – was born. And here's a flagpole flying a flag with a few quick lines unmistakeably delineating the famous Joey Smallwood sly (but not shy) heart-shaped face, with bow tie and glasses. And there are some wooden benches to sit and enjoy a spectacular wilderness view, of islands, forests, lakes, and rivers – and, just a bit over the horizon, Bonavista Bay and the Atlantic Ocean.

We are meant to believe that, at moments when great decisions had to be made, Joey would just skip up to this lookout and contemplate eternity. This is uncannily similar to the Sir Walter Scott Lookout in Scotland, an equally superb but more rolling and less wild view, and Sir Walter also is said to have often stolen away to that spot to contemplate problems with money, women, and twists of plot. And here's the Joseph Smallwood Interpretive Centre. And the more I read about that guy, the more interpretation he needs.

In Newfoundland they have a friendly competition between weather broadcasters. Each tries to be more surrealistic than the other. Today, for instance, a humorous lady was giving the times-temperatures-tunes on the Gander radio station. The morning temperatures (in Celsius) all around the island ranged from 1 (in the east) to 13 (in the west), but she refused to believe the reports. She was telling everybody in central Newfoundland that this must be last month's report she'd been handed, it couldn't possibly be that cold this far into spring. She seemed to be joking, but she resisted making it obvious, and she definitely had this listener balancing on the sharp edge of doubt. . . .

In fact, all over Newfoundland, she said, kids are swimming in the ponds. Listen. And she put on a tape of a mess of kids splashing in the water and squealing with glee. She said she knows Newfoundlanders are hardy folk and not the kind to be cowed by wintry storms. But they also like their children and wouldn't let them go swimming on a day with temperatures like this. So she told the world to disregard the temperatures she'd just given, she was right now (zip-zip-zip) taking off all her clothes and getting into her polka-dot bikini, so she could go out and join the kids frolicking in the waves. Click. Meanwhile, St. John's is expected to reach a high of 6 today.

We're approaching Glovertown (rhymes with Clovertown), and it's getting colder and wetter. As we close in on the Avalon Peninsula, the towns seem to get larger, and the highway busier. Excuse the "royal we," it's actually just me and my lucky naked baby foot. There's The Doctor's Inn Guest Home. Maybe it's actually run by a doctor and you get free medical advice: "That prostate feels a bit swollen," "Have you had a relaxing enema lately?" or "How often have you had sex since arriving on The Rock?" You can also get home-cooked meals and view people getting tickled in the Tickleview Restaurant.

For the next few miles, the Trans-Canada Highway runs through Terra Nova National Park, with its numerous wilderness views, guaranteed to please the grouchiest tourist. A solemn but ambiguous government sign announces the entrance to the park and warns of the danger of moose: "Number of Moose-Car Collisions This Year: XXX." There's space for a number, but there's no number there. It's either been stolen, or lost, or maybe eaten by a moose, because it certainly hasn't been a collision-free year. And even if there were a number, you wouldn't know if it meant in this park, on this highway, in this province, or in the world, and if by "car" they also meant motorcycles, trucks, and buses.

There's a Charlottetown in Newfoundland too! The population of the more famous Charlottetown, capital of Prince Edward Island, is 35,000. The population of this Charlottetown isn't currently available, but it does have a Howard Johnson's, so it would probably be about the same population as Square Island, Snug Harbour, or Comfort Bight. Both Charlottetowns would have been named at the same time, 1763, at the end of the Seven Years' War, when France's vast colonial empire in North America (including Newfoundland and Prince Edward Island) came under official British control, and crazy old King George III's queen, the even crazier Charlotte, went on a campaign to have places around the world named after her. So now there are Charlottes, Charlottevilles, Charlottetowns, and Queen Charlotte Islands all around the known world, even in the United States, which hadn't yet cleverly taken advantage of George III's insanity to declare their independence. There's even a Charlotetown (deliberately misspelled to avoid confusion, no doubt) in Labrador.

In the otherwise-excellent *Colony of Unrequited Dreams*, Wayne Johnston is not always the most reliable narrator. For instance, he says from certain points along the Isthmus of Avalon you can see both Placentia Bay to the south and Trinity Bay to the north. At certain locations you can see Trinity Bay, at other spots you can see Placentia Bay, but all the way along the isthmus I never stopped looking, and my head never stopped swivelling, from north to south, anxious to find the spot from which one could see both bays. But I had to admit defeat. Maybe he was speaking metaphorically. It does seem as if you should be able to see both from the same spot.

Come to think of it, Johnston's narrator was on a train at the time, and maybe from the lower level of the railroad, views of both immense bays would, on occasion, be available simultaneously. Also, that would explain how the train-bound narrator might not have noticed how incredibly steep and deep the valleys of the isthmus are, how precipitous the mountains, and how squeezed together they are, as if two land masses have had a massive head-on collision on the highway of deepest time.

The Isthmus of Avalon unites the two Newfoundland twins at the stomach. One twin, known as "the outports," is area-strong and population-weak, while the other, the Avalon Peninsula into which we are heading, is area-weak and population-strong. Approaching the Avalon, the landscape becomes more complex, with narrower and more frequent valleys and chains of hills, and with extended families of great shimmering ponds, which at this time of year are full of clear, black shining water and surrounded by pale yellow rock and wintry tundra stretching out to the horizon. Some of the ponds have at their sides remnants of great snowdrifts frozen into place in the most graceful manner. We seem to be descending into a lower level, and the sky seems to be descending as well. The road descends into dense fog, then ascends way above trees and fog, almost to the other-worldly granite outcroppings at the tops of these mountains, where there is not enough soil to grow a dandelion, and where there are vast glacier-like sheets of hard-capped ice. Glimpsed through the

fog, these appear to have been there forever, but they'll have disappeared (temporarily) in two weeks or so.

This stretch of road not only goes up and down, but also way up and
way down, and sometimes even way way up and way way down – no
way around it, because of the narrowness of isthmuses. It must have
been an interesting road-building experience. Anyway, it's just an
isthmus, and sometimes an isthmus is just an isthmus, but this
isthmus is as crinkled as a Colorado cordillera.

"Time and temperature," squeals the radio, "three-forty-five plus
four."

Fifty miles from St. John's, and the fog is thickening like a Charles
Dickens plot. Yes, the world has become foggy, foggier than even the
vilest villain would like it. We all like it a little foggy, but not this
foggy. It's been nine days now, and the fog is so dense people are
getting a bit tense. If a football game had been scheduled for today it
would have to be postponed on account of fog.

Of all the major Canadian cities, St. John's is on record for being
the foggiest, snowiest, wettest, windiest, and cloudiest. It also
suffers the most avalanches. On February 17, 1921, a fellow named
James Delahunty died in an avalanche on Signal Hill, in the city of
St. John's, and when his body was recovered it was noticed that he
had died with his lunch pail open and a sandwich halfway to his
mouth. That's how fast death can come, folks. So get those wills
made out.

St. John's also has more days with freezing rain and wet weather
than any other Canadian city. Yet the residents say they love it!
Nobody would lie about love, would they? Who can blame them for
seeking consolation in physical intimacy with spouses and/or dear
friends an amazing 8.35 times a month?

You can't beat Environment Canada's *The Climates of Canada* for
such interesting statistics, coupled with poetry. For instance, each year
an average of 250 icebergs drift down on the Labrador Current, only

to come to grief on the Grand Banks. These "majestic, wintry ghosts" (Environment Canada is a hotbed of junior Gordon Lightfoots) "worry mariners more than pack ice, chasing drill platforms off site or barricading fishermen in the many bays and harbours."

The Labrador Current, known affectionately as Iceberg Alley, is a sort of Gulf Stream in reverse, bringing frigid waters and massive chunks of ice from the west coast of Greenland down along the coast of Labrador to Newfoundland. (They should call it Nofunland, except for that remarkable 8.35-times-a-month statistic.) Nobody ever counted icebergs until the sinking of the *Titanic* in 1912. Since then, they're counted every year, and yearly extremes (the food of statisticians, just as earliest dreams are the food of poets) have ranged from a minuscule none in 1966 to 2,202 in 1984.

At one-fifth of a mile an hour, it takes an iceberg three years to get to Newfoundland from where it was calved high up on the west coast of Greenland.

Out of my way, they seem to be saying. I'm a majestic wintry ghost!

Those fellows at the bar last night were the sons and/or grandsons of the people who voted for Confederation. The people on the Avalon Peninsula voted against it. It was 1948. The premier was Joey Smallwood. The official word was that you had to vote either for "responsible government" (as favoured by the businessmen of St. John's) or for becoming Canada's tenth province (as favoured by Joey). The wealthy Avalon Peninsula went for responsible government (66 per cent), and the fisherfolk of the outports went for Confederation (70 per cent). There was bitterness among the businessmen, who expressed contempt for the "ignorant and avaricious outporters." The latter, who with the help of Joey saw right through the "responsible government" propaganda, had, according to the merchant classes, abused their right to vote by handing Newfoundland over to Canada "as a free gift."

"England didn't want us," said those guys last night, "so when Canada wanted us, my son, we went for it."

And they said, "That Joey Smallwood is a saint, my son."

"Is?"

"Saints, dey never die, my son. Did you not know dat?"

And they said, "We don't give a hoot what anybody says, whenever you travel anywhere like we have, dey know dat Canada is de best country in de world, dere's no doubt about it, de best, de best, far far far above any udder country . . . and we be awful glad Newfoundland belongs to Canada, don't ever think for one split second in eternity we're not."

As a Canadian raised with strong pro-Canadian feelings, tears flooded my eyes. One was not likely to hear such sentiments expressed in a lot of rural areas of Canada, especially in parts of Alberta. But here it was in full bloom. The artsy-fartsy, hip-and-with-it intellectuals of Corner Brook and St. John's would of course pooh-pooh such chit-chat toot sweet. They still favour the Union Jack, even if they happen to be descended from Irish Catholics, and they speak of "going to Canada" or "Dave here, he's from Canada," but they make a point of never being nasty about it. Marc Lalonde (formerly a major cabinet minister in Trudeau's government) was three Tuesdays ago quoted in the *Toronto Star* as saying Albertans and Quebecers have to have someone to hate. To which he might have added, had it served his purpose, that Newfoundlanders have to have someone to love. The same someone. Strange world.

Cosmologists say there are eight billion planets exactly like earth (environmentally speaking) in this galaxy alone. I often feel like a fellow who has spent an entire lifetime on each of these eight billion planets. But only this week have I arrived in Newfoundland.

And there it is, come down a hill and around a curve and it's my first glimpse of old St. John's, and by golly it's a handsome sight, one of the Milky Way's great little cities. Would that be the harbour over there? Yes, I believe it would be, especially with all those boats, and all that water, and the horseshoe-shaped ridge of rock protecting it from the wild Atlantic. Turn the heater up a bit. They're calling for snow this weekend, so this must be the coldest spot in Newfoundland, and the reason would be because St. John's is right out in the open Atlantic. It's smack dab in the middle of Iceberg Alley, which affects the Avalon Peninsula quite unlike the manner in which the Gulf Stream affects western Ireland and the Outer Hebrides. Around here they are blessed with a late-start-to-summer, early-start-to-winter sort of climate. No long, hot, lazy summers up here.

And the fog has started to lift.

More on that 8.35 times a month later. . . .

THE BOYS OF POUCH COVE

St. John's • Pouch Cove

Saturday, May 19–Tuesday, May 22. Word Play is a venerable old bookstore in the heart of St. John's. It's a two-storey stucco-and-stone building on a large lot, and with a Union Jack flying above it, as if the front of the store were the stern of an eighteenth-century sailing ship. On the renovated second floor is a private gallery, where local painters and artists-in-residence get to show their work, some-times to great cries of outrage from members of the public who might wander in off the street and be unwilling even to try to understand what the artist is trying to accomplish.

Lynn Donoghue dared to exhibit some of her richly textured and carefully observed penis paintings here, and managed to handle the resulting fuss with serenity. I told her I liked them fine, but they were a bit too direct (and erect) for your average faith-based male in the street. She already knew that. A few years ago, some locals had thrown stones at one of the artists' residences – the one that Lynn and her colleague Maureen Lynette (both from Toronto) were now staying at in Pouch Cove farther north. But everything has been peaceful since the stone-throwers were taken to court and had to endure the judge calling them a "bunch of arseholes."

The store and gallery belong to James Baird, who combines dynamism with wit, flashing eyes with generosity. He's also a scion of the famous old Baird family of St. John's. "My family was against Confederation, and thinking of Newfoundland as a country is in my genes," he says. "Newfoundland is probably more a state of mind than anything else."

Jim also runs the Pouch Cove Foundation, which offers month-long residencies in Newfoundland for painters from anywhere, the farther away the better. His business card says "Artists Desired."

"The only good thing about the area was the view," says Jim, "and the only people who appreciated the view were the artists. So we invited one. She enjoyed it and told others. So here we are."

There were three painters in residence at Pouch Cove, they were all friends of mine from Toronto, and they kindly invited me to stop by when I got up there. I spent a few days in one house, right in the community of Pouch Cove, but with panoramic views of the actual formidable and magnificent cove, which is not really a cove, since it can be more treacherous than the open sea when a storm's brewing. Maureen Lynette and Lynn Donoghue's shared house was a mile or two down the road, conveniently near a grocery store, but with less spectacular views. The hospitality was wonderful, especially since I wasn't even a painter.

> *"All Newfoundland boys have adventures, but not all Newfoundland boys survive them."*
> – Norman Duncan,
> *The Adventures of Billy Topsail* (1906)

Pouch (pronounced "pooch") Cove – population just under two thousand, at the northern tip of the Avalon Peninsula, eighty klicks north of St. John's – had received universal attention recently, but not for the good work of the foundation. It was rather for a greatly tragic event that had caused an immense outburst of sorrow in the community, and all over Newfoundland and the rest of Canada. Three boys – Jesse Elliott, eighteen, and Adam Wall and A.J. Sullivan, both sixteen – were chasing each other from iceberg to iceberg in the cove when they fell into the sea and drowned.

It was on March 7, just over two months ago. The boys were playing a traditional game called "following." There were no witnesses, but it appears one boy fell in, and the others instinctively jumped in and died trying to save him. Or maybe all three were on the same chunk of ice and it was hit by a big wave, or by another chunk of ice, or maybe it just slid out from under them. In some ways it would be preferable to die trying to save your friends, no matter how bad the odds, than have to stagger home and break the news. Many Newfoundlanders over the centuries have died trying to save their friends.

David Bolduc, the third painter from Toronto, told me that the mother of one of the boys used to clean the house we were in, but she won't do it any more. It was easy to see why not. The large front window looks down over the exact spot where the boys died.

The owners of this house, currently on loan to the Pouch Cove Foundation, are Gabrielle Alioth, the Swiss novelist, and her husband, Martin Alioth, who is a mediaeval historian and broadcast journalist, with a special interest in Irish affairs. The two of them have collaborated on numerous radio programs, including one on the novelists and poets of Newfoundland. This little white house, with its amazing views of sea and rock, was tucked in among numerous other little white houses that constitute the community of Pouch Cove, and it didn't look out of place at all. The accident and the resulting press coverage were still in the air, and Bolduc and I felt like wretched interlopers in a horrible family tragedy. There was great gloom everywhere.

But life goes on, and a little red-haired boy, about four, named Joshua, dropped by to show us how he was coming along on his new bicycle.

"Brown hair, not red," he said.

"Looks awfully red to me," said Bolduc.

He looked doubtful.

"How old are you?" I said.

He held up four fingers.

He drove by at full speed and slammed on his brakes, then turned around and pointed at his rear wheel. "Look," he said. "No trainer."

My stay in Pouch Cove was a welcome rest in preparation for the next phase of my exploration of Newfoundland. From May 19, when I turned over the car to Ann Shigeishi, to May 23, when I rented another little Japanese car, this one red and new, I didn't spend a minute thinking about my book. But now it was time to get working. . . .

COURAGE AND COWARDICE

Ferryland • Fermeuse • Renews • Cappahayden

Wednesday, May 23. The southern segment of the Avalon Peninsula, less populated than the north, is riddled with old churches and historical landmarks. On the walls of the Colony Café in Ferryland are several portraits of pirate-ship captains and colonial entrepreneurs, as well as historical murals and old framed maps of the general area. Somehow it manages to avoid that insipid touristy feel. Even the prices on the menu are geared for the Newfoundland market.

But I'm having trouble getting down my first-ever taste of cod tongues and cheeks, even if they have been lightly sautéed to perfection, and even if I did grow up on massive daily doses of cod-liver oil. I think I prefer the tongues to the cheeks, but I'm not sure. The cheeks are the big ones, right? Silly question.

"Right," says the waitress, "and there's more jelly in the cheeks. It's the jelly or something that, uh, that sometimes, er . . ."

"Makes certain people a bit nauseous?"

"Exactly, sir."

"Oh! I see. The cheeks have the jelly in them."

"Yes. They has the jelly in them. It's the tongues that has the meat in 'em."

"Just like in human beings."

"Just as in us. Right you are, sir."

Looking down at me as I struggle with my cheeks and tongues is a portrait of George Calvert, Lord Baltimore (1580–1632), a dapper-looking Yorkshireman, who founded the Ferryland colony in 1621. But this was just practice for his founding of the Maryland colony thirteen years later. Lord Baltimore was a Catholic, but of the closet variety. Both colonies were Protestant.

On the window ledge by my table someone has left an inexpensive camera, with a name on it, Jonathan Cohlmeyer. "Don't worry about it," said the waitress. "This'll be three summers it's been here. When he comes back to pick it up, he won't be able to remember who it is the pictures will be of."

Immediately outside the café, you're in the sacred grounds of the old colony. Wall remnants have been found, composed of flat stones on top of each other with no mortar, so that's the style that has been adopted for recent recreations of the little buildings.

There are several bare rocky islands a mile offshore – they have odd shapes, and one tall one seems to have been sliced in half by a celestial thunderbolt at the beginning of time. Cowardly French warships, filled with lusty pirates and murderous privateers, would anchor behind these islands, hidden from the view of the Ferryland folks, and would patiently wait for the perfect moment for a surprise attack – sometimes in the middle of a storm.

One mural shows a French ship bouncing up and down in the waves and firing cannon shots at the pretty little colony, while lightning flashes across the full moon. The French first came here in 1504, then left temporarily, but they forgot to leave a note saying they'd be back. When they did return, the English had taken over, so the French had a temper tantrum. The ruins of a house that had taken a direct hit from a French cannonball have been excavated.

This happened in October 1696. The house was right on the sea, and it's not big, only about twenty by forty feet, but the fireplace took up one entire twenty-foot wall.

Lord Baltimore built a fabled mansion here, but was driven out after only one year by hostile pirates, French fishermen – and maybe even by the now-extinct Beothuk, who were known to be in the immediate area. The site of it awaits discovery. I'd wager it's directly under the modestly handsome gothic Holy Trinity Church, halfway up a high grassy hill overlooking the seaside settlement.

The area around Ferryland is studded with large wooden houses of the flowery gingerbread style popular with members of the "merchant class," as they call it in St. John's, or by the "shipbuilding class," as they call it in the outports.

Today's Ferrylanders seem a devout and well-organized little group. They received half a million dollars from the provincial government for the restoration of Holy Trinity Church, for instance. The warmth and vitality of the support the people of these small communities give to their churches takes the mind back to previous centuries.

The wind picks up and starts whistling, and dozens of little kids on a field trip start imitating it, running around like the wind, whistling and screaming.

Nothing is happening in the village of Fermeuse, except two small women are walking along the road, one wearing a red jacket and the other a peach-coloured jacket. Nearby is Fermeuse's near-rhyming neighbour, Renews, boasting a Unisex Haircutting Salon and the magnificent Renews River, which is full of giant salmon leaping six feet in the air, and either my glasses are dirty or they're wearing little top hats and monocles, carrying canes, and singing "Salmon-Chanted Evening."

Renews was the birthplace of a great hero, Captain William Jackman. On October 9, 1867, the *Sea Clipper* was going down in a gale off Spotted Island, Labrador, with twenty-seven aboard. Jackman, in twenty-seven furious swims over six hundred yards of icy water each way, rescued all twenty-seven people from the sinking wreck. He survived to have two lengthy poetic ballads and a stirring limerick written about him and was decorated with a silver medal from the Royal Humane Society. He had been told not to bother about the final person to be rescued, it was only a woman, and she was ill and wouldn't survive being rescued. "Living or dead, I'll not leave her there!" he cried, then jumped back in and rescued her anyway. When he got her back to shore, she thanked him for his kindness with her last gasp, then died. His father later said, "I would never have forgiven him if he had left that woman on board."

Much of the southern quarter of the Avalon Peninsula is covered in treeless, tundra-like bog, with numerous dream-like herds of wild white caribou. I was seized by an alarming optical illusion: for a brief moment the world turned upside down, the sky turned into the sea, and waves seemed to be breaking over my head. This was on the downward approach to Cappahayden, and after some analysis I convinced myself that the illusion, though dramatic, was caused merely by the sharp angle of my approach to the sea and the eerie late-afternoon absence of horizon. In other words, I lost track of the horizon and found myself looking out over the tops of trees farther down the slope. So I mistook the sea for the sky, and then great whitecaps seemed to be breaking above me. Just for a moment. . . .

If ships, like illusions, can take on lives of their own, the *Florizel*, which came to grief off this coast, had a strangely haunted one. On October 4, 1914, five hundred members of the Newfoundland Regiment, the "Blue Puttees," boarded HMS *Florizel* at Pleasantville and sailed to England. The ship was taking a break from seal-slaughtering expeditions. The Blue Puttees were the fearless fighting men of Newfoundland, and 732 of them died in the July 1, 1916, battle of Beaumont–Hamel, on the opening day of the Battle of the Somme. There were six hundred thousand casualties at the Somme, but no country bled as badly as Newfoundland. Beaumont–Hamel is very near the top of the totem pole of Newfoundland history, just as Vimy Ridge is for Canada's sense of itself. Both sites have been marked with magnificent commemorative statues, the less known one at Beaumont–Hamel depicting a bronze larger-than-life male caribou standing on a high rock, with his head upraised and bellowing agonizingly to anyone with ears to hear.

The *Florizel*, a sleek, handsome ship with a single smokestack, was called "the pride of Bowring's Red Cross Line." It had seen duty as an icebreaker, a sealing ship, a troop ship, and a passenger ship. Four years after carrying the Blue Puttees to their deaths, it left St. John's at 7:30 on the stormy night of February 24, 1918, carrying 138 civilian passengers and crew. Just as those Blue Puttees never should have been ordered to advance against the vastly superior German position, so the *Florizel* should not have been sent out into that storm, which got worse and worse. Far off course, she smashed into Horn Head, off Cappahayden.

Numerous would-be rescue ships were unable to get close to the wreckage, or turned back, certain that no one could be alive. It wasn't until the storm started to ebb twenty-seven hours later that it was discovered that, of the 138, seventeen passengers and twenty-seven crew members were crying to be rescued – which they then right promptly were. If you're ever in Bowring Park in St. John's, you'll see an elaborate Peter Pan statue commemorating the death of *Florizel* passenger Betty Munn, a little girl who was "torn from her father's arms by the wind as he knelt to protect her."

To air a bit of Newfoundland's dirty laundry, there is still a controversy raging over the *Florizel*. Some maintain the Cappahaydenites stood on the icy shore watching sullenly and doing nothing to help the rescue attempt.

Others say they helped a lot.

And some say, when the rescue was all complete, the pride of Cappahayden manhood sailed out to the wreckage and sneakily stripped it clean as a chipmunk's tooth.

Others say there's no evidence for that at all.

When night falls, the wild caribou become white flames standing silently, scarcely moving and without flickering, as they graze in the moonlight or lie on the ground resting. They look much smaller than they should be, too delicate to survive the winter, and with coats that are not heavy enough. They have little humps on their backs, and sometimes their eyes shine in the moonlight.

Ocean View Home Away from Home seemed like a nice name for a guest house, and so I marched in, hoping for a room for the night. But I made a terrible mistake. It wasn't a guest house, it was a nursing home, one of many such motel-like homes for the aged one finds everywhere in the Newfoundland countryside. The elderly get excellent care in this province, so Newfoundlanders tend to take good care of themselves, and they do drive carefully, especially when they're sloshed.

We, too, could some day be like this living desiccated photographic cardboard cutout of an old woman sitting at a kitchen table in front of a cold cup of tea. Her eyes were open but she was staring into nothingness, not a whisker or a jowl was twitching, although the drop of moisture on the underside of the tip of her nose was quivering a bit in the subtle air currents.

It was just another of McFadden's many mistakes, and I was directed to a guest home up the road a bit. It was an ordinary but slightly outsized bungalow, with a few extra rooms tucked away here and there, but it had a carefully handpainted sign on its roof, saying in huge block letters eight feet high NORTHWEST B&B. Why would a guest home with a name like that be located in the southeastern part of the island? It seemed likely the explanation wouldn't be as interesting as the mystery, so I didn't ask. Or maybe I just forgot.

SERENITY, STORMS, AND SLOT MACHINES

*Trepassey • St. Shotts • St. Stephens • Branch
Cape St. Mary's • Placentia*

Thursday, May 24. Marilyn Kenny had three different brands of Puffed Rice to choose from on the table, and white toast with margarine, and a pot of coffee. We talked for the longest time, and it was a soulful talk. Her husband, Ambrose, was out in the garbage truck. Every few minutes the phone would ring and she'd pick it up, pause, then say, "Ambrose is out in the garbage truck." But sometimes she would say Ambrose is out *on* the garbage truck. You never knew what she was going to say next, *in* or *on*. It was spring, you see, time to get the town tidied up.

A highlight of my Irish trip in 1990 was visiting Sneem just after they'd won the Tidy Town Award. They now have that in Newfoundland, too, and Trepassey was hoping to win it. They've got a long way to go, but that's why Ambrose was out with the garbage truck, making the town a bit tidier, though it will never look as tidy as Sneem on that lovely spring day in County Cork.

A glance at today's paper signals the important news that the

U.S. spy plane has been brought back from China in pieces, and Kellogg's Raisin Bran now has 25 per cent more raisins. On the wall is a photograph of the three handsome Kenny boys, all three now working in London, Ontario, in three different construction trades, though they look as if they should be models for *Gentlemen's Quarterly*.

Marilyn was proud of them, but something was wrong. The serenity of sadness was in the air, an air of resignation. She had a round, plump face, with a small upturned nose and thin lips. She was born in Trepassey and so was Ambrose. The two were born and raised on the same street. What an unusual difference in family backgrounds – Marilyn was an only child and Ambrose was the youngest of fourteen. But that was a long time ago, for they're both in their mid-fifties now. A couple of Ambrose's siblings have died of cancer "of course" (as she put it, ruefully). Of the survivors, one is in Texas, but most of them are still in and around Trepassey.

Then she told me that they had a daughter as well, their only little girl – cute, funny, bright as blazes – but she had died years ago of a brain tumour. Even now you could sense Marilyn's sudden pain, as if simply admitting that her daughter no longer existed cracked her serenity and caused her heart to be stabbed anew. She knew I wasn't in a rush, and so she told me many details surrounding that long and painfully drawn-out tragedy. From the moment they first started to notice something was wrong until they could get her diagnosed was just short of a year. The doctors used to tell them they were crazy, there was nothing wrong with the girl, and the psychiatrists would question Marilyn about her parenting abilities. Also they demanded to know why she was working at a job, as she was at the time, instead of being a full-time housewife.

Something about the nature of the tumour, she wasn't sure what, caused her daughter to be happy in spite of her illness during her last few years on earth. She was radiant, euphoric, never depressed, and always fun to be around.

Marilyn said her daughter felt pressure in her head at times, but she never complained of anything, certainly not of pain. Her hair all fell out, but she was still perfectly happy, not even slightly embarrassed about it. One day she was vomiting in the toilet, and she came out and said, "Oh mother, I'm so sick I think I could die." Her mother naturally gave her a concerned look, and the little girl began laughing her head off. By relating these details for me, Marilyn was revivifying her memories, and keeping them sacred.

She was saying that she and her husband are getting health-conscious. About five years ago they both quit smoking. She says she suspected for a long time that Ambrose might be smoking in the shed, so she would sneak up on him and burst in unannounced. There was never any trace of him having been smoking, but she kept doing that for quite some time. She would get suspicious.

Ambrose Kenny really is out with the garbage truck. I caught him at the side of the road on this early spring morning with blue skies and cool breezes off the sea. The Trepassey people put their trash in recycled lobster traps, now that the lobsters are gone from the south shore. Ambrose had collected all of that, and now he was cleaning up a winter's supply of garbage from the old ball park/open-air concert hall. Then he was going to give the fire hydrant a fresh coat of paint. All this was in preparation for the Tidy Town competition.

I gave him a brief report on three old hot-water tanks rusting away in a vacant lot. "I know where you mean," he said. "We'll get on that right away."

I mentioned the Tidy Town awards in Ireland, but he seemed to know all about it. He said that's where they got the idea. After all, this is one of the largest Irish populations in all Newfoundland, here by the Southern Shore as it's called, or the Irish Loop as it's known in the tourist industry.

There are many little clouds in the sky, black clouds, grey clouds, white clouds, but there's also a lot of sunshine, no fog, and all in all it's a lovely morning to be alive in Naked Newfoundland. Why do I call Newfoundland Naked? There's an "I am what I am" feel about the province. You immediately know everything about everybody you look at, at least everything important. Shy as they may be, nobody has anything worth hiding, and they can fill in the details for you any time you want.

Beyond Trepassey, a quiet secondary road leads down to the tiny fishing village of St. Shotts. Three white caribou are grazing close to the road. As I approach, one becomes startled and bolts, but the other two merely stop grazing and stare after him, wondering what all the fuss is about.

At the end of the road is the placid sea, with tiny pond-like ripples all the way to the horizon. On the barren hills, flocks of sheep browse among the gravel. This seems to be part of the Mary Queen of the World Parish, and there's Our Lady of Fatima School. From a hill above the harbour at St. Shotts can be seen the L-shaped cement pier, and one boat with three men in it, a small blue boat with a little cabin. It looks as if they're going out to do a little cod-jigging, perfectly legal for those with a licence. We can't come home with a boat overflowing with fish like we used to, but we can still do a little cod-jigging now and then and hope for a nibble.

The southern tip of the Avalon Peninsula throngs with bird-watchers in the fall, as this is an important migratory meeting place for American golden plovers. Billions of these tiny perfect birds select the Trepassey–St. Shotts area as a major resting spot before their long flight straight down to South America. When they take off from the Irish Loop, it's overseas all the way, straight down to northern Brazil. The adults leave in the early fall, and the immature ones stay till the last minute, as late as late October, presumably to build up their wing muscles for the great feat of endurance ahead. These birds are great little flyers, covering something like twenty thousand miles a year, but sometimes an American golden plover will stray off-course and end up in England, where they're known affectionately as Bloody Yank Goldies.

It's so beautiful here, with the blue sky, the different shades and subtle tones of natural colours, the ponds, the winding half-frozen rivers, and the winding road with no traffic whatsoever. The road is clear all the way up to the horizon I'm heading towards, not a piece of traffic on it.

Little iron crosses stand way out in the bog, each cross with a circle symbolizing the cyclical nature of life. Sometimes the cross will be painted yellow and the circle painted white. Being buried in a bog must be for those free of religious affiliation and/or bank accounts. There's a little river still entirely blocked up with ice.

Marilyn this morning told me that, when a mother loses a daughter, it's a huge, life-changing event. You lose your fear of death after that. You also lose your fear of dying. If your innocent little daughter could handle it, you can handle it too.

It also has a tendency to shake us out of our religious ideals, some of which seem a bit sentimental and inadequate after a lousy experience like this. Yet she became more religious. It wrenched her out of her fundamental creed and left her with a profound experience of the religious sense of the world, its beauty and brevity, its mystery and history. It gave her some unexpected serenity. More likely a real lot of it. Serenity and grief sometimes go hand in hand.

The south-shore communities, full of single-family dwellings with white vinyl siding, have a prosperous look about them. But Marilyn told me the look is illusory. Unemployment rates are so high nobody has any cash. Their only equity is in their house. Keeping that equity in a good state of repair is imperative, for the house has to last until the owners are so elderly they have to sell up and move into Ocean View Haven. Also it really doesn't cost much to keep your house shipshape, mostly time and whatever paint or brushes you can borrow. As for the ubiquitous white-vinyl siding, the price was low for the protection it afforded, and it was widely said to be cheaper in the long run than either the dearest of the long-lasting paints or the cheapest of the early peelers and fast faders. Clever sales pitches were offered, with lines such as "You'll always feel it's the best thing you ever spent your husband's hard-earned money on."

A fellow was pulling off the main road onto the St. Shotts Road. He was going home, he'd been to the bank maybe, and he braked and started rolling his window down, as if he wanted to talk. He wanted to tell me a funny story the bank manager had told him. There's probably some other guy in St. Shotts with a little red car, and he thought I was him. But then he saw my face and he looked shy and embarrassed, and he took off in a big hurry. He thought he knew me, and it's a ritual in these remote parts to roll the window down and say things like "How's your mom, Ed?"

St. Mary's Bay is a proud daughter of the Atlantic, which on the map gives the southern coast of the Avalon Peninsula the look of a cloven hoof. St. Stephens, one of many small communities on the shore of said bay, is an interestingly scattered collection of small white houses. The two-storey ones resemble a large cube of sugar – as long as they are wide as they are tall – and, to add to the effect, the roof is either flat or only slightly slanted. They're plain, but pleasing to the eye. They seem to be outnumbered by the more svelte and rectangular single-storey houses, somewhat less Newfoundlandish to my eye, and with sharply peaked roofs so you're not in danger of the roof collapsing under thirty feet of snow – it just slides off.

There's more to the symmetry of these two-storey houses than their cuboid shape: there's a door on the main floor, perfectly centred, with a window on each side perfectly squared. There are three windows on the second floor, the two outer ones directly above the downstairs two, and the middle one directly above the door. And sometimes, when there are only two rooms upstairs, there will be only two windows on the second floor, one over each lower window, and nothing over the door, so that each house looks like a face with two eyes looking out over the sea, still searching for those whom others have long forgotten.

Across the Holyrood Pond Causeway and farther north for a few miles, the houses are more likely to be freshly painted than to be vinyl-sided – and the colours are wild. The people here seem to be rebelling against the pale, frigid monotony of the all-white communities. First off there's a snow-white house with a bright and extremely vivid purple trim. Smashing! A cloud spreads its feathery wings and a sunbeam shines straight down on the house. As the cloud shifts farther, the sunbeam moves on to another, this one a smaller, snow-white house with a bright blue trim. What an eyesore! Just kidding – actually it's quite the treat after all these vestal-virgin villages. And check it out, here's a canary-yellow house with a lipstick-red trim. And there's a paler yellow house with an enamel-like trim the glossy brown of the glaze on a chocolate eclair.

From all over the province, from Port aux Basques to Pouch Cove, from St. Anthony to St. Alban's, thoughtful people with civilized and subtle minds phone in to the radio show to discuss in great detail the performance of their elected representatives. Character, integrity, and being in touch with home base are the virtues required of the successful candidate. Political philosophy or position on the political spectrum is just so much baloney if you're not there to offer assistance when the harbour is blocked with ice or when the church steeple gets blown away in a storm.

An old gentleman, on the phone right now, wants to know if the radio-show host is old enough to remember the "poorhouse" (pronounced "powerhouse") that used to be in St. John's before Confederation. "The people who lived in this powerhouse looked better than the poor people today," he says. This is his subtle and civilized way of suggesting the provincial government might consider providing more social benefits for the poor. Why should the rich get them all? My hopes that the host would ask the old guy more about his memories of the poorhouse were dashed, however, as the host just wanted to get it over with fast.

"Remember dat, d'ye remember dat?" the old fellow was saying.

No, the host wasn't old enough to remember that, but when he was going to broadcasting school, his mother used to say, "If you keeps spending money like dat ye'll have me in the poorhouse." And before the old fellow with the dangerous ideas can say another word, the host adds, "Well, Angus, thank you very much fer yer point, old friend. 'Bye fer now."

Newfoundland Newsflash: On the two o'clock news a young woman in Stephenville is "very pleased" to have won the $10-million lottery – and she hopes this will mean her husband will come home from Alberta, because the kiddies miss him something fierce.

A friendly old fellow who filled my tank at his filling station wanted to know if I was from Toronto. He said he could tell, because he used to live up around there. The wind was bitterly cold, but his wife was eating a chocolate ice-cream cone with a psychotic look in her eye.

During the 1940s he'd worked near Toronto, managing a string of pool rooms. He managed to raise enough money to buy a two-hundred-acre farm near Milton, Ontario. There was a deep thoughtfulness in his voice, as if he thinks about those years a lot, but doesn't get to talk about them much. They farmed a few years. Then they got homesick. They sold up and returned to Newfoundland.

That was forty years ago, but there was a sense in the air that she's glad they came back, and he suffers in silence.

Now she was looking at her ice cream as if she wished it would hurry on and start melting, because it tastes better that way. She had the look of a serious chocolate ice-cream addict. She'll have to go cold turkey like a cool cat or be found dead in a walk-in freezer somewhere. I know what I'm talking about. I used to be one. But I licked it.

Last year they decided to hop in their car and take a sentimental journey down to Upper Canada. They could hardly find the old farm, but when they did they were shocked to see that the farmhouse had been torn down, the farmlands had been torn up, everything was an awful mess. What had been terrific farmland, woodlands, and trout streams is all apartment buildings and gravel pits now.

He liked my suggestion that Newfoundland today would be like southern Ontario in the forties, when you could still breathe the air without a care and drink from the tap without mishap. "Dat's de way I remembers it too," he declared. "And ye know what else? I seems to remember there was a bluebird on pretty near every fence post."

It's low-slung, multi-gabled, red-roofed, hexagonal in shape, storm-proof, and painted white, with recessed entranceways. It sits high on a green cliff over the silvery diamond sea at the Cape St. Mary's Ecological Reserve. It's a squat and angular interpretive centre, where the gannets, black-winged kittiwakes, common murres and thick-billed murres, great cormorants and double-breasted cormorants (known locally as shags), black guillemots, Murray snowbirds, pelican ducks, mergansers, and sea eagles go to find out about human beings. It's known as the Dr. Leslie M. Tuck Centre, named after the famous naturalist and ornithologist from Shoal Harbour. You'll have noticed the lack of puffins in that list. No oversight. They don't nest here. Never have.

"No puffins. Puffin flybys is about it," says the young fellow with the round, soft, smiling, handsome face of the official spokesperson. "They don't nest here, for the soil's too rocky." He said this was arctic terrain, this was tundra we were standing on, the southern-most example of it. If you want to see puffins, you go to the Witless Bay Seabird Ecological Reserve (on the eastern shore of the Avalon

Peninsula, just north of Ferryland) and they take you on a boat tour. You see 'em that way; it's just too rocky around here.

> *"An egg of the Great Auk is not to be had for a song."*
> – Lewis Carroll

Paul Harris was the fellow's name. We were standing next to a stuffed great auk (*Pinguinus impennis*), looking as if alive. The auk family includes the common puffin, the dovekie, the razorbill, the common murre, the thick-billed murre – all North Atlantic species – and another dozen in the North Pacific. But the great auk was the only species of the auk family with wings too short for flight. And it is now the only member of this family to be extinct, the last one having been butchered in 1844. It is not known if their wings had become too small or their bodies too big. But something went wrong, and flightless auks have proven not to have had what it takes to survive the *Homo sapiens* takeover of the planet.

Paul Harris is a likeable young fellow, and he is a student at Memorial University in St. John's, studying criminology and biology. Yes, they had a two-for-one special, he says, with a deadpan look that gets us both giggling. He enthralls me by demonstrating how the eggs of the great auk were narrower at one end, so that, if they rolled, they would roll around in circles and not roll straight off the rock. He had me full of amazement and admiration for the evolutionary intelligence of that poor extinct creature that could swim better than most fish could fly.

But a few days later I would get thinking and realize I'd been conned again. All bird's eggs are narrower at one end. Some of us may be fooled easily by smart young whippersnappers like Mr. Harris, but not for long. Then again, he may have been repeating the story his professor had told him. Perhaps he had not reflected upon it himself. But I doubt it.

Prior to sending me off on my expedition to the scary high cliffs, he told me what to look for, and how to identify the major species and so on. He gave me a brilliant little series of birdwatching tips, then directed me to a point thirty feet from the gannet colony.

"Looks a bit scary, Paul," I said.

"It is, so be extra careful," he solemnly advised. "Try not to get too close to the edge. We're about three hundred feet high most places around here."

There was a notable lack of railings, and it was hard to believe nobody had ever slipped off this amazing precipice out of a Wagnerian opera. All sorts of drops like this are found on the west coast of Canada, and people are forever falling off and being killed on the rocks below, or falling to their deaths when the cliff they're sitting on, drinking in the view, collapses with no warning.

"Once you're out there," said Paul, "if you look to your left, you'll see these guys, the smallest member of the gull family." He pointed to a picture of the black-winged kittiwake. "We've got ten thousand nesting pairs out there. They haven't laid any eggs as of yet. The gannets have, but not the kittiwakes. So if you see a gannet that's sitting for a long period of time, keep watching it, have a little patience, and if it lifts up you may see an egg underneath."

That would be nice, I thought, but I'd rather see a whale. "No whales yet. The whales generally move in close to the cliffs when the capelin come in, which is usually the first week of July around here on the south shore, but it varies from year to year, depending on weather conditions, climate, temperature, and what have you." He switched back to his first love real fast. "These guys, the common murres and the thick-billed murres, can be seen on the bottom-most ledges. . . ."

These are the auk look-alikes?

"That's exactly right. The only difference between the common right here, and the thick-billed right here" – he was indicating pictures on the wall – "is the thick-billed has a white stripe extending from the bill. Other than that, it's exactly the same colour, the same size, what have you."

And they don't have anything to do with each other?

"They generally keep apart, but occasionally you'll see them swimming together."

The way to the nesting grounds is to the east, across an unspoiled stretch of cliff-top tundra that has been ground zero for many dramatic storms since before time began; in fact the Cape St. Mary's Lighthouse, to the west of the Centre, is said to have been torn apart by storms three times in the early years.

I'm not sure how they define tundra locally, but there must be permafrost down a few feet. Anyway, this is the southernmost patch, and the shrimpy-but-hardy spruce "trees" along the edge of the cliffs get their nutrients from the spray from the fifty-foot waves smashing into the scary cliffs and from the supersaturated sea winds. But every time the spruce puts up a little vertical shoot, along comes a rough wind and nips it off. The ground is alive with spruce trees, and some are five hundred years old, but their only option is to grow sideways, and they never get more than a few inches off the ground. A human being is the tallest thing in this environment, a flat, natural waste-land suddenly plunging straight down to the savage sea. At the point of the plunge, there is a sudden outcropping of warm-blooded life, what seems like a billion birds, all going through the rituals of co-operative domesticity (one little family in each cliff-side condo).

The wildflowers are everywhere in profusion, but there is no sign that any of them are about to blossom. Each little bud is curled up as tightly as a hard ball of rubber bands, patiently waiting for the sun to tap it on the shoulder and ask for a dance. Wild irises are everywhere, but they're not even showing a hint of their colours.

I still can't believe that tourists haven't been swept off the cliffs and into the sea around here. Frankly, I have to screw up my courage just to look through the field glasses, because I'll lose track of my proximity to the edge. What did Paul mean by "too near the edge"? Am I too near now, not near enough, or what? And the wind is so powerful that, if it suddenly stopped, one might just get sucked right over the edge like a mannequin in a movie. Would a falling human scream out a song of farewell, or would he just fall quietly with a smile of resignation?

At the edge of the cliff I have a bird's-eye view of a zillion birds all breathing and breeding as one. It's like being an American golden plover looking down at a city full of people. The wind is powerful, but I'm keeping a strong grip on the stunted spruce trees to infuse my soul with a semblance of serenity. I was listening to the babel of the gannets, and just for pure appearance there is no lovelier bird to look upon brooding, or just walking around stretching its wings, or flying too, but I was too focused on the drop to make a definitive study of their nesting habits. And I didn't really give a hoot if I saw an egg or not.

When I returned to the Centre, Paul took me into the screening room and put on a nature documentary that had been shot in the area, with lots of Irish-like music. I was the only one in the audience, but I'm sure that, as the season progresses, business will pick up. One thing that sticks in my mind is the reference to a storm in the 1940s that "swept away" forty fishing boats and all the men in them.

Placentia is a large old town (pop. 5,013), famous for its lift bridge (the only one in Newfoundland), its waterfront boardwalk (one of many in Newfoundland, but a particularly nice one), and its no-nonsense coat of arms, with the word Placentia on the top, Plaisance (the original Basque name) on the bottom, and logos representing the cannon (for history) and the lift bridge (for progress).

That lift bridge, it's really something, and it certainly gives Placentia a touch of pizzazz. It's special. Many stay-at-home types may live and die without seeing another. When it was built in 1961, Placentia felt more connected to the world. That's been the recent history of Newfoundland: isolated communities suddenly finding themselves connected, by road, ferry, train, telephone, computer, lift bridge. . . .

Placentia is full of character in a pleasantly messy, sloppy, laid-back, down-home way. It's a town with tons of testosterone and enough history to keep a team of writers writing till Doomsday. It was the capital of Newfoundland for a time, but that was before the Treaty of Utrecht. . . .

All those cars filling the vast parking lot out front would make one think Harold's Motel and Lounge would be all booked up. But *au contraire*; the manager almost fell over when I asked for a room. When she turned her back momentarily, I checked the book, and it appears I'm the first (paying) overnight guest since last Christmas. You can't judge a hotel by its parking lot. It turned out all the cars were for the slot machines and the bingo game downstairs, with some overflow from the Mary Brown's chicken franchise next door.

The slot zombies and the bingo maniacs must be keeping the place going. They love sitting in front of their slot machines day and night, with friends bringing them potato chips and Pepsi, the breakfast of slot champions, so they don't have to budge from their spots by the slots.

The bar was empty. Booze doesn't mix with bingo and slots. Mostly the slot addicts are sweet old-timers. All their lives, they've been devoted to family, church, neighbours. But lately they've changed alarmingly. They get in front of a slot machine like dogs guarding a bone. If you put a gun to their head they'd just keep playing. Even if they do win a big pot, it will all go back into the slot.

It all delivers the same message: the way they stand or sit in front of the machine, their silent communion with flashing lights, bugle calls, ding-dong bells, funny little organ chords. They can push all the buttons on the slot machine, but if they could only push the right buttons inside their own hearts, they wouldn't be lining up outside the bars in the morning.

There was also a bingo going on that night, downstairs in the dining room. The players were sitting erectly at rows and rows of tables and chairs. At first it looked like a bowling banquet, though they did seem a bit cramped for dining, and all they had was potato chips. And their body language showed they were concentrating really hard, as one must do if one wishes to win at bingo.

Meanwhile, I said to a row of people at the slots, "Any winners here?" Nobody said a word, but the lady who runs the place was walking by and said, "They're *all* winners." She arched a brow to show she meant winners in the same way that pretty well everyone in jail is innocent – which makes it tough for the ones who really are.

"Don't get addicted to this now," I said. Two elderly ladies looked at me blankly, as if they hoped that didn't mean I had come to take the machines away. A middle-aged player who was still a slot virgin, still a bit conscious of his surroundings, said, "Oh not me. I've got this number on the wall." No idea what he meant by that. I glanced at the number, but didn't catch its significance. One would think he would have two numbers on the wall, and quit when he went above the high number or below the low number. But of course this scheme, like a finger in the dyke holding back the floods, never works for long; your dirty little mind finds all kinds of reasons for going over or under the limit. Oh life, oh nature, oh joy! It's amazing the numerous ways we've devised to separate the poor from the little they have. If they give heroin addicts methadone, what kind of drug would help the slot addicts? It would have to be something they could depend on to break their addiction without causing a new one – and, of course, not too pricey.

But let's not overlook the religious aspect to this addiction: although they haven't consciously taken any vows of poverty, the slot addicts are becoming penniless faster than Saint Francis. Also, their money is going to charity. At least a small percentage of it is. Theoretically.

Now dig this, hepcats. I'm up in my room, in my pyjamas, I have a beer and a sandwich, I flick on the TV, and what do I see? The

Placentia Lions Club is sponsoring a bingo! The flickering black-and-white image of a fat lady dressed up like Eleanor Roosevelt barks out bingo letter-number combos in a snarling monotone, with split-second pacing, like a perfect percussionist. Isn't that odd! All day people have been lining up at the pharmacy to get their bingo cards, and now it would appear that everybody who isn't downstairs playing bingo, or the slots, is at home in front of the TV with their cards out, playing bingo.

It's not a character defect that turns you into a slot zombie. It's the machines. They're programmed to program you. You just have to stay away from them. If slots had been around in T.S. Eliot's time, he might have been hooked. Then he'd have written:

> *This is the way the world will end:*
> *Bingo and slot machines.*

KEEPING CANADA COMPANY

Placentia • Argentia • Come by Chance
Gloverton • Burin Peninsula

Friday, May 25. Today's weather is the same in Baffin Island as it is in Newfoundland: 4 degrees Celsius and clear skies. Harold's Motel and Lounge looks as if it's been here forever, except that it was brand new once, and people would get dressed up and come from all over the south shore to gape at it, back around 1947. Imagine, a two-storey nineteen-room motel! Placentia is really going places!

This morning Placentia's lift bridge was the scene of a bad spill. It's a tall, handsome, beautifully proportioned, and much-photographed two-lane structure that can be seen from a bend in the main highway ten klicks up the valley. But a fellow was going a bit too fast in his pink-and-white rusted-out Cadillac with tail fins; as he drove over the bridge, which was sitting about three inches above the road pavement, he hit that three-inch ledge with just enough torque to break his front axle. This caused his old car to come screeching to a halt half on the bridge and half on Highway 100, with its left wheel sticking out at a terrible angle, like a spilled skier with a broken leg. I was a minute too late to witness the accident, but arrived in time to see the driver in the car, sobbing. I was on my way down to Argentia and decided to keep going. Many others were ready to help him get straightened out.

But when I came back, two hours later, the car was still on the bridge. The driver, who seemed from a distance to be wearing a fake beard, had stopped crying and was pacing back and forth talking to himself. For some reason they couldn't tow that car in, but a tow truck from the garage was parked on the bridge, and a mechanic was trying to replace the entire front axle on location, with traffic lined up for several blocks, as vehicle after vehicle squeezed its way through, like drops of glucose in an intravenous tube. There was no horn-honking, but everybody looked exasperated, as if they were in a terrible hurry, and this was the last straw. So even Newfoundland people can be rushed and stressed out when little things happen like a breakdown on a bridge.

It may be that the tow truck had been back and forth trying out different axles for this rare old car and was having trouble finding one that would fit. And I don't want to get anyone in trouble here, but it appeared that the accident was caused by the bridge not being properly seated, or the lift mechanism might have been switched off prematurely, leaving the bridge surface a few inches above the road surface. I'd be sure to check out the bridge operator. He may have seen this guy coming along in the old Caddy and innocently lifted the bridge a notch just to give him a little jolt, just as a friendly joke. Oh well, nobody was killed.

Out of Placentia on the way to Argentia there's a handsome new log-cabin convenience store at the side of the road, and something told me they'd have good coffee. They didn't actually have any for sale by the cup, but we got talking, me and Dan Pomroy, and his photographer wife, Darlene, who has put a pot on. Soon the aroma of coffee fills the store, with the aroma of frozen sticky raisin buns defrosting.

Like Marilyn and Ambrose before them, Dan and Darlene have known each other forever. Darlene bills herself as an "innovative photographer." Her studio is incorporated into the store, which sells local crafts, hip waders, fly swatters, tricycles, crayons and colouring books, blue jeans and jackets, belts, winter parkas, hammers and saws, canned goods – and, in a modest sort of way, almost under the counter, Darlene's excellent photographs, either in frames or matted.

Her work is truly innovative, but without a hint of pretention. She just takes pictures, with her heart, of things that interest her – the Placentia lift bridge, for instance. She was up doing some aerial photography and has a really good shot of the bridge from the air, along with pictures of the numerous interesting buildings in Placentia, including the long, low-slung Spanish-colonial–style Sacred Heart church, with its sturdy white tower and its red tile roof. So there's a lot of recognizable local shots that she's admired for, and also still lifes, photos of piles of lobsters, and so on. Each picture is a microcosm of her world view and a testament to the fullness of her heart. The next time I see a pile of lobsters, or the Placentia lift bridge, it'll be at least partially through her eyes, thanks to her photos.

So this isn't a traditional convenience store and she's not a traditional photographer. In fact the first day in photography school, she vowed never to do weddings. She didn't want to imagine her work being torn up in anger in years to come.

As with all artists, it was easy to get Darlene talking about things other than her work. The seal hunt? "They're sayin' there's no fish here. Well, the seals are eatin' the fish. And if you take one seal eats ten fish a day, that's a lot of consumption when you've got millions of seals." That's an opinion heard more often lately, but she has others. For instance the decade-old cod moratorium might have a sinister side to it. What exactly are those giant trawlers doing out there on the horizon?

"The trawlers are out there and heaven knows what they're taking up. So it's an issue that's got to be put forward and proven that it's the seals that are destroying the cod fishery, or the fishermen are destroying it, or the trawlers are destroying it, or maybe it's a bit of everything. Those trawlers could be taking more fish than ever."

She had a legitimate suspicion that every ton of cod that wasn't being caught by Newfoundlanders was now being caught by foreign trawlers. And there wasn't much the Canadian government seemed to be doing about it.

"And you take the herring boats," she said. "The herring boats go along with a vacuum, they suck up everything that's on the bottom of the ocean – for herring. Now what does that destroy? They're getting the herring, yes. Right? But then what else are they getting with it?"

By this time the three of us were in the back room drinking coffee. Then Darlene's dad popped in for a visit. "Good day! Come in, come on in here." She giggles like an affectionate teenager. "Now here's my dad. He'll tell you about huntin' an' fishin'. Dave, do you hunt an' fish?"

Dad comes in shyly, but with a big smile on his little face. He's always happy to be alive, says Darlene. I compliment him on his fine daughter and son-in-law and ask what he did to deserve such luck. He chuckles shyly. "I don't know. I musta done somethin' right, I guess." He's a retired auto mechanic, retired fifteen years, and he's pretty sure he's got all the grease scrubbed off now. He started talking about the different shades of opinion on the seal hunt and how certain he was that, in any referendum, the people of Newfoundland would vote to "stop, er, support the slaughter." His interesting half-slip suggested that, deep in his heart, he knows it's wrong to kill seals for their coats, unless you have no choice.

Dan, whose chief trade is carpentry, was the more forceful and more natural speaker, so he silently appointed himself major spokesman, leaving Dad and Darlene to listen quietly. He insisted there'd be little support among Newfoundland voters for banning the seal hunt. But even Dan seemed to have a little private part of himself, sitting in a dark corner somewhere, that would like to see the ban put in place. I didn't say anything about the inner doubts I sensed in them, but after a while Darlene switched over to the animal-rights position – and fairly strongly, too. Not all the way, but over half.

Dan figured the seal hunt couldn't be banned "because of the cultural an' historical aspect," which seemed a weak argument. The issue about the seals killing off the cod was stronger. The seal population didn't increase in the same curve the cod decreased, but the seals are on the increase. For instance, all three of them agreed that Placentia Bay never had a large seal population in their long memories, but now they're even finding seals on the road and way up the rivers.

Darlene: "One time you'd never see a seal in the ha'bour, and now they're in."

Dan: "They're in all the time. They're on the highway!"

Darlene: "Yeah! And they're up the rivers!"

Dan: "But there's too many seals. I mean they're really truly immensely abundant. There's no predator for the seal. So they're not manageable. Man was controlling it, but now there's no seal hunt, no large-scale seal hunt, right?"

Meanwhile, the Newfoundland writer Ray Guy has always been opposed to the hunt. "The only virtue salvaged from a couple of centuries of seal killing was stoicism in the face of misery and calamity," he states somewhere. And he claims the value of the seal hunt to Newfoundland's economy is about the same as cuckoo-clock manufacturing to the German economy. Tourism could kill the seal hunt in a flash if enough visitors stayed home in protest, but it's getting so that seal issues aren't huge in the public mind these days. The tourist industry is worth $500 million, according to Guy, while the sealing industry's worth is, though a tiny fraction of that, not easy to pin down. The Canadian government claims it's so many millions of dollars a year, the International Fund for Animal Welfare (IFAW) claims it's one-tenth that after accounting for government subsidies, and the Canadian Sealers Association says it's worth twice what the government claims.

I was surprised I still hadn't found anyone in my travels fundamentally opposed to the cruelty of the seal hunt. Then it was Dan's turn for the sort of slip of the tongue that reveals a deeper opinion: he insisted that I'd been talking to the "wrong" people, when obviously he meant the right people, the ones who agree with him, the ones who aren't opposed to the hunt.

Dad plunged in with great passion for an old guy, even though Dan kept trying to cut him off. "If you ban the hunt, you'll have no fish," said Dad. "You'll have no trout if you did dat. Nothing. Those seals right now, around the mouths of the rivers at the spring of the year, with the salmon running down the river, and in June and July when they run up, they're catching everything, you know. There's hardly any trout left in the ponds or salmon even way up the rivers."

As for the natural predator of the seal, Dan brought up the polar bear, but Dad said polar bears around here, unlike humans, "are scarce and not that plentiful." Dan suggested the whale, but Dad said whales prefer small fish like the capelin. "Dem whales," said Dad, "dey're big beasts but dey got good table manners."

"And den for all der size dey has de small froats," said Dan.

"Exactly," said Dad.

Dan tackled the cruelty issue by calling it both emotional and fashionable to be against the hunt. He said, "What could be more cruel than veal?" He defined the term nicely: "An animal that's put in a cage and raised without movement. Tsk."

I wanted to know why, rather than brutally skinning them alive, the hunters just didn't shoot the seals nice and neat with a twenty-two handgun at close range.

"In one ear and out de udder you mean," said Dad, who had definitely conquered his shyness.

Then Dan, after telling us it's an emotional issue, got emotional. He said the sealers do shoot the seals rather than skin them alive.

Dan: "Dey do dat. De cruel part, dat's not de bulk. Dat's de ones dat dey manage to capture on video. Dat's not de average, dat's not de run-o'-de-mill sealer, I don't think. Dere's not many human beings dat cruel. Dat's just what's get exploited."

Dave: "I'm hearing you."

Dad: "No, I mean nobody wants to see that."

Dan: "No, I mean dere's cruel people in every society, no mind where you come from, we know dat. Dat makes headlines. Dey's de ones dat makes de headlines, not de responsible ones."

Dave: "So are these bashers and skinners trying to save a bullet or what?"

Dan [pauses to think]: "Naw, I don't think so. I think it's nudding only cruelish foolety, I mean foolish cruelty, an' a lark – an' I know one of de videos dat came out a liddle while ago, it sounded to me an awful lot like it was staged." I think he was alluding to one produced by the IFAW. "An' dey got people gullible enough for a few bucks and dey get caught up in it. An' I watched it, and I know two people, him and her" – he points at Dad and Darlene – "dere's nobody in de world wid any more respect for animals dan dem, believe me, to treat animals right. My wife couldn't even watch it on television."

The building that houses the store, the studio, and the kitchen was obviously of recent construction and was built of richly varnished cedar logs and planks. The three of them built it themselves, with friends, and when they finished, the first thing they did was have a big party, right in the store, and they didn't even have any Mainlanders there to ask stupid questions and raise suspicions.

So then Dan got suspicious and wanted more information on the kind of book I was writing. He wanted to know if I was maybe under disguise, and the whole book was going to be about the seal hunt. He finally blurted it out. "You're not with the IFAW, are you?"

"Not yet, but I might just join after this trip."

Darlene said she was a member, "an' it makes it a bit confusing at times."

Dan said, if I wanted the last word on seals, they knew someone I should check out. "He's a good guy and as a matter of fact he's from our hometown here. Rex Murphy. A well-educated man. Do you know Rex?"

"Not Rex Murphy, that bloodthirsty seal-basher from the CBC?"

"That's him!" squealed Darlene, who was definitely softening her pro-hunt stance.

"Now, now," said Dan. "He's not that bad last I checked."

Dan was being terribly blasé about being on familiar terms with the one-and-only Rex Murphy, a veritable Canadian icon. "Oh, that Rex!" he says. He casually points out the window. "It was over de hill dere in de community of Freshwater where he was born and reared. And one of de best times I ever heard Rex, in language we all understand" (Dan shrewdly acknowledges Rex's propensity for obfuscation at times) "was when he took on Rick Smith of the IFAW, in a straightforward no-holds-barred debate. Nobody could hold a candle to him, cuz every point Rex had him. He knows, he remembers. I guess it's his livelihood to know what's going on in public and current affairs, eh?"

Meanwhile, I sense that Dan and Darlene must have a good marriage, because she belongs to the IFAW and he likes Rex Murphy. I suggested a pro-hunt–anti-hunt "mixed marriage" in Newfoundland would be almost as bad as a Catholic–Protestant marriage in Belfast.

But Darlene didn't marry Dan for his politics, and Dan thinks Darlene's a honey bunch: whatever she says is right, even if it may be wrong. In fact, he can be more pro-hunt than he ordinarily would be in order to compensate for his wife's anti-hunt stance. No problem. To me, that's a Newfoundland sort of thing. Just because you and your partner have opposing opinions on all the big issues of the contemporary world, there's no reason to quarrel.

At one point Dan was talking about last year's shrimp wars with Prince Edward Island. There was so much upset at Ottawa's new shrimp quotas, some Newfoundland grocery stores refused to stock P.E.I. potatoes. I asked him to explain the problem, and he came out with a spontaneous iambic-pentameter couplet to rival Shakespeare, one of those fiery couplets at the end of a sonnet that sums everything up so neatly:

We can't go over dere and get it from dem,
But dey come over here and get it from us.

When we got talking about the lobster situation, Dan got excited
again and came out with another heroic couplet that wouldn't look
out of place in *Hamlet*, if the place names were changed:

De lobster dat dey catch in P.E.I.
Is not even a legal lobster in Newfoundland.

I'd asked Marilyn Kenny, and now I was asking Dan Pomroy: why
does everything and everybody look so prosperous in spite of the low
average income?

"Well, how would this happen on the Mainland what happened
with this building, as an example?" he said. "I didn't pay no labour.
That don't happen on the Mainland. If you want someone to shovel
your driveway, you pay. If you want someone to do anything for you,
you pay. And you pay dearly."

Unlike his wife, Dan was raised on an isolated island in Placentia
Bay. The population never reached four hundred at the best of times.
Everybody was part of an extended family that interlocked with all
the other extended families. And everybody helped everybody else.
Working for your neighbour was the same as working for yourself.

"You see, that's the way you had to do, cuz there was no subsidies,
there was no social services, and if you had a family member that was
down and out or the husband died, well everyone had to chip in to
keep that family afloat. Right? That type of thing? But other than
that, I couldn't explain, it's different. You wouldn't drive along the
highway and not stop to help someone. . . ."

"Arf, arf," said a big black mutt named Nellie in the corner, then
resumed snoring. All of a sudden I shivered, realizing we were standing on a rock in the middle of the North Atlantic.

I mentioned that earlier today I'd been in a little "department store" in Placentia. There's a chain of these, called Riff's. The cashier mentioned I'd really cut my face bad this morning. I said it served me right, because I was trying to get one more shave out of my last blade. She said I should get an electric razor. I said do you sell them? "We only have the one kind here," she said, "and it's no good."

I rolled my eyes and gave them a "Nothing like this has been known to happen in Toronto for forty years" look. Darlene and Dan hooted happily.

"Oh, you'll get that around here," they said.

"She said get the Philishave, that's the kind my husband has, but we don't have them here. I said that if she said something like that working in a store in St. John's, they'd fire her. She said she wasn't moving anywhere, she liked it here just fine."

"Maybe we're too old-fashioned," said Dan, suddenly depressed. "Maybe we're too trusting, I don't know."

Darlene lived in Toronto for a year. Same old story. Nobody would talk to her. Yet when Toronto people come up here everybody stops and talks to them.

I told her Torontonians wouldn't stop because they were in a hurry to get to the bar for happy hour. I told her I'm always friendly to Newfoundlanders, wherever we cross paths. And I added that they sometimes make snide comments such as "At last, somebody dat speaks English."

"Yeah," said Dan. "But I mean dere's more people on de streets of Toronto than there is on welfare in Newfoundland – and we're classed as a welfare province for far too long." He knew for sure there were no homeless people in Newfoundland and fewer people on social services than there are homeless in Toronto. "And no matter wheres you go to you get social services, right? That's the thing about it. I mean you [meaning the federal government] traded off our fish fer de wheat, so if you hadn't got to make that wheat deal how many out west'd be on it [social services], havin' trouble? Oh we've been the kicking can of the country fer too long."

I laughed. "Did you say you've been keeping Canada company for too long?"

"Yeah, that too," said Dan. "And what's this happy hour ye were mentionin'?"

"Oh, that's where you get two glasses of Screech for the price of one."

"That's what they told us when we voted to join Canada."

Dan told me, "You'll do okay if you want to go up to the northeast coast for the icebergs, if ye've got any fondness for icebergs."

"I've been fond of one or two in my time."

"Not that kind, Dave. The big white ones wif only de tip above de water."

"I think they're really cool. Somebody should make vodka out of them."

"I cannot believe dis guy!" says Darlene.

"Er, we already do dat, Dave," said Dan.

"Oh yeah, I forgot."

Darlene said it was lucky I didn't go to all the trouble of applying for a patent. I still don't know if they think I was joking or not. I was – in fact, I even buy a bottle of Newfoundland iceberg vodka from time to time.

But thanks, Darlene, Dan, and Dad – it was definitely a 3-D experience. And don't worry about double negatives or whatever. As long as you have a double positive in your heart, that's the important thing. With a bit of effort you could have everybody in Canada talking Newfoundlandish. It would further distinguish us from the Yanks.

Here's a little girl who's walking along the highway with her mother, and she's on one side and her mother's on the other, and as they walk they both have their eyes glued to their respective roadside ditches.

What are they doing? Well, like many others all over the island, they are searching for refundable bottles and cans or anything else of value. Poor things. They look respectable, they're clean, and they take good care of themselves. But they definitely don't look happy. Daddy is ahead in his suv, waiting for them to catch up before he moves on ahead for another mile. Somebody's got to stay with the vehicle, right?

If Newfoundland is such a fisherman's paradise, why don't they just get a string, a hook, and a worm, and catch some trout? A creel of trout around the waist would look better than a creel of old beer cans. Maybe it's because they don't lack for food, but they need some cash money fast to make a payment on some loan or they'll be foreclosed.

Anyway, the little girl was about thirteen and looked embarrassed as I drove by. This was a little-travelled (but well-paved) highway. The girl was hoping there'd be no traffic at all before they finished. The mother didn't care, though. She was frowning in profoundly determined concentration and only had eyes for the ditch.

Come by Chance is a famous Newfoundland town, right up there with Corner Brook and St. John's, but it's a tiny place, there's nothing to it. I know there's the world's smelliest oil refinery down a bit, but I can smell it from here and have no desire to see it. There's not even a sign saying "Come Again" when you leave. It has what may seem to some a naughty name, but of course it's a local nautical term. There's a Chance Cove down the coast a bit, and you can either come by Chance or come the other way.

With all these convenience stores along the main street it could be described as the convenience town for the entire isthmus. I went in one after another, hoping to get a coffee to go, but nothing resembling such a thing was available. In one store, I'd just been told no coffee, then another shopper came from the back. She was the prettiest creature, and with lots of character too, with luxurious blond hair to her shoulders, a face like an eccentric intellectual angel who is currently memorizing *Middlemarch* in case great literature is banned in the New World Order. She looked like such-and-such a star in such-and-such a movie. Make that Veronica Lake in *Sullivan's Travels*.

But she was wearing camouflage trousers with a big hunting knife in her belt and a leather jacket, and she had left her car running outside. It was a little red car like mine, except with a large hand-painted image of the Road Runner on the back. So, as I went toward the door *sans café*, she called out, "What was it you were looking for?" So I says, "Just a coffee, I'm fading fast." Then she says, "Just go up to the Irving station, they have coffee there. What way were you going?" West. "You shouldn't have come to Come by Chance, you should have kept going, just a bit longer, and you would have had your coffee by now."

She paid for her cigarettes and a six-pack of beer. I looked deeply into her eyes and said in my best Bogie voice: "She smokes, she drinks!" She said, with a laugh, "Oh, this isn't for me." We walked out together. I said, "Enjoy your party." She said, "Oh, it isn't really a party." She got into my car, I got into hers. Then we both realized our mistake, laughed ourselves silly, and switched cars.

I had this sudden Woody Allen fantasy that she would pull into the Irving station behind me and we could have a coffee together. But by the time I got to the Irving station, she was way up on the Nevermore Peninsula somewhere, giving the beer and cigarettes to their rightful owner, and not having a party.

There's something about a beautiful woman with a hunting knife in her belt that makes me feel like a young bull in springtime. But to her I'd be just another grizzled old veteran of seasons long forgotten. Besides, she was expected back with that beer and cigarettes.

It's 7:20 p.m., and the setting sun is blinding me as I drive west along the Trans-Canada Highway toward the Burin Peninsula cutoff at

Goobies. There's a pull to head north from here to Trinity, where they're making the movie version of *The Shipping News*, a novel set in Newfoundland and by an American, apparently not a book that's well liked in Newfoundland, but adored everywhere else. I should head up there and talk to the star, Kevin Spacey, tell him how much I loved him in whatever previous movies he was in, and see if he'd be interested in some novels I'd like to see filmed – novels not only set in Canada but written by Canadians – terrific older ones such as Hugh Garner's *Cabbagetown* or Patricia Blondal's *A Candle to Light the Sun*, then maybe some really good newer ones as well. So I pull off into the big town of Clarenville (population 5,000), near Shoal Harbour where the late Dr. Tuck, the famous naturalist, was born. I need to do some thinking and have a bite to eat.

The federal MP for this area is the Liberal cabinet minister Brian Tobin (who would soon announce his surprise resignation), and the biggest sign in the mall is the one advertising his riding office. It's right next to Rod's Restaurant, with its smaller sign saying "Eat In – Take Out – We Serve Breakfast."

Rod's has a good reputation, but it was my first dining dis-appointment in Newfoundland. The fish was deep-fried to an alarming degree, with batter half an inch thick, and the french fries came from a freezer. It never occurred to me fish would be done like this in any federal riding anywhere in Newfoundland. No wonder Tobin resigned. I scarcely touched it, but I paid for it and left quietly. It would appear to be cod that had been exported to New York for processing and then sent up to the frozen-food section of the supermarkets of this amazing province, where good restaurants abound.

The waitresses (two tubby teens) were taking a little rest, so I asked them about Brian Tobin. Does he ever come in?

"Yeah, he was in yesterday," they said.

What did he have?

"He didn't have anything."

Was he just popping in to see if everyone still likes him?

"That about explains it. He comes in now and then and smiles a lot and shakes a lot of hands."

Do you like him?

(Pause.) "He's okay."

Now my heart is telling me to avoid movie sets. The tug I felt toward Trinity has been replaced by a much more powerful pull to Goobies, and then down the Burin Peninsula to the southernmost tip of the island. It's hard to explain, but leaving the Trinity Bay area for later will somehow make for a more symmetrical trip, a less wintry trip perhaps, and a better chance to see more icebergs and maybe even a whale or two.

So now I'm heading due south on the "Heritage Run," more popularly known as Highway 210 – or the road to Marystown, Grand Bank, and the ferry to Saint-Pierre. The sky is a fuzzy-feathery peach tone (like a gannet's head) on the sides, from the horizon to a third of the way up all around, with long thin pink-and-yellow cloud-strings, like a giant harp stretched across the dark background grey of the zenith. The sun is down, and a tiny shivering sliver of a silvery moon is floating in the spot where the sun would have been two hours ago. A rabbit the size of a German shepherd (it's probably an arctic hare) runs directly in front of my car with no warning, but somehow it doesn't get hit. . . .

The peach colour is now restricted to a long, thin band resting on the western horizon, but above that, an exquisite light green has formed, and above that a darker green, and then a blue, and then a darker blue, and all the little ponds dotting the dark landscape are shining like sapphires and opals, each reflecting a subtly different tone from the sky. This is a landscape to die for, and many have done so. How could anyone raised in this area ever leave for Toronto or New York?

The peachy strip of light has disappeared beneath the western horizon, leaving a strip of green, and then a whole sky full of darkness, with a brilliant new moon with the old moon in its arms, and thousands of stars blazing away like mad. There are no towns, no motels, no filling stations, I'm on empty, and just as I'm about to pull over and prepare to spend a cold night sleeping in the car, a dream materializes out of thin air on the lonely road: King Arthur and His Court. Yes, that's its name, and I'm saved! Here's everything I could desire: a filling station, with a bar, a restaurant, slot machines, pool tables, and rooms.

King Arthur and His Court is under new management and has changed its name from Wander Inn. But the Knights of the Round Table did love to wander, so there may still be a subliminal connection. A plump, smiling lady comes out to tell me how pleased they are to see me, what took me so long? And yes, they have rooms, and yes, they have everything I could possibly need, and then some. I was so happy I gave her a hug, and she was so happy because I was happy she hugged me right back.

FRIENDLY HENRIETTA
AND HER FRIENDS

Burin Peninsula • Red Harbour • Marystown
Grand Bank • Fortune Bay • Point Crue • Lawn
St. Lawrence • Lamaline • Burin

Saturday, May 26. That was Rhonda who gave me such a warm welcome last night, and another woman could be seen through the open door of the kitchen – an outport fashion model of a woman in a waitress's apron, a filling-station attendant's blue shirt with top button fastened, and a commanding appearance. She was shooting daggers at the hubbub at the front desk. This was Henrietta, and soon she'd be every bit as friendly as Rhonda. For instance, when she served dinner in the dining room, she kept calling me "my love," which Rhonda never did. So I asked why she had been glaring so disapprovingly. She denied having any disapproval in her heart, but she confessed to a pang of jealousy. She felt left out. She wanted a hug, too. So, as a gentleman of the old school, I had no choice but to stand up and give her a tender little embrace.

It was a spacious dining room, but the only other diners were four men from the tiny French island colonies of Saint-Pierre and

Miquelon, off the southern tip of the Burin Peninsula. They seemed to be government office workers, or accountants, on a trout-fishing holiday, and they were drinking claret and nibbling at desserts and coffee after a large meal. As Henrietta and I embraced, all four turned and watched with amusement and envy. Their little islands were all that was left of what was once the great French overseas empire.

"I'll have a bottle of what they're drinking," I said.

"Sorry, dey brought all dat wine wif dem, demselves. We've got everything but de wine."

I kept feeling flashes of joy at stumbling on a place like this so late at night. To be saved in such a charming manner, just when you think you're going to be shivering in your sleep all night in the car . . . it was a miracle. Even the meal was good. The garden salad had been nicely tossed, the cod had been grilled with delicate herbs and spices, and Canadian beer was the perfect substitute for French wine.

When Henrietta was taking my order, she said I could have beef stew, even though it wasn't on the menu. The reason for this was that the plan-ahead Saint-Pierre fishing team had ordered it well in advance. You have to admire that sort of paramilitary precision. All four would know exactly what they would be doing at any given time. There would be no need for any kind of serious thinking on this once-a-year pleasure trip, away from the women, away from the office – ah, let's not let anything spoil even one minute of it. On a timebound trip like that, planning is imperative.

It's amazing how well Henrietta suits her name, being exactly the kind of woman I think of as a "Friendly Henrietta" (a private archetype, no doubt), whatever her real name may be. A Friendly Henrietta in my mind is about forty, usually a Nordic redhead, with blue eyes, broad brow, narrow chin, a bright, fast mind, twinkling eyes. She's a bit imperious, but in a friendly way, and she gives you her entire attention. Friendly Henriettas are usually over average height, slightly lanky, and a bit awkward in their gait.

I had a drink later in the bar, with the versatile Henrietta doubling as bartender. She right away needed to know my date of birth, sex, and mode. What's mode? It's either pessimistic, optimistic, normal, or sadistic. I said I'm masochistic. She said it had to be one of those four. I said normal. She said she'd look it up on the Internet and tell me in the morning how long I had to live. But I might not survive the night, I said. She insisted I would.

The offshore fellows also came into the bar. Three of them had been born in Saint-Pierre and grew up there. Their English was a lot better than their drinking habits. They were sloshed. It was the last night of their holiday. Back to the ball-and-chain tomorrow. The fourth guy, who was innocent of English but appeared to be enjoying himself one minute and then full of despair and ennui the next, was a recent arrival from Paris. What crime had he committed to be transferred to such a lonely colony? Maybe he'd requested the transfer, but now regretted it and has bouts of serious homesickness – especially when visiting the vast non-French wasteland of Newfoundland, where his mother tongue has become useless for the first time in his life, perhaps. The three others were confident and competent in both French and English.

They seemed unable or unwilling to make Saint-Pierre sound alluring or even mildly interesting. All they could say was that one gets there by passenger ferry, no cars. Maybe I'll pop over – wander around town, buy a beret, a loaf of bread, a case of wine. I'll get to practise my French. Maybe I'll fall in love with the place and stay forever. It's only ten klicks off the tip of the Burin Peninsula if you have a load of contraband and need to row your own boat. If you have nothing to fear from the customs inspection, it's about a forty-klick ferry ride from Fortune Bay.

The four Frenchmen seemed to know little about events in Canada, and they even had a bit of an argument over whether Quebec had achieved independence yet. Two said no, one said yes, and the fellow from France anguished over the question but couldn't make up his mind. But if they'd really wanted to find out they would have asked me, because they knew I was from Upper Canada and would therefore be unable not to know.

The barroom here was much smaller and more intimate than the one at Burnt Berry, and a recently installed large window overlooked a black lake rippling with moonlight. Could this have been where the boys of Saint-Pierre had fished? No, they were fishing a river farther north in the Burin Peninsula. As for the bipolar Parisian, this was his first fishing trip ever, and he couldn't catch a thing, though the others were doing well. It was as if he just didn't have the knack. In my judgment, he'd be a fellow sensitive enough to worry about the feelings of the fish being hooked and pulled out of the water to die. Unwittingly, the spirits of the river sense this and arrange to keep the fish away from his hook.

In a lot of places in Newfoundland, the bartender will pour the beer into the glass, then serve the glass and stash the empty before you can see it. Often it's so quick and automatic you may wonder for a few sips if what you're tasting is what you ordered. It's said the practice of putting the empty away fast is intended to cut down on flying beer bottles in case of fights. But everything's been as peaceful as sin so far. Perhaps this is just me, I have no proof (except of course the shockingly high statistical rate of intercourse – that 8.35 times per month), but Newfoundlanders are lovers, not fighters. I sense a spark in the air and in the eye that would indicate that most everybody has either just done it or is about to do it – or both. They have hot sex here more often than we have hot meals in Toronto. Except of course for the Pentecostals and Salvation Army people. If it weren't for those spoilsports the frequency rate would be even higher.

Rhonda was now one of four people playing the slots. It's almost impossible to find an unattended slot machine anywhere in Newfoundland. Wherever there's a slot machine, some poor bastard is feeding twenty-dollar bills into it. Eventually one of the players would cash out, and it would be like musical chairs, with everybody angling to fill the one vacated. Slot machines aren't exactly a spectator sport, so the only reason several people seemed to be watching the players play was to be able to slide in fast when the opportunity arose.

With Henrietta getting busy on the bar, the spell of the slots catches up with me. I put in a twenty and win big in the first game. Aha, here's my chance to be smarter than the average slot addict: instead of continuing and losing all my winnings, I'll just cash out. So I took my ticket to Henrietta and received thirty dollars – for a ten-dollar profit. But then I felt cheated somehow. Something in the human heart does not like to quit when it's ahead. I couldn't resist putting a five in this time, and with that five I played for two satanic hours, winning sometimes but never much, losing sometimes but never much. And when the slots automatically shut down, as they're programmed to do every morning at 2:30, Henrietta returned me $4.85 of my $5.00. You get a little lift when you win and a little fall when you lose, and it's altogether stupid and mind-numbing.

At one point the player at the slot next to mine was none other than Henrietta herself. Sounds peachy, but there was a little impediment. Dudley, the supply bartender, a younger guy with a big beer belly and acne, seemed to be the jealous type and deliberately hovered over the Friendly One to prevent us from glancing sideways at each other now and then. Soon they were taking turns playing, and whether or not he was playing, he insisted on angling his body so that it broke the sacred sightline between Henrietta and me, like a big black cloud hiding the moonbeams, as if he thought the little flower of friendship between Henrietta and me should be firmly nipped in the bud.

Dudley had already told me he'd been to Saint-Pierre "just the once," and he wouldn't go back unless he "had no choice." But when I asked him what he disliked about it, he was as evasive as the three trout fishermen plus one. It was as if he couldn't believe I didn't know there was only one reason Newfoundlanders go to Saint-Pierre. All I could get out of him was that he was "up to no good" down there. Eventually he admitted he was trying to make a modest dollar by smuggling three bad things: cigarettes, booze, and pills. But something went wrong and he didn't want to give me the details. I suspect he got caught. In fact, he might still be paying off his fine. And maybe the judge told him the next time it'd be the Hacksaw Hotel.

But that was last night. My room was definitely not soundproof. I heard every ugly word of the fight the husband and wife in the next room were having. They fight all the time, this couple, a bright-eyed Friendly Henrietta tells me this morning. They even bounce each other off the walls and floor from time to time. She says she used to get involved in trying to stop things like that, but had learned the hard way not to interfere in domestic squabbles. It's a man and woman who are staying here for a week – another fishing holiday.

And when the two of them go fishing in the morning, they kindly lock their nine-year-old son in the room with the TV on, and the remote control to keep him happy. Lucky kid! Daytime TV all day every day. And the programs he's watching are amazing. I can hear them through the bathroom wall. Right now the Wicked Witch is telling all the little kids that their parents are stupid, and you shouldn't pay attention to anything they say. Excellent advice. I hope the kid's listening.

Friendly Henrietta tells me the two go fishing, and they're all lovey-dovey all day long, then they come home and start screaming at each other.

"Can't be good for the kid."

"I should say not," she says. "I'd rather be divorced."

"Which of course you are."

"Never married."

Also this morning, as promised, she tells me my Personal Day of Death. It's . . . Wednesday, July 23, 2014. So I have six million seconds to go. Sounds good to me. Time to slow down and stop making plans.

My only firm plan today is to pop into Marystown (which the tourist board calls the "Jewel of the Burin Peninsula") to get my specs fixed. Everything else is like the weather – notoriously hard to control. (As Isaac Bashevis Singer maintains, making a plan is simply a signal to the demons to see who can be first to thwart said plan.) The sky is blue, except for a few long, threadbare, shopworn grey clouds in the west. The ponds are sparkling with a blue much bluer even than the sky. It's the southernmost part of Newfoundland, and on the map the Burin Peninsula looks like the left hind leg of the arctic hare. This hare is taking a desperate leap from Europe across the Atlantic and has almost landed in the middle of the Quebec land mass. Port aux Basques is the nose, Stephenville the eye, the Northern Peninsula the oversized and erect ears, and the Avalon Peninsula the fluffy unkempt tail.

The newscaster on the Marystown radio station reads some little item on South Africa, then says: "Nelson Mandela spent twenty-seven years in prison for defending apartheid." Things like that always happen, when you try to make do without an editor.

On the quiet Burin highway, a group of fifteen women and girls are standing in the road. At a distance they seem like standing stones coming up through the pavement, because they are standing so straight and so still. Close up, they seem like apparitions, with little smiles on their faces, and they are dressed up like Mennonites, in early-nineteenth-century homespun dresses and bonnets. They're wearing no makeup and no jewellery. But then they start to drift to and fro, without seeming to move their legs, and I drive slowly around and between them. Not one of them glances at me. It's as if they don't notice me at all.

I asked about them when I got to Marystown. But no one had any knowledge of such a group of people. There are a lot of strange people in the world, they said. But no one knew of any Mennonite or Amish types on the Burin. So it seemed best not to ask around any further. In my mind, it was a ghostly apparition. The popular literature of

Newfoundland is full of the most powerful ghost stories – gripping and hard to pooh-pooh out of hand. Those women and girls couldn't see me, but even though they may have been from two centuries ago, perhaps standing on that spot on the Burin Peninsula long before the highway was built, I could somehow see them. I'd had no inclination to stop the car and speak to them. My only desire was to keep driving.

That would have been near Red Harbour. The Burin Peninsula is solidly Catholic, for what that's worth. As I entered Marystown, the first thing I saw was a stone wall with DAVE AND MADONNA painted on it in white letters three feet high.

Interview with middle-aged woman in the info kiosk at the Main Marystown Mall:

Dave: "Is there a glasses store in this mall? I need to get my specs fixed."

Kathy: "Yes dere is, but it's closed today."

Dave: "Oh no!"

Kathy: "Dere's one over in d'udder mall."

This mall is almost empty, but for some reason an older woman, busty, and wearing a musty tweed coat, has come up to the kiosk and is standing so close to me the front of her is touching the rear of me, and she keeps sighing with loud impatience. She keeps trying to bump me out of the way, or get me to step aside and let her go ahead and buy her lottery ticket. But I feel uncharacteristically stubborn – perhaps a bit of psychic inflation brought on by the Red Harbour apparitions.

Dave: "Can you give me a little room? Thank you." [To Kathy] "It's over in the other mall, is it?"

Kathy: "D'ye know where it's to?"

Dave: "No, but I'll find it."

Kathy: "Are you shore?"

Dave: "You think it will be open?"

Kathy: "Yes, but I'll give them a call if you wants."

She gets out the phone directory.

Dave: "Thank you very much, Kathy. I appreciate this immensely."

More sighs from the older woman, who has started poking me with her chest and bumping me with her hips again.

Kathy: "Yer welcome." She flips through the phone book. She's not rushing. More sighs of impatience from the rear.

Dave: "Please don't touch me."

Older woman: "Okay, okay."

Kathy: "It's in the Peninsula Mall." She seems to be going slow deliberately, just to annoy the pushy broad behind me. "Clear Focus it's called."

Dave: "Clear Focus. I like that." Turns to older woman. "What about you, lady? Do you like it?"

Older woman: "It's okay."

Kathy phones and finds out they're open till five and they're expecting me.

Kathy: "There you go. Now, where're ye parked to?" Older woman sighs.

Dave: "Right over there by the Canadian Tire."

Kathy: "Did ye see the bowel park when ye came in?"

Dave: "Bowel park? The one with the bowel diamond and bleachers?"

Kathy: "Roight. Well, yer turns left dere and den yer sees a booncha lights. Yer gotta go through der lights, an' den yer looks to yer left an' den yer sees a great big building an' dat's der mall. An' I tried my best to explain it t'yer."

Dave: "You did a good job, Kathy – and I'm going to recommend you for a raise."

Kathy [beaming]: "Thank you very much, sir."

Dave: "And if I get lost I'll come back here."

Kathy: "All roight!"

So then I felt guilty, because the older woman's transaction took about three seconds. I could have easily let her butt her way in. But I just didn't feel like it, and I sensed Kathy also thought the woman was being rude and deserved to be stonewalled. But in retrospect, even her sighs were nothing but innocent attempts to notify the Blessed Virgin Mary that here she was living her faith by the saintly practice of divine patience. Her anxiety would have had something to do with the fact that the longer she stayed waiting the more likely it would be that the priest might come by and chastise her for spending her limited gambling money on the lotteries when she should be spending it on the bingo over at the church hall. "I didden see youse at de bingo last Saturday, and now I sees you buying a loddery ticket. What's Jesus going to say about dat?"

Interview with a young lady who runs a used bookstore in the Marystown Main Mall. Her name is Phoebe Peach, and she is small, about four-foot-eight, with a high-pitched and piercing voice, and one of her legs seems to be out of commission, so she has to drag it behind her. She could pass for sixteen, but seems about twenty-three. Her store is called Phoebe's Books and contains an assortment of maybe four thousand paperbacks, in excellent condition, nicely categorized, and placed on dust-free shelves in perfect alphabetical order. What was she currently reading?

Phoebe: "I'm not a book reader myself, but I listen to all the book programs on the CBC, like *Between the Covers* and *Writers and Co.*, and all that, with the interviews with the authors. And they have authors reading from their books, and that's what I listen to instead of reading. But I like the business part of this, and the people part of this. Some of what people have been reading? Um, the Newfoundland stuff is really popular. We just recently got in this one, *St. Lawrence and Me* by Ena Farrell Edwards – she lives just down at the end of the peninsula – and this has been quite a good seller. And this Robin Cook is popular, he writes a medical-thriller-type book."

Dave: "There was a movie version of one of his books. *Coma*, it was called. You get to see the living corpses hanging by hooks from the ceilings."

Phoebe: "Ayee! I'm not into scary stuff. No, I like a good tearjerker myself. I like to have a good bawl now and again."

Dave: "Harlequins?"

Phoebe: "Yeah, sometimes. An' I also got in a Jeffrey Archer yesterday. And Robert Ludlum is another one. And John Irving. And Michael Palmer. And Jean Patterson is another popular one, but we don't often get her books in. And John le Carré."

Dave: "Margaret Atwood's a huge fan of his, I hear."

Phoebe: "Thanks, I'll remember that."

Dave: "Is this your own store?"

Phoebe: "Yup, I'm the owner."

Dave: "You look so young to have your own business."

Phoebe: "Well, my folks helped out and stuff."

She said she'd had the store five years now, and she was doing well with it, and it was a nice little way to make a nice little living. "But the thing is, when you're in business for yourself it's not the money aspect I find, it's the people – and I'm here to serve you. I'm not looking for any benefits as such for myself."

In a large, boggy, undeveloped public-park section of Marystown, an environment-friendly boardwalk has been built to allow people to experience the pleasure of strolling out over the wetlands and around Jane's Pond without getting their feet wet. Clumps of trees sit on little grassy hummocks. Nicely built boardwalks are not at all rare in Newfoundland, often going along the beach, or sometimes built in steps up the sides of steep hills for easy access to romantic lookout points. If that's not a sign of civilization, what is? But – hard to believe – I've yet to see anyone walking on one. This one is billed as a "nature walk and exercise park." Here it is, a Saturday, the first warm Saturday of the year, and nobody is using it, nobody is walking on the

Marystown boardwalk, nobody is either obeying or disobeying the sign saying PLEASE RESPECT THE ENVIRONMENT – no young people, no old people, no lovers, no poets, no madmen, no beautiful weeping middle-aged women lonesome for their mates off in Toronto, no young mothers happy pushing strollers. Where is everyone?

Across the street from the Sacred Heart church, there's a vast memorial garden, containing a great circle of crosses eight feet high. As I stand in the centre of the circle, the crosses resemble basketball players standing at attention for the national anthem, gazing blindly down at me, they're so tall and slender and still. They're painted white, and they represent the stations of the cross.

These stations are particularly beautiful. They even had me thinking of converting – especially so hard on the heels of the Red Harbour Apparitions. First off, they are simple and unpretentious in the extreme, two qualities notoriously rare in the field of twentieth-century ecclesiastical art, with its tendency toward vain abstraction and unintentional ugliness. Without trying to appear to be from an earlier era, these have been set up with all the passion and concentration of a Michelangelo, if he had been chained to a rock in the wild North Atlantic.

In each station there's a sort of gothic window, and the scene inside is carved in wood and delicately painted in various hues of high-gloss enamel, then encased in weather-tight clear plastic boxes. Christ is condemned. The cross is being lowered onto his shoulder.

There's the first fall. Oh, God, this must be so moving to a devout believer, and these are the best stations of the cross I've ever seen, more moving than even the great cathedrals of Europe. Each figure has a face that, with few strokes, allows you to read in it all you can handle. Anything more would be distracting and draw undue attention to the artist, for the anonymity of the artist often bestows a special kind of halo on a work of sacred art. And perhaps Newfoundland is one of the few places on earth where such a powerful work of art would remain anonymous. The folklore is full of examples of poor fishermen making huge Christ-like sacrifices, and should there ever be the mildest recognition of their courage, devotion, generosity, or whatever, they would be embarrassed.

Jesus is only three inches tall, but he's carrying the cross as if it were almost weightless, he's turning his head to smile sweetly at the crying women, and the soldiers seem at first sympathetic to his unimaginable plight. As if for the first time, I feel the special cruelty of forcing a convicted political prisoner – an idealist, a mystic, a pacifist, a man famed for saying "Blessed are the peacemakers" – to carry his own cross up a hill where he knows he'll be nailed to it.

Jesus has fallen again; the seventh station marks his second fall, and the soldiers, sympathy forgotten, are now whipping him when he's down. They're wearing little plastic helmets. The soldier who is actually doing the whipping is wearing a cape, but the cape is spreading open with the exertion, exposing flesh as naked as Christ's.

As Jesus is being whipped, there's a fly buzzing inside the plastic box. The fly's weakening fast, but he's still looking for a way out. Judging from the litter of dead insects in the bottom of the encasement, he's not likely to make it.

Gulls squeal as they circle high above the Memorial Garden. In the next station, Christ is on his feet, but he has an ugly look on his face, and he's pointing to heaven. Now Christ has fallen again, he's pretty well had the biscuit. Of the two women, one is gazing passionately at him, and one is glaring sternly at the soldier who again has his whip raised, but his clothing is no longer in disarray.

Jesus is the suffering innocent individual, while the Romans represent the world, which is a cruel place out to get you. At station eleven, his right hand is being hammered to the Cross, to test the sincerity of his contention that it's best to "resist not evil, but whosoever shall smite thee on thy right cheek, turn to him the other also." He has his eyes closed and looks as peaceful as a Buddha sitting under a tree. In station twelve Jesus dies. I've never been so moved by the stations of the cross, even in Ireland, where they have them all over the place, in the woods, by a stream, by a well, or along a series of sluices and waterfalls designed and built by an anonymous farmer and his wife.

In station thirteen, seven friends take Christ's body down from the cross. Strange that I almost wrote "helped him down" – a silly mistake, as if something in me doesn't believe that Christ is dead. Can one be a believer without knowing it, without even trying? Is this a state of grace?

"Christ has no body on earth but yours," says the memorial plaque in the middle of the circle formed by the stations, with a vast grave-yard of small white headstones stretching out behind the circle.

Marystown is a large, spread-out community, a post-Confederation amalgamation of four fishing villages. It claims a population of 7,700, but it's hard to see where all those people are. Even the two large malls are rather quiet for a Saturday afternoon, the sort of day when you're not sure if you should wear your parka, your jean jacket, or maybe just a T-shirt.

Those long, thin arms of your glasses that stick out and fasten to your ear, do you, gentle reader, know what those arms are called? If you don't, please don't feel badly, because until today even yours truly never knew. If you thought they might be called churches, syn-agogues, mosques, places of worship, you'd be dead wrong. . . .

They're called "temples."

And if they'd never been invented, or if we were born without ears, we'd have to go around in contact lenses all the time.

The fellow at Clear Focus told me that. He also took my glasses off my head, threw them in the garbage, gave me a new pair, same style, charged me five bucks, and I could see better with them both for distance and reading. In Toronto you have to go to the Portuguese area for service like that.

Even with the blissful landscapes of the Burin Peninsula, its low population density, and ever-present silence, certain problems can be seen around here that are similar to those in the city. I'm particularly thinking of not having time for anything, the sense that time is going too fast, and the sense of not being able to get anything done. The roads aren't busy enough for road rage, but the seeds of it can be seen. The population is getting older and time is speeding up.

People drive sensibly. If they see someone crossing the road, they don't accelerate and honk their horns, and they seldom feel the need to roll down their windows and scream obscenities at elderly pedestrians in crosswalks, or other drivers, etc. But even in peaceful, laid-back Newfoundland, you'll often see people on the verge of panic because of a little lineup at the cash register in the convenience store.

For instance, at the checkout corner of the supermarket in Marystown, people with welfare coupons kept coming in from outside and being served, apparently on compassionate grounds, before the people standing in line with groceries and credit cards. And the line kept growing and we were all losing our patience, sighing and shuffling our feet to demonstrate how well we were suppressing our anger.

One lady came in. She was a sad-looking specimen of humanity, and things had obviously not been going well with her since God knows when. With her big, round, unfocused eyes and grey emaciated face and body, she looked three-quarters dead. She was clutching a handful of food coupons and asked the cashier to help her find the food she needed.

So the good-hearted, well-raised cashier kindly got out the current advertising flyers and went through them, showing her what food she was entitled to, and then carefully showed her which aisles the food would be found on.

Meanwhile, the line at this normally speedy four-items-or-less checkout counter kept growing and growing, and people in spite of their good nature were getting steamed. Finally the little guy ahead of me was being attended to. He started waving a brand-new ten-dollar bill he'd just received in change. "Has ye seen it yet?" He was jumping up and down. "It's de new ten dollars wif Joey Smallwood on it! Joey his self on de new ten-dollar bill!"

The tension in the lineup instantly vanished. Everybody had been holding their breath with that terrible impatient feeling, and suddenly they were all screaming with laughter. I was there and didn't quite get it, so it's okay if readers don't get it. One guy started choking on his dentures, but he recovered and laughed some more. I didn't realize the notion of Smallwood on the Canadian ten would be so hilarious to Newfoundlanders. Anyway, there were no takers. Nobody looked to see if he was really on there. They'd be happy if he were, though. I'd be happy too.

And of course Joey would have insisted that the welfare people be served first. At least he would have in the early stages of his political career, before he found it convenient to jettison his socialist ideals, like many democratic socialists before him. But he didn't entirely jettison them, for toward the end of his career, he liked to pepper his speeches with lines from Oliver Goldsmith, such as "Ill fares the land, to hast'ning ills a prey, / Where wealth accumulates, and men decay. . . ."

Later I eyeballed the new ten-dollar bill close up, and at certain angles Sir John A. Macdonald does look a bit like Joey Smallwood. But it's definitely Sir John A. on the bill, and not Joey.

South of Marystown, history abounds. Here's the seaside well where fishermen in the eighteenth century would come for fresh water, and the beautiful forested and deserted islands out there, which were heavily inhabited in the nineteenth century. In fact to a certain extent they were inhabited right up to the post-Confederation resettlements.

A government plaque nicely notes of the islands that they were "the settlement of choice for our first permanent residents," and that "isolation was not a factor, for the ocean was the principal highway." In fact it would have been the only highway till about the late thirties, when the first roads began to connect the villages along the Burin Peninsula. By the early fifties, Premier Smallwood was saying that isolation had become the "curse of Newfoundland." He envisioned a highly industrialized province, and that would require centralization. Starting in 1953, he offered off-shore families $150 – it was later raised to $600 – to leave their homes and move into large towns on the Newfoundland mainland.

By 1965 the island communities of the south shore had ceased to exist. Strangely, that would be just about the time when island communities were springing up everywhere else in the known world. Since the 1960s, for instance, real-estate values have skyrocketed for even the less well-known of the Gulf Islands of British Columbia. Maybe it will happen here yet.

"Welcome to Burin – A Blend of the Old and the New." Every town around here has its special slogan, usually one that expresses a sentiment that will appeal to everyone in town, be inoffensive to visitors, and be free of any taint of irony. Burin is a small harbour town on the side of a hill, with dazzling views, a coat of arms with two crossed swords, and a history of European settlement going back at least to 1718 – the same year the French founded New Orleans, the population of New York was seven thousand (of which 10 per cent were African slaves), and Alexander Pope translated Book 4 of the *Iliad* by Homer.

Would it be possible not to notice a giant silver fishing lure fifteen feet high standing straight up in an old fellow's backyard and flashing in the sun? As I drove by he gave me a look that seemed to indicate he wished someone would stop and chat, and so I did. He was one of those guys so old that he's been left cruelly alone by the various deaths of his coevals. Probably lots of people drive by without noticing.

This is the most amazing piece of Lawn Art of all time – certainly right up there with the Baie Verte homemade front-lawn iceberg, or even with Claes Oldenburg's "Giant Hamburger" at the Museum of Modern Art. This is a giant cod jigger fifteen feet high, standing on end, and painted silver aluminum. I'm finding the old fellow's English hard to follow, but I think I have this essentially right.

The jigger was made by his son, Rodney Beck (pronounced "Bay" or "Bake"). Apparently Rodney has been teaching English in South Korea but will be coming home at the end of July. The old fellow himself every year repaints the jigger from top to bottom. It looks like a giant minnow, with a trinity of giant hooks coming out of its head. It stands tall and slender on a luxuriant, well-tended, spring-green lawn. He's already put this year's fresh coat of paint on the jigger, and he's now in the process of touching up the large, silver-painted stones that surround it at its narrow base. Simply beautiful!

Apparently he gets the silver paint cheap in the winter at the local paint store and keeps it in his garage till the spring. Everything about his home is extremely neat and well cared for. Here's a man who loves his home the way a home should be loved. Whenever I would refer to the paint as "silver," he would say "aluminum," as if he didn't want anyone to think it was worth stealing and smelting down.

And then, out of the blue, he stuns me by touching on a whole area of great pain and bitterness in his life: "I had a brother killed overseas. Bill Beck. He was in de navy, de British navy, and he had five children over dere in Scotland. I never hears from nobody. I don't know if his wife is dead or alive, or she's married again, or . . ."

He looked into my eyes and saw I understood. I shook my head in sympathy and told him it'd probably still be possible to track his five nephews or nieces down. They'd probably be pushing sixty. They'd be interested in hearing about their long-dead dad's brother, George Beck, of Newfoundland, and maybe find out interesting facts about the early life of their father. There was also a chance they wouldn't be interested at all, but that seems unlikely. I suggested he contact his member of parliament for assistance in the matter. MPs are always looking for interesting little problems to solve for their constituents. He liked that idea.

On November 18, 1929, a 7.2 earthquake occurred off the coast of the twin towns of Grand Bank and Fortune, on Fortune Bay. It ruined twelve transatlantic telegraph cables and caused a tidal wave that killed twenty-nine people.

Grand Bank is the birthplace of Senator Eugene Forsey (1904–1991), a pioneer Canadian socialist, who studied at McGill and Oxford as a Rhodes scholar. Along with the Baptist preacher Tommy Douglas of Saskatchewan and the poet Frank R. Scott of Montreal, he founded Canada's first national workers' party. He also had a hand in the powerful political document known as the Regina Manifesto, the first line of which goes, as every Canadian school-child knows (I wish):

> We aim to replace the present capitalist system, with its inherent injustice and inhumanity, by a social order from which the domination and exploitation of one class by another will be eliminated, in which economic planning will supersede unregulated private enterprise and competition, and in which genuine democratic self-government, based upon economic equality, will be possible.

Grand Bank is full of beautiful old wooden houses, complete with widow's walks, the name Newfoundlanders give to those windowed turrets at the top of the house looking out over the sea. These would have been built to enable the women of the house to scan the horizon to see if their husbands were coming home, or, as some say, to make sure they weren't on their way.

Some fortune hunter has put up a huge billboard outside the adjacent town of Fortune: "The Old Lady says: Do you have a Planned Fire Escape in your home?" But from the size of these homes (nothing higher than two floors), I don't really see how a fire escape would help. Someone is under the mistaken impression that Newfoundlanders are easily spooked.

Snook's Barber Shop is closed on a Saturday afternoon. Mr. Snook is probably descended from the local Snook who helped Captain Cook navigate these waters 240 years ago. That same Snook also told the good captain that spruce beer was an excellent preventative for scurvy. He gathered spruce boughs for the captain and taught him how to make beer from them, thereby spreading the word and saving lives. He would also be related to the merry family of Snooks who were so helpful to the semi-fictional York Mackenzie and his young friend when they holed up in this area for several months in order to escape from private investigators in *Helmet of Flesh*, by Toronto writer Scott Symons.

The entire population of Fortune seems to be done up in suits and ties, new hairdos, fancy dresses. Must be a wedding. Pretty well anywhere in Canada, according to my observations, when a municipality is on the skids financially, the last stores to get boarded up are the ones that sell wedding dresses. But I didn't see any stores boarded up in Fortune, nor were there any stores selling wedding dresses.

Also, in the interests of fair play, I should announce the appearance of new styles of Lawn Art as they appear. In Grand Bank it's store-bought Afro-American jockeys and boys fishing. In more sophisticated Fortune, it's all dories – nicely renovated and varnished full-sized dories on lawns and backyards, and toy dories on porches, railings, and window ledges. This is to remind us that this was once a great fishing centre and all-around hub of industry. It's still a vibrant little town, huddled around the dock where you catch the ferry to Saint-Pierre and Miquelon. But I just don't feel like going; Newfoundland is enough for anyone to write a book about. In fact I've decided not to go to Labrador either. They'll just have to wait till next year.

From Heritage Park, off the road way south of Fortune, at a place called Point Crue, at the southernmost tip of the Burin Peninsula, my field glasses scan tiny, low-lying Saint-Pierre (which seems to have a lot of snow on it). Its larger sister islands, Little Miquelon and Great Miquelon, joined by a thin isthmus and pretty well uninhabited, are much higher in elevation, yet no snow can be seen on them, at least from this angle. The islands are clearly visible, even with the naked eye. In fact there is just the right amount of mist rising from the sea to create the illusion you can see right through all three.

Terrible storms strike with little warning all the time down here at the southern blunt end of the Burin Peninsula, which is shaped a bit like Italy, with a shoe at the bottom and a thigh at the top. Just a few weeks ago a roaring winter storm came up out of the Gulf of St. Lawrence and killed two elderly people in the community of Lawn, which I'm passing through right now. A cat is making a beeline for the school bus, even though there's nobody in it – and that's about the only activity in Lawn just now.

All right, I'll confess. When I first heard of that storm, I pictured the old couple being swept away while sitting on the Lawn in their Lawn chairs. In Lawn, every chair is a Lawn chair really. If they had a bowling alley, it would have to be called Lawn Bowling. That cat is now sitting at the closed door of the school bus, looking annoyed. I think he wants to go for a ride. Or maybe he feels uncomfortable because he's carrying too much fur for a warmish day like this, so he's sitting in the shade of the school bus, but it's not much cooler.

The people aren't that bothered by springtime temperature shifts. In fact, there goes a woman in a black fedora, a black parka, and a pair of black bell-bottomed jeans. Yet she's carrying a naked, fully exposed child in her arms. Ten years ago everybody would have been out mending the nets and patching up the boats, but that's all history now.

Another storm, on February 18, 1942, took the lives of 204 sailors, when two U.S. destroyers came to grief in this area. The ships were en route to the naval base at Argentia. The USS *Truxtun* broke in two on the rocks of Chambers Cove, two miles away, and the USS

Pollux hit the beach at Lawn. People from surrounding towns sprang into action and rescued 168 of the sailors from certain death.

Most of these tiny communities I'm going through, like Lawn, St. Lawrence, and Lamaline, for instance, if you were to take both your hands full of dice, about twenty or thirty of them, and toss them on a rough up-and-down surface, where they landed would resemble one of these villages. And in just about every town you'll find a young man or a young woman just sitting on the step gazing into infinity, wondering whether they should move to Marystown, or St. John's, or Toronto, or London, or Paris, or New York, or just marry their local sweetheart and stay put here for the rest of their lives.

APRIL AND MINNY

Burin Peninsula • Goobies • Gambo • Wesleyville • Cape Freels

Sunday, May 27. I wasn't expecting to return to King Arthur's Court so soon, if ever, but Henrietta seems to have intuited correctly that I would be back tonight. She said they'd had a busy day. The only room still vacant was the one I'd had last night. So this is still a place of little miracles as far as I'm concerned. The room wasn't even made up. I insisted they leave it that way. She insisted she'd fix it up specially for me, which she did, as I stood around awkwardly chatting with her and watching old newsreel films about Newfoundland during the Great Depression on the island's own network, NTV. Also, she took the time to show me how to use a rather complicated satellite system they have, called ExpressVu.

What a treasure she was. She had time and a kind word for everybody, she was never rushed, yet she was a really good worker, and she got weary after a twelve-hour shift, but never stressed out or snappy – always Madame Kindness. But when she finally gave me the hang of how to work the ExpressVu, she clicked her tongue at me for not having been able to figure it out on my own. "It's de simplest thing in de world," she said, with a cute smile that almost made me blush.

After watching *Acorn the Nature Nut* for a while after she left (John Acorn is said to "enjoy every living thing he comes in contact with"), I switched channels to *Hannah and Her Sisters*, and it struck me that Michael Caine from fifteen years ago looked a lot like Dan Pomroy from a couple of days ago. Both of them have a bit of theatricality about them, and both know how to deliver their lines.

It's Sunday morning, and the four French fishermen are sad as dishrags to be packing their fishing rods up, for it's time to head back down to the ferry in their Renault camper with the French licence plates. It's fun to see these big, heavy-set fifty-year-olds sitting in such a tiny vehicle, loaded down with fishing gear, hip waders, nets, rods, and a pair of canoes on the roof racks.

Last night, when the three Saint-Pierre–born fellows were in their room snoring away, the guy from France was in the bar, busy exploding everybody's stereotype about the French being civilized drinkers. This guy was plastered. He was perched on a stool and playing a slot machine, while on the verge of sliding down and curling up on the floor.

Maybe all this was unusual behaviour for him. Maybe it seemed a rational response to being trapped for another night in Newfoundland. Maybe he'd been posted to Saint-Pierre as a punishment for drunkenness. I pondered for several moments about the most polite way to approach him on this subject. But every time I tried to strike up a conversation, in my lousy French, he would say, in a sour tone, "Atsa poppa, atsa poppa, I'm a poppa too, blap." And I thought he didn't know a word of English!

Henrietta and Rhonda are weary and about ready to go home. They worked the bar, the kitchen, and the slot machines till closing time. Then they worked all night in the kitchen cooking up meals and throwing them in the freezer. Luckily they get paid by the hour.

"What did you do with Mr. McFadden's bell?" says Henrietta to Rhonda. She means "bill" but it's pronounced "bell" in the Burin.

Do Rhonda and Henrietta work together like this every night?

"No," says Henrietta. "We're not in here every night. Like, usually, we're never here together. She works one day; I work the next. We work twelve-hour shifts."

"That's easy to remember."

"We're the coo-icks. But we do everything else when we have to. Let's see now, one-two-three beer."

"My French is rusty, but I'm getting to understand the Newfound-language real good."

"The Newfie twang," says Henrietta.

"Like up in Canada we say cooks, you say coo-icks. We say good, you say gude."

"Gude!" shouts Henrietta. We laugh. "Good!" she shouts, demonstrating her command of my language, too.

"Oh, you can do it if you want!" I observe.

"I kin do it real good," she says, slyly, "if I want to."

"Speak like a Mainlander?"

"Oh no, not that." Then she sighed and fired off a zinger: "It's hard to change when you live it all your life."

"Excellent excellent excellent gude excellent," says Henrietta. "That's what her report cards always say." She's talking about her twelve-year-old daughter. "She's doing real gude and real good too. She's in grade six, and she's a grade-A student."

"Says a lot about her. She's smart," I declare, with piercing insight. "And she's well-adjusted, and she's happy. Right?"

Big pause, while Henrietta looks at that from all angles.

"Ah, she's lovely," she says.

Then she gets serious again, for Henrietta is a serious person with a lighthearted way of speaking. She bounces back to her natural state of seriousness quickly. She's blond, and she likes to wear pink. She goes a bit overboard with the cosmetics, and by the end of a shift it's flaking and fading. You could imagine her in knee-high rubber boots milking a cow on an old-fashioned dirt farm, if they had them around here, or maybe collecting the eggs in the morning and feeding the pigs. I'm trying to imagine her in an evening gown, but it just doesn't work.

"My daughter, she doesn't do anything," she says. "She's . . . she's laid back, she never studies, she has an exam she won't look at a buick" (Newfoundlandish for "book") "but then she'll go to school and she gets ninety-seven or ninety-eight on an exam."

"You better work lots of hours; she'll want to go to university."

"Her dad can do that."

"He's around?"

"Not with me, but he's around."

"And there'll be scholarships for her."

"Dere's been talk already."

"Look like you?"

"Nope. Not at all!"

"Look like her dad?"

"Like her dad's sisters."

"They smart?"

"Not overly."

She'd already told me she'd never been married to her daughter's dad, it was just one of those things. "Sounds like an interesting life you're living," I say.

"It's nothing I can't handle."

Here's what a great place the former Wander Inn is. Henrietta is going through the receipts and says, in a soprano peep of surprise: "You never had any supper last night."

"Er, um, I ate farther down the peninsula before I realized I was coming back here."

"Oh!" She seems disappointed that not coming here was an option, and she is probably right. She might have even been imagining me, God forbid, down around Marystown, looking for someplace cheaper, or fancier, or something. Or she could have been imagining a lot of things. Maybe in her deepest heart she was used to men driving all day without stopping to eat, so eager are they to dine at Henrietta's.

And then she says, "And you didn't say when you came in." She is scolding me! I haven't been scolded in decades. It's wonderful. "I mean to say, I would have got your supper. No matter what time you came in, you'da still got yer supper."

What a treasure! A bit of sweet-talking seems in order: "I know, I know, Henrietta. This is a wonderful place. You don't find places like this in Ontario. Finding it was like Grandpa Bush striking oil."

I wasn't fooling. This was a great place, and I knew it would be as soon as it appeared out of the pitch-dark night when I was using up my last dewdrop of petrol, and it looked as if I was going to have to sleep in the bog under a blanket of peat like the Kennewick Man.

She got a bit choked up, and so did I. I glanced deeply into her eyes. She wasn't used to being appreciated for the fine human being she was. Or maybe she thought I was alluding to the people around here being a bit primitive, with their old-fashioned, warm-hearted approach to running a business.

"We're good people though."

"I know."

"And the total is $55.69. That's right, you had your three beer last night, you had your paper, and your room for the night. You thought you had more beer than that, didn't you?"

It later occurred to me they thought I was a nice guy, so they charged me Newfoundland prices. If you want to go through life lightly, just make people laugh – but be ready to duck a punch.

I told Friendly Henrietta that she was a wonderful lady. She looked at me. And I wished I had two or three like her at home. "You wouldn't need no two or three, one would be enough for the likes of you, no doubt."

Henrietta isn't her real name. She understood I was writing the book. She urged me to keep it serious and don't identify her too much. She said she can always tell people it's really her if she wants to. Just so that people in the area would know who it was if they read the book, which they probably wouldn't. They don't read books by Mainlanders much around Newfoundland. But she asked me to send her a copy for sure.

In the otherwise spit-and-polish village of Goobies, at the intersection of the Trans-Canada Highway and the Burin Peninsula Road, there's a sprawling Irving truck stop. The coffee shop is full of married couples the size of linebackers, wearing black leather vests on which are pinned and sewn all kinds of decals-badges-souvenirs, all designed to show that they belong to the Married Couples Moderately Christian Motorcycle Club (MC3). It's a forty-hog caravan on a holiday tour. Let's see where would they be from – aha! Newfoundland!

I'm outside, gazing with wonder at all these motorcycles. Every single one looks so shiny and new this must be their collective first outing. Most of them have their owners' names swirlingly painted on them in the most delicate tones: Fred and Arlene, Ozzie and Tweet, Kevin and Carly, Gord and Elsie, Graeme and Peggy, Ed and Pauline, and so on: man's name first, and the man always drives, with the woman strapped in behind. They communicate with earphones and mikes and a two-way speaking system.

Does it sound like fun? I bet it would be. Unless you were cursed with the need for solitude, which none of these people seems to be – or if they are, they're not saying anything. And it could be awkward if the woman kept shouting sarcastic remarks into her microphone such as "Slow down, I don't feel like hitting a moose this morning," when you're already going so slowly old men on Vespas are passing you with a light-hearted tip of the beret.

One of the owners came out to say hello and to show me some of the amazing features of these machines. I asked if women ever drove with the men on back. "That's not allowed," he said. "I don't like it back there."

"You guys are so frigging macho."

"Oh, we gotta be in the driver's seat."

He shuddered to think of the kind of husband who would let his wife drive his motorcycle – and even worse, with him on the back. He knew of another club that signed up a few single women with their own motorcycles, but no guys would ever ride on the back with them.

So it turns out this is the local Honda Goldwing MC3 Club. You have to have a Honda Goldwing to get in. They have these clubs all over the world. And it's almost always mom-and-pop deals. For instance, the guy I was chatting with was a dentist from St. John's, on his holidays, and his wife was a dental assistant, also on holidays.

Every motorcycle is exactly the same. Slightly different colour. So they'd soon get tired of checking out each other's rigs. I bet it's a front for a big wife-swapping circle. What would they do if all forty of them were running down the Trans-Canada Highway in two ranks, and they came across the Ontario chapter of the Honda Goldwing MC3 Club on an outing to Newfoundland? Would they do battle or have a lovefest? Or both? You decide. I wasn't asking the dentist.

These Newfoundlanders are amazing consumers, some of them. They've each coughed up $25,000 for their motorcycles, which they can't ride in the winter, and the winter lasts ten, eleven months. If snow fell tonight, they'd be screwed.

And the motorcycles are so luxurious, it's almost like sitting at home in front of the TV, as they head north towards the beautiful Bonavista Bay coastline, where they'll watch whales leap and icebergs melt in the spring sun, with their stereo speakers in their helmets pumping out Beethoven's Ninth, for instance. And when the whole team stops for a rest, and they remove their helmets, they can still hear all their favourite string quartets blasting out of the alternate speakers tucked away under the armrests.

Do they ride in two ranks along the highway?

"We won't ride side by side, because the bikes are so big. So we'll stagger 'em, y'know. Sometimes we'll go side by side but not often, because it's too dangerous. Like, if you come around a turn and hit a pothole, it could be a problem if you're too close to the next guy."

It's the third time I've seen the old Joey Smallwood Lookout at Gambo, but something new has been added since I was last here: a handsome hot-dog stand, with a giant Italian umbrella. Harold is the name of the smiling fellow behind the counter, and he has the stand located at a perfect spot so it can be seen for miles both ways on the Trans-Canada Highway. Also, there's a parking spot here big enough for thirty cars, in honour of it being Joey's Lookout. Harold attests that he hasn't yet been asked for a vegetarian hot dog, but he figures it's just a matter of time – and, when the time is right on that score, he will definitely yield to public pressure. This man is a good entrepreneur. And he's got Joey's statue looking over his shoulder for luck.

Harold had an important job in Toronto, but he missed home something fierce, so he bought up somebody's hot-dog stand, tied it to the back of his car, and drove it all the way back to the unforgettable haunts of his youth. Now it's a well-known fact that hot-dog season isn't as long in Gambo as it is in Toronto, but a lesser-known fact would be that here the licence is $150 (and you have your pick of wonderful scenic spots to set up your stand), while in Toronto it's $3,500 (and you almost have to hire goons with brass knuckles to defend your claustrophobic little corner in front of Union Station or SkyDome). Plus, in Toronto, you have to keep dishing out free dogs to the homeless and elderly panhandlers who just beg and plead and pull at your heartstrings till you can't say no. There definitely are poor people around Gambo, but they're shy, you don't see them much except in bottle-gathering season, and they'd rather starve than ask for a handout.

Harold is wearing a blank white T-shirt, jeans, and a Foodland ball cap. He also has signs farther up the road both ways, saying SAUSAGES HOTDOGS COLD POP 2 KLICKS AHEAD.

I asked him what he did in winter, and he said he watches TV – and sometimes he goes out and cuts a little wood.

As for the Sir Walter Scott Lookout in Scotland, I described the terrain to him in great detail, and you could see him imagining his hot-dog stand there. I assured him it'd be a lucrative spot, since the Scots are right now losing interest in traditional fast foods such as blood sausage and haggis and are discovering hot dogs.

He'd not only never heard of the Sir Walter Scott Lookout, he'd never heard of Sir Walter Scott. So I gave him a few little tantalizing stories about old Sir Walter, and he got excited and promised me that next winter he will read all ten of the Waverley novels. I told him I'd try to get by in the spring to ask questions.

All the advertising signs around Gambo have a silhouette of Joey Smallwood on them. It's a corporate logo instantly recognizable, like the Alfred Hitchcock profile. Praise the Lord, it's Sunday in Gambo, Joey's hometown. And all the people are coming out of all the churches all at the same time.

At the drugstore, in the recently amalgamated series of communities of little white houses and churches now known as Wesleyville, on Bonavista Bay, an hour north of Gambo and the Trans-Canada Highway, the pharmacist, perhaps wishing to get out of the store for a few minutes and check the shining, white, rock-bound sea for whales and icebergs, said he knew exactly where my old friends April English and Sam French lived. Rather than just point me in the right direction, he insisted I follow him in his truck, which I did, and he left me sitting in the driveway of April and Sam's house, at Cape Freels, a bit north of Wesleyville, on the Atlantic's rocky shore. There was nobody home.

An hour later, a little red Volkswagen Cabriolet (perhaps the only convertible in Newfoundland) pulled in, with April behind the wheel and no Sam to be seen. April was squinting to see who was in her driveway, and so was Ben, her white Bedlington terrier.

Slowly, and ever so dramatically, I rolled the window down, until nothing was between my face and theirs but thirty feet of fresh Atlantic air. Ben looked away in disgust. April is not one to fake anything, and she seemed genuinely pleased as, in wide-eyed silence, she mouthed each syllable of my name.

I shook my head and said in a slow, solemn tone, "You can't get rid of me that easily." Ben's ears shot up. April did her unique, deep-throated "Ha-*haaah!*" – which she utters whenever she feels that something seemingly comic may need to be filed away and thought about at leisure.

I later found out that Sam was in Toronto struggling to get a highly paid architectural commission finished by deadline, and no one had warned either of them that I was going to be in Newfoundland, and/or that I might be searching them out. However, without getting into private matters, several people had insisted I seek reconciliation by popping in on April and Sam on my tour – even though I'd been a bit hurt because they had moved to Newfoundland without telling me. I know, I'm paranoid. They just didn't get around to telling everybody.

You see, two years ago, after a harmonious twenty-year friendship, April and I had a falling out, over something far too stupid to write about. It was a professional matter, but it affected our long friendship, as these things will often do, and we were both stubbornly waiting for the other to call. Sam, of course, knew of the dispute but seems not to have felt any need to take sides, or, quite possibly, he was on my side but it wouldn't be prudent to say so. I don't hold grudges, but I hate to apologize when I genuinely consider myself blameless, which I seldom do, except in this case.

April was friendly, which is almost as good as forgiving, and insisted I sleep over before leaving for Change Islands and Fogo tomorrow. She took me on a two-hour tour of the barren and rocky territory, gazing at icebergs, scanning the horizon for whales, and pointing out the homes of interesting people such as the famous Newfoundland painter David Blackwood, who was down in St. John's at the moment, "checking out the competition," as April put it.

When we got back, April's new friend Minny Lorry (a.k.a. Small Truck) had come over, as instructed, with her powerful outport accent, and was waiting for us to show up. It was interesting to see her and April interrelate. They'd become close, in spite of their extreme differences of temperament and background. April is strictly from the exclusive Rosedale section of Toronto, so much so that she laughingly admits that what she misses most about Toronto is the upscale department store Holt Renfrew. Minny is the essence of homespun down-home shrewdness. She's travelled off-island, but as for the myths of elegance and taste, in her they run in a folksier manner that cannot really be described but can only be appreciated and that complements April's style nicely.

April had to go to the local historical museum, which she is currently renovating with Sam, to do some last-minute things before she forgot, and Minny and I took the opportunity to zip down to the lobster dock, where we chose a pair the size of dachshunds – males, as specified by April.

Then Minny had to get home to her husband, Ron, who wasn't able to visit, because April is a big smoker, while Ron has an "acute bronchial disconfiguration" and is apparently wasting away while on sick leave from his teaching job.

But Minny lingered on a bit, as I had asked her to, since I couldn't kill the lobsters and suspected April wouldn't want to either. We had the water boiling in a big pot.

"Ron's a man who's been around," revealed Minny. "And he knows people. He tells it like it is, and some people don't like that. New Yorkers tell it like it is, and so do the people from Boston, and Newfs don't like that." Ron is from the United States but has been in Canada for ages.

"Would you do the honours?" I said to April after she came in and blinked approvingly at the lobsters. She looked at the boiling pot.

"No," she said, shaking her head in a how-could-you-ask tone.

"Well, I can't boil these babies alive," I said. I did it once, decades ago, and have managed to avoid this nightmare-generating experience ever since.

It doesn't go with her style generally, but April has a tender heart. In fact on our way home from checking out icebergs, she swerved her car and almost lost control – in order to avoid a cat that was already dead.

She didn't use to be like that. I think it was dog ownership and vegetarianism for health reasons that have made her so sensitive to the lives of animals.

"You're getting to be a soft-hearted person," I said.

"You mean the way I swerved to avoid that dead rabbit?"

"It was a cat."

"Oh, I thought it was a rabbit."

But Minny Lorry was still with us, so April and I sat tensely at the big, round, oak kitchen table, with queasy looks on our faces, as Minny tossed the handsome giant lobsters into a pot of boiling water, because we Mainlanders were too cowardly to do it for ourselves, but nevertheless wanted it done. We were like Richard III, commissioning Tyrell to kill the two little princes in the Tower of London.

As the awful seconds ticked, she kept poking the lobsters with a long fork to hasten the end and to keep them from leaping out at her and biting her nose off. Minny was so kind to do this, paradoxically speaking. Ron was expecting her at home. Maybe he had a couple of lobsters for her to kill as well.

The three of us drank a glass of champagne, then Minny ran home. April and I tore open the most wonderfully intricate food-packaging job in the world and began gorging ourselves like half-starved seals. "She's been killing lobsters all her life," said April, "so why should we do it and upset ourselves for weeks after? Let her do it. She likes to do it. It doesn't matter at all to the lobsters who does it. They always sensed that their turn would come."

ONE LAST LOOK

Cape Freels • Dildo Run • Toogood Arm
Twillingate • Farewell • Change Islands

Monday, May 28. With my field glasses, I'm sitting on the deck at the rear of April's house, looking out over the rocky, treeless islands that hug the shallow, shelf-like, rock-strewn shore, searching for the line that separates Bonavista Bay from the Atlantic Ocean. There isn't one to be found. But if there were, it would go from Cape Freels, which is just a short walk north of here, on a straight line south-southwest to Cape Bonavista, where somebody else is probably sitting. Everything southwest of that line is Bonavista Bay, everything northeast is the Atlantic.

Some of the treeless, yellow islands immediately offshore have dilapidated old shacks on them. They used to be known as fishermen's shacks, but since the cod moratorium, they've come to be known as poachers' shacks, even though none seems inhabited. A rock far out on the horizon has a lighthouse on it, way out so far all you can see is the lighthouse, not the rock it's standing on, and then only with the field glasses.

Minny shows up. She's a night owl, but she also loves to be up early, so she has a good long nap in the afternoon. Ron, who is her second husband, is a teacher at the high school, and a big reader. He's got her reading seriously in such fields as psychology and how the mind works. Ron is Jewish, from Boston. "Oh yes," she said. "I've come a long ways with Ron."

They have two Briard sheepdogs, named Tovah and Chaim, on whom she dotes. "You like animals so much," I said, audaciously, "how could you have been so beastly to those poor lobsters last night?"

She let me have it: "It's like dis, see? Youse guys wanted ta eat de lobsters, right? Well, I had to do what I had to do. It's just a chain of events dat kind of happened."

I asked what Tovah meant. She said Bible. I said isn't that Torah?

She thought about that for a minute. "Maybe Ron's pulling my leg. I'll skin him if he is."

We got talking about the mating habits of lobsters. "I watched a program on de TV," she said. "Dey mate. You should see dem mate. It's amazing. Like he'll be just like a man, all lovey-dovey, when he wants what he wants, and den when he's finished he just goes on his merry way, right?"

"They don't mate for life?"

"Not de lobsters. Maybe de lucky ones. Just like people. A lot of us don't mate for life, but what about when yer really old, wouldn't you want somebody dere wid you? Truefully?"

"Some of us are born to be wild."

"I think a man like yerself needs somebody around, if only for de companion-type thing. I'm old-fashioned too, I guess, but dere comes a time in yer life when you don't even need sex!"

At one point I mentioned having heard, on this trip, a bitter complaint or two about the wave of infantile "Newfie" jokes that became popular on the Mainland in the years following Confederation. It was like telling the Newfoundlanders, proud to have become Canadians so recently, that they weren't smart enough to be Canadians. But Minny pooh-poohed the idea. The jokes never bothered her.

"A lot of times you can take things too serious too, right? And I thinks Newfs are overly sensitive, some of them. It's like de term Mainlander. Ron had this student who wanted to know if everybody from the rest of Canada was a drug addict. So Ron had to say it's not Mainliner, it's Mainlander."

Minny was not short for Minerva; it was her given name. She was one of nineteen children, all of whom survived into adulthood, and most of whom are now in western Canada. In fact, Minny recently visited her Victoria siblings and has decided that, of all the cities in the world, that's the one she most wants to live in.

I was absent-mindedly going through my shoulder bag and pulled out a little item I wouldn't be needing. I held it up and said, "Does anybody want, absolutely free of charge, the audiotape of an un-expurgated historical romance, set in the Lake District of England, at the time of the great Romantic poets, Wordsworth et cetera, called *The Maid of Ellesmere*, written by Melvyn Bragg and beautifully read by Victoria Hamilton?"

Instantly, Minny made a lunge for it, saying "I'll-take-it!" Maybe she's listening to it right now as I type.

But now it was time for April and me to abandon Minny and take off in two separate cars for the Farewell ferry up Twillingate way. We had lots of time, so we stopped en route to contemplate the icebergs.

"There's nothing like an iceberg washed up against the shore to spread an aura of charm throughout the entire landscape."

I knew April had been feeling exactly that way herself. "Make sure you put that in your book," she said.

Even the dreary graveyard with a faded picket fence and a large sign proclaiming that God Loves His Dead Saints can be charming when there's an iceberg in the background.

Something tells me not to look up, but I do anyway, and there in the sky is my lobster from last night, in the form of a cloud coming straight at me with evil intent. Or maybe it's April's, and it's really coming at her. Whatever, it's got two perfect dark eyes, each just a bit smaller than the full moon would be. It also has two long skinny arms reaching out in our direction, and at least on the right arm there is a definite claw on the end.

"That lobster has gone to heaven but hasn't forgotten the brains behind its assassination," said I.

April grabbed my arm. "L-l-lucky we're l-l-level-headed and not p-p-prone to p-p-panic," said she.

At Dildo Run and Toogood Arm the sea is full of thousands of odd-shaped iceberg fragments. Photographers focus on the giants, but the fragments are more twisted. One looks like a robin pulling a worm out of the earth, another like a kangaroo sliding down a fireman's pole. There's a perfect snow-white mushroom about five feet high. On shore, the brave little snowdrops and buttercups are beginning to blossom. They don't have the weather channel to tell them it's okay to open up now, so this is courageous of them. There's no going back.

May is the month in which it's most likely a melting iceberg will get close to shore and discharge a half-starved polar bear, who has managed to climb aboard somewhere along the Labrador coast before finding itself drifting too far out. If it decides to make a swim for shore at a highly populated Iceberg Alley tourist-town such as Twillingate, it can be dangerous. Sometimes an arctic hare will come ashore from an iceberg. The hare will just bound off into the woods and be forgotten. But one doesn't forget a hungry polar bear in the neighbourhood.

And so, all the way around the north shore, there are stuffed polar bears on display in courthouses, gift shops, museums. Tourists often get upset to discover the polar bears were shot, after finally setting paw on land after their long ordeal, and so, as April tells me, the official cover story is that the bears die of heart attacks while being chased away from areas of human domesticity.

"Would you like to go to the Lighthouse Museum?" said April, merrily, as if it was a terribly mundane thing for us urban sophisticates to be doing. I would, and we did. But it was all locked up. Day off.

In a little midtown alleyway in Twillingate, three teenagers were waving their arms and all talking at the same time. One was African in appearance, the first of that proud and intelligent race I'd noticed in Newfoundland. His friends were a sly-looking young girl and a fellow with hair in multitudinous and multicoloured ringlets down his back.

They stopped and smiled in such a manner I was struck by their beauty. I couldn't help saying to the one fellow, "What do your parents think about your hair?"

"They never say anything about it." His hair may be a scandal, but his English was excellent.

"They probably think about it, though, wouldn't you say?" said the African-Canadian fellow, who was a bit taller than the others, but they were all about the same age, and equally radiant.

The girl was laughing prettily. She was wearing bobby socks, saddle shoes, and a calf-length, calfskin skirt which was hoisted innocently over her skinny knees as she squatted between the two standing fellows.

"Sorry to interrupt your argument," I said with a friendly smile as I turned to walk away. April was waiting in her car for me to catch up.

"We weren't arguing," said the black Newfoundlander.

"We were just talking about the future," said the white girl.

"Very excitedly," said the Technicolor boy.

"You've got a lot to look forward to."

"We were sort of hoping so," said the dark-skinned, bright-eyed guy.

There's something special about this new generation, born around 1984. They seem to respond so well to a kind word in an unkind world. Kindness and understanding – could it be about to blossom globally?

Will the Change Islands change me? April feels I'm overdue for a change, but I think I'm perfect the way I am. April's never visited but wants a full report when I get back. She stands with me as I wait to board the ferry at Farewell. Does she remember when she was little, the thrill of being taken on trips and discovering for the first time that the world isn't just your own little neighbourhood? She remembered this warmly. I confided in her that I had been reliving those childish thrills inexplicably all through this trip, at least as soon as I left St. John's. I couldn't understand why.

This made her thoughtful and silent. Then she said, as she had said before, "I hope you're going to put that in your book."

Still, I don't know about reconciliation. I've looked down all the usual trap doors for my guilt in this situation, but haven't found it. She's certain I made an "unforgivably egregious error." I'm sorry if I hurt her feelings. But I don't say much about it. I try to take my hits with a laugh. It's the only way.

Sign on the Farewell ferry: "Welcome to Change Islands – Settled in Early Seventeen Hundreds – The Original Squid-Jigging Grounds."

April looked at me. I looked at her. She sternly enjoined me to phone the minute I get back. It was definitely not a Second World War farewell, but there was a tinge of sadness.

There were only three other passengers on the ferry, and all three were Salvation Army men returning home from a meeting in Gander. I right away went for a coffee and started chatting with the young fellow behind the counter of the tuck shop. He'd been born and raised on Fogo Island and was dying for a change. He was sick of working on this stupid back-and-forth ferry. He wanted to get away, do something with his life. Did I have any suggestions?

He was a good-looking young fellow, but I decided against suggesting he go to Hollywood and be a movie star, because artistic aspirations have to come screaming from within. For years he'd been thinking of heading down the road to Toronto to try his luck there. Lately he'd been thinking of joining the navy. . . .

He informed me there were no hotels or guest homes on Change Islands, and this was the last ferry for the day. But he assured me I didn't have to worry about a place to stay. When I was tired, all I had to do was "knock on any door," and they'd take me in for the night. And if by some fluke they couldn't take me in, why the people next door would do so for sure. They do it a lot. They're geared for it.

Our voices apparently had carrying power, for the ferry captain showed up with a big smile on his face and pointed at the Salvation Army guys. "That big fellow over there, I told him about you, and he'll put you up," he said. "You won't be lonely either," he said, his smile broadening alarmingly. "They'll take real good care of you."

The young fellow in the tuck shop was listening, so I quietly said to him, "Just like the navy will take real good care of *you*." Then I went over and introduced myself to Mr. Fred Fancy, retired fisherman, sixty-five, dressed in a Salvation Army uniform. He said he'd put me up for sure, and that's all there was to it.

But then I got talking to the much younger Salvation Army minister, and he was an interesting young fellow. He was wearing a hockey jacket, but he'd taken off the Toronto Maple Leafs crest and replaced it with a Salvation Army crest. The third guy shyly looked out the window for the whole trip, but now and then he would laugh at something funny.

The Salvation Army has retained more of an emphasis on the religious aspect in Newfoundland than in other parts of Canada, and indeed the world. Thus spake the earnest, level-headed, and fair-minded minister, about thirty. In the rest of Canada, for instance, the emphasis was on help for the poor and homeless, food banks, and that's about it. But here in Newfoundland more emphasis is placed on prayer, forgiveness of sins, and generally getting straight with

God. Elsewhere evangelism is understated, but here it's paramount.

He had a good mind and was extremely well informed on a variety of subjects, including Canadian politics, and the politics of other countries as well. In Alberta at that time there was a mindless political stampede around the person of a right-wing fundamentalist Christian named Stockwell Day, who wanted to scrap social benefits for the greater glory of Jesus. He appeared poised to take over the country, but this fellow predicted otherwise. Day was in over his head, he said. Nobody liked him around here, not even the Pentecostals. About two months later, Day would be unseated by his party, and the minister would be proven right. He had many insights into Canadian politics that seemed more penetrating than the best columnists for the top papers. He also told some amazing stories about local Newfoundland political scandals of the recent past, involving politicians I'd never heard of.

This Sally Ann pastor was a dedicated man. He'd graduated from Salvation Army College in St. John's, learning how to be a minister. He gets a bit of an income, but not much. He smiled the smile of a man who needs little financial reward for what he does. Stockwell Day and his ilk would say that, if he prayed, the money would come rolling in.

"Well," he said, "I pray, but not for money. I pray for people whose income is even less than mine." It was easy to tell his heart was on the left. But he bad-mouthed nobody, and his worst criticisms of the worst politicians were delivered politely and respectfully, without a hint of malice. A lot of professional politicians would envy him for that talent alone. Unfortunately, I forgot to ask him about his sources of information. And I forgot to ask his name, darn it. There's a leadership convention coming up for the New Democratic Party, and I wish he were running. Maybe next time.

At Mr. Fancy's quaint, quiet, old, quasi-puritanical two-storey fisherman's house (shingled rather than vinyl-sided), I was introduced to Mrs. Fancy, a woman who gave the peculiar impression of trying to be less effervescent than was natural for her. Now and then a bubble would escape and float up to the ceiling, but she kept the lid pretty tight. She was sixty or so, and she had a mildly cynical look in her eye. These two definitely weren't Bible punchers, but they weren't partyers either, and they seemed to be following the teachings of the church.

The house was at the pointy end of a narrow, arrow-shaped inlet. A large window gave a classically panoramic view of both arms running off into the sea, and with similar small old homes, most of them not as well maintained, lined up along both arms.

The Fancy house had been sitting here 150 years, unchanged except for the occasional sag or bulge. They'd enlarged the seaward window, perhaps at the enthusiastic suggestion of a guest. But the house seemed in excellent shape, warm and livable. The principal items of decoration, after the monster TV, were framed family photographs.

Family photos have long been a fetish of mine. My desire to study these, however, was stifled by big beefy Fred Fancy, still in his Sally Ann outfit. He insisted on taking me on a tour of "the island" – meaning both Change Islands, now that they've been married by a causeway and have become more like one than like two. He pointed out everything he thought would interest me: there was the Bethel Pentecostal cemetery, the Anglican cemetery, the United Church cemetery, and even the Salvation Army had a little cemetery all its own. Apparently Catholics are in short supply up here – so there is no Catholic cemetery, no Catholic church, and the inhabitants feel not at all snubbed by the lack of papal visits down through the years. Wouldn't there be a priest in the summer to look after tourist emergencies requiring last rites and extreme unction? "No way," he said. "The Catholics are all over in Fogo."

Mr. Fancy even pointed out the A.R. Scammell Academy, a kindergarten-to-grade-twelve school named after the poet who wrote, at age fifteen, the unofficial Newfoundland national anthem, known round the world as "The Squid-Jiggin' Ground." You know, the one that starts with the resonant line, "Oh dis is de place where de fishermen gadder," and ends brilliantly with: "And if you get cranky without your silk hanky, / You'd better steer clear o' de squid jiggin' ground."

Scammell (born 1913 in the Change Islands) was also an oral historian with a special interest in the tales of the last of the island fisherfolk, and in their way of telling them. A fisherman friend of his once said that, while others might excel in finding needles in haystacks, Scammell's gifts were such that he could find rubies in dunghills.

Back at the Fancy stronghold, Mr. Fancy had schlepped a giant box of chicken over on the Farewell ferry from Bartlett's on the Mainland. I had a breast, a leg, and a cup of tea. It was better than the Colonel. Also I tried Mrs. Fancy's homemade bakeapple jam, bakeapples being – forgive me if you know – sweet Newfoundland berries with crinkly skins that make them look like tiny baked apples.

What was Mr. Fancy's favourite television program? When you see a large, gleaming, thirty-two-inch, state-of-the-art TV set like that, with a satellite dish and immediate access to every program in the world, you know you're dealing with a fellow who likes his telly. He beamed with pleasure at my question and said, "I has two favourites: I likes *Jeopardy*, and I likes *Wheel o' Fortune*."

On the floor next to the television, a large Bible sat on a low wooden stand. It looked as if it had been sitting there ever since Mr. and Mrs. Fancy had got religion – and nobody had ever opened it. How could I be so sure? It was still shrinkwrapped. Too bad. There would be a lot of nice pictures in a Bible like that.

This was Mr. Fancy's second marriage. He had been married earlier, and they had one child, but it only lasted one year – the marriage, not the child. It would appear his wife took the child away with her to the bright lights of some big city, maybe St. John's or Toronto, leaving Mr. Fancy bereft, bitter, and confused.

But not for long. Mary, his second wife, had also been married before, and her husband died under rather mysterious circumstances just about the time Mr. Fancy's wife and child took off. Mary and Fred soon straightened each other out, with some help from the Sally Ann.

They both had strong roots on the islands, and I soon became absorbed in the rich bouquet of interconnected human faces in the framed family photos. Intrigued by the similarities and differences, I tried matching siblings and choosing a face to try to follow through the years.

But one old black-and-white photo stood out. It showed a serious and intelligent-looking man in his thirties, looking off into the distance. A beautiful woman in her twenties gazed adoringly at him. I picked the photo up and stood there staring at it in silence, mesmerized by the face of the man as much as by the adoring female.

Complete silence as Fred and Mary Fancy watched me looking at the photo. I looked at it a long time. Finally Mrs. Fancy spoke up. "That was me and my first husband." He had sharp cheekbones and a do-it-yourself haircut. He looked like a rugged, more intelligent, more weatherbeaten version of the movie star Dirk Bogarde. He had an air of modesty but a touch of genius. He definitely had a certain star quality about him. If you saw a book with this photo on the back, you'd want to read that book. He didn't look schooled in any formal way, but it wouldn't have surprised me if he was a great reader of all the great poets and philosophers of his day. He may have had a special interest in W.H. Auden, H.G. Wells, D.H. Lawrence, E.J. Pratt, or Madame Blavatsky.

He was a beautiful man; he had a deep and seasoned look about him, and he died at forty-two. They'd had four children together. He was out one day with his twelve-gauge shotgun, said Mary. He'd driven the kids somewhere, dropped them off at the ferry slip. On the way home, alone, he spotted a seal, out on the ice. So he put a shell in the shotgun and went to shoot it. But the seal chose that moment to slide off the ice. He decided he didn't have a good shot, and he didn't feel like walking out on the ice, so he put the gun in the vehicle, and I'll be darned if it didn't go off and blast his stomach and liver to bloody bits.

But he was still alive. Mary got the news via phone and ran all the way down to the ferry slip just in time to join her husband in the emergency boat that had arrived to take him to the hospital on the Mainland. She was telling me all this while trying to subdue the sobs of sorrow that kept bubbling up from her heart. It was sad, and I felt an odd sense of deep connection with the entire event. Conscious, and in unimaginable pain, he died while holding her hand and staring into her eyes, just as the boat was docking on the other side.

Then she started sobbing without restraint. "At least I got to say goodbye to him," she said. She had told herself that many times, and it was always a bit of comfort.

So she got married to Fred Fancy, whom she'd known all her life, and who lived just down the road and around the bend, and who was just recently divorced.

Crab fishermen take their traps out 150 miles, Fred was saying. I asked how long it would take to get out there, and he had to confer with Mary, who seemed to feel better now. They finally decided it would be eighteen hours each way. It's a long and dangerous trip in their tiny boats, but, oh boy, there's a lot of money in crab, he enthused. "I has t'pay ten dollar a pound fer crab," he declared. I'd hate to think if it would be less or more for others.

"You do not," said Mary, sternly, having caught a bit of a smile on my face. I couldn't think of her as Mrs. Fancy, for she had the sorrows of Mary in her heart.

"No, no, no," he said. "Yer right, I pays nine dollars a pound. But it's ten dollars on the Mainland."

She gave him a little smile. She's still a handsome woman, but in that photo thirty years ago – wow! – what a pair those two must have been. Dynamite, day and night! And I don't recall seeing any photos of Fred in the huge collection on display.

Another striking photo was a head-and-shoulders portrait of a girl in her middle or late teens. She had an unsmiling, heart-shaped inverted triangle of a face, with thin lips, a long narrow nose, and eyes that seemed a bit too sad and knowing for her age. This photo, and the photo of Mary's first husband, shared a quality that I've always found rare – their eyes were not just open and looking at the camera or whatever, but they were also fully conscious of the moment. They knew exactly who they were, what they were doing, where and when they were, and why. And they also knew they were having their picture taken, not an everyday occurrence on Chance Islands. Would it be okay to ask who she was?

Before I could decide, the front door opened, and in walked a little girl about eight. Her name was Clara Jean. She was Fred and Mary's granddaughter, and Clara Jean spends a lot of time over at Grandma and Grandpa's place. She's quiet, said Mary, and she likes to watch TV. She definitely was quiet, but she wasn't watching TV this evening. She just hopped up on the sofa right next to me and kept quietly looking at me, as if I'd just been beamed down from the Dog Star with a litter of pussycats in a wicker handbasket. I had the feeling she had taken an instant liking to me, and I had to her as well. Except that she didn't seem to have learned to smile yet. But that was fine. Kids shouldn't have to smile.

I showed her the photo and asked if this was her big sister. She said no, that's me. What? Yes, Mary confirmed it. I looked closely at her face. She didn't seem particularly old for eight. And yet in the picture she definitely looked pretty well all grown up. Funny the way the camera never lies.

Then she got out some crayons and drawing paper. I asked her to draw her grandfather. She sat down on the floor and drew a picture, then handed it to me. It was a good likeness. I was very surprised and very moved. She hadn't looked at me once when she was drawing. I thought for sure she was drawing Fred.

"It's you," she said, softly.

"I know. Thank you."

She was sent up to bed, and I stayed up for an hour or two, as Fred amused me with incomprehensible stories about chickens, eggs, and holy water, and the day ten guys managed to paint the whole interior of the Orange Hall. What colour? White. And his stories about the Catholics, the Salvation Army, the Orangemen, and so on. Then it was time for me to go to bed. As I climbed the stairs, I was pleasantly startled to see Clara Jean's face staring at me, from her bed, with the door open just enough to get a good view as I'd be coming up. She knew she'd be gone before I was up in the morning, so she wanted one last look – at me, from me, or both.

AUTOBUS WRECKS
AND THE
FOUR ELEMENTS OF
THE UNIVERSE

Change Islands • Fogo Island • Fogo • Farewell • Burnt Berry

Tuesday, May 29. For breakfast this morning, the house, which was a bit on the under-ventilated side, was full of the smell of burning bacon fat, so I kept my head under the covers for an hour. Everything was in its place and sparkling clean. You'd have a hard time finding a dustball in this house. Everything shone with scrubbing, as if they somehow knew there'd be someone coming over on the ferry. A little cross-ventilation would have been welcome, but it didn't seem right to fiddle with the windows without asking.

With my head still under the covers, I could gradually hear a nasty fight from downstairs. It was the two big people against the one little person. I felt badly for Clara Jean, but was also proud of her. They wanted her to do something, and she didn't want to do it. No, it was the other way around, they wanted her to stop doing something, because all of a sudden she raised her voice quite loudly and said, "My mother does it!" Shocked silence from the big folks. And then, even more loudly, in tones of embattled repugnance, if that's not too strong a phrase, she added the coup de grâce. "My mother lets me do it!"

By the time I got down, Clara Jean had gone. So I missed her.

"Here, take this. Some good Catholic eggs sprinkled with holy water," said Mr. Fancy.

"How will I know that's real holy water?"

"Faith, my son."

Mary smiled. Everything was fine, except that my brain had to scramble to figure out what a Catholic egg was. I think he meant he bought them from a Catholic.

"Yes, I got Catholic eggs, and Protestant hens. I sprinkled 'em with holy water and never received a chick. And a Salvation Army man owned the hen." These were jokes, and I laughed, appreciatively but with little comprehension.

He told an Orangeman joke. "An Orangeman came by and wanted to know how the eggs he gave me were coming along. 'No good,' I tells him. 'They're both roosters – and no good for anything.' And you know what he said? He said, 'That don't say much for we. Haw haw!'"

We both laughed. I said, "You mean you were expecting hens but got roosters?" He paused, stopped laughing, and said, "Yes." The punchline had a nice ambiguity to it and could be taken as a comment on the uselessness of the male sex in general or of the ineptitude of whoever had sexed the eggs.

Mary had cooked up huge batches of fried eggs and buckets of fried bacon this morning. They really tried to push it on me, but I didn't want any. The cooking smells and the quarrel were still bothering me. Again, they insisted I eat at least a piece of toast. They didn't understand that some people eat when they want, not when others want them to. There was a huge platter of bacon there, and each time I declined a serving, Fred would pick up another slice and gobble it down. Finally I saw him eyeballing that last crispy black slice, his twitching nose pointed straight at it, and so did Mary.

"Eat it, Fred," she said, as if he were a well-trained family dog – and *ka-boom*, the last slice of a former mountain of greasy bacon was gone! Then he started looking around the kitchen as if hoping there was some chicken left over from last night. But he'd eaten all the chicken before retiring.

"Maybe I will have some bacon after all," I said, as he wiped his lips daintily with the back of his hand. A joke! They laughed merrily.

But I did have the tea, and they served it, like last night, in an interesting manner. I guess they've been doing this all their life, and their parents before them. There would be a cup full of hot water, and a dry teabag on the lip of the saucer. When you wanted the tea, you dipped the teabag in the hot water, stirred it, added sugar and a healthy shot of Carnation Condensed Milk, and bliss was yours.

But at first I didn't notice the teabag – and, since the water was so dark with sediment (a problem with tap water in Newfoundland, as elsewhere), I picked up the cup and started sipping. My watchful hosts corrected me before it was too late. I dropped in the bag, jigged it like a cod-jigger, and then like John Candy in one of those *Second City* programs, I pointed out the window and yelled "Whale!" As they ran to the window and peered out in vain, I whipped up the carpet and emptied the cup in a soggy pool under it.

"Would you like another cup?" they asked.

After breakfast, Mary went for a walk, and I remembered a sad dream. Beings from another planet were reading my poems, which were projected onto a huge screen, and they were moaning and groaning and saying things like "How banal! How simplistic! How commonplace!"

Oh well, maybe I needed that. I found myself telling Fred Fancy about it at breakfast. He was sympathetic and seemed to understand perfectly what that dream meant. In the dream, "I" was A.R. Scammell, as well as all the other homespun poets in places not normally noted for their sophisticated rhythms. The critics from outer space were snotty tourists from the big city, laughing at the quaint ways of the islanders. That dream was a warning from that great Dreammaker in the sky. I can observe and record all I want, but appreciation, encouragement, and support are better than passing heartless judgments.

For instance, table manners were fine, but last night I had started eating my chicken with a knife and fork. Fred stared at me with a look of disbelief on his face. "That's better," he said, when I switched to the more natural finger-feeding.

Fred resumed telling stories about holy water and ducks, and would occasionally slip in a reference to his belief that it was necessary to be constantly punishing children – for their own good and the glory of Jesus, I presume. He thought it was "out and out outrageous" that you can't say the Lord's Prayer in school any more. He understands that there are lots of different religions in the world, but no matter how many there are, you still have to say the Lord's Prayer in school. He always had to say the Lord's Prayer in school, and they even had to read the Bible, so there was no doubt in his mind that all future generations should have to do the same. I told him he had me convinced, and I'd begin spreading the word as soon as I got back to the Mainland.

I noticed a very handsome ring on his finger. Was it a Salvation Army ring?

"No," he said, "that's a Mason's ring."

Oh you're a Mason too? I didn't know Masonic rings had crosses on them.

He flashed his ring and said, "Dis is what ye gets fer being a Mason."

How high are you?

"Oh, I'm as high as you can get."

Thirty-three degrees?

He shook his head, a bit deflated. "Not that high. I'm at the Red Cross level."

Then he went on about the shame of how you can't even beat your kid any more. "Many's de times I got hit upside de head. And it didn't do me no harm no way at all." He said he used to get lashings and beatings. "And I'm a better man for it."

Mary agreed with him and, having returned from her walk, jumped in by saying it's getting so bad that you can't even talk nasty to your kids any more. You can't even chastise them.

They were trying to find out if I'd heard the early-morning battle of wills or how much of it I'd heard. I wasn't going to say a thing. But . . .

"Odd how you can beat a kid but not an adult," I said. Nothing original there, but it seemed to register somewhat, as if he'd never heard that idea before.

"But you can't discipline your kids any more," said Fred, "and that's why there's so many undisciplined kids running around. And they're all going to grow up to be undisciplined adults."

"The Nazis were disciplined," I said. "Do you want your kid to be a Nazi?" I know I was exaggerating. But I couldn't bear thinking of little Clara Jean getting bounced around by big people.

Fred's cat's name was Whiskers, and what a lovely grey cat it was. It was one of those cats that respond well to love. It would stalk me and, as soon as I sat down, it'd be in my lap. "He's poppy's pet. He lies outside for hours, and if a mouse comes by, watch out. Oh, he's a good mouser all right. But he can't catch birds. They fly away on him. I was born with a cat in the house. Always had cats, never cared for dogs." It was interesting to know that about him. Who would have guessed he was a cat fancier?

And sitting on top of the corner china cabinet was a large stuffed rat someone had sent him from Labrador "as a joke." Apparently it's considered hilarious in Labrador to mail a stuffed rat to a Salvation Army captain. Speaking of Whiskers the cat, the whiskers on this rat were so thick and long and greasy, I got the impression that, if you put a match to just one of them, the rat would blow up. Maybe that was why the rat had such a worried look in his eye. I wanted to turn him around so he could look out the window at any sinking ships there might happen to be out there, but they preferred to have him facing the corner, as if to punish him for being a rat. This was no mousy little rat, this was a Labrador rat of nightmarish girth and length.

Just as the Salvation Army is less secular in Newfoundland than just about anywhere else in the world, so are the Masons. Fred belongs to two churches, he tells me, and in no way do they conflict with each other. I said I knew a bit about the Sally Ann, but what did the Masons believe in?

"See that Bible there?" He pointed at the big beast beside the base of the TV. "You want to know what the Masons is about, you just take that whole Bible and read it all the way through from Jenny's Sis to Revolutions, and that, my son, that's what the Masons is all about."

"Is that the only book you own?"

"It's two books – two books in one – the New Tasty Mint and the Old Tasty Mint."

"I'll just have to read them some day," I said, with fingers crossed. I'd already read all the good parts.

"That'll be the best thing you'll ever do, my son," said Fred.

The Masons and the Salvation Army – they've no doubt played a great role down through the years in the Newfoundland fishing communities. Burying. Marrying. Consoling. Christening. Saving souls. Helping out with the groceries when needed. And teaching people that, no matter how thirsty they may be, leave that bottle alone.

Fred Fancy also goes collecting a lot, banging on doors all over Change Islands and Fogo, asking for donations to the Salvation Army's Red Shield Campaign. He even knocks on doors when he knows the people are Catholics. And they donate generously too, he said.

Occasionally someone will slam the door in his face, or tell him they don't want to have anything to do with the Sally Ann. He swallows these slams like a saint, and says, "I don't wish them any trouble, but if they ever do run into trouble, I want to be the one to take them a basket of groceries, or a cheque, or winter coats for the entire family, or help him buy a new car, or help rebuild his house."

It gave me a thrill to hear him say that. If only the entire world could be run in the same way that the Salvation Army runs the former fishing communities. Quietly, and with great moral integrity, let's face it.

I made my last visit to the Fancy washroom and wondered anew at the sign saying NOTICE DO NOT FLUSH THIS TOILET UNLESS ABSOLUTELY NECESSARY. When I was paying up (they refused to tell me how much, but were glad to accept whatever I could afford) and saying goodbye, Fred said he had to plant forty onion bulbs today, and he had to collect the day's crop of eggs from the chicken coop. He said there always had to be somebody home in case someone came around wanting eggs. He also said he used to drink like a fish, but he saw the light. We'd been talking about the term Newfs or Newfies, and his attitude was the same one Minny had espoused. It depends on who's using the term and what kind of tone they're using it in.

As a young man, before he got religion, when he used to be on the boats, one time he was in some crummy dive in Montreal, drinking like a fish and stewed to the gills, and "this French-Canadian lady" got mad at him and referred to him as a "stupid Newfie." And he replied, "Don't you call me a stupid Newfie, you fucking French-Canadian frog." He gave me the eye to see my reaction. My smile told him I was a little surprised to hear a Salvation Army captain use such language, but it denoted a refreshing absence of clerical hypocrisy. Mary's smile and twinkling eye indicated she felt the same way.

Maybe we were wrong, though. For instance, I'm sure if he heard Clara Jean say that word, he'd horsewhip her. Jesus would be upset otherwise.

I'm alone on the tranquil Change Islands ferry dock, scanning the watery wastes of Hamilton Sound for the ferry, as well as rocks, islands, churches, lighthouses, whales, icebergs, sinking ships, herds of seals, a solitary caribou making a beeline for the nearest point of dry land, German U-boats, and, as always, owing to a solemn childhood vow, damsels in distress. The ferry will soon arrive and take me over to Fogo Island, semi-famous in some quarters for being one of the four corners of the earth.

I know vividly from much personal experience that, when someone dies tragically and in good health, surviving family members will all their lives hang on to differing versions of how the death took place and of the events leading up to it. Such different takes on serious events need not cause rifts in the family, because the different versions are all operating in the same cause – personal healing. It's like a religious belief, or even just a nuance of a belief; one must feel free to believe whatever one wants to believe, as long as it doesn't become pathological.

This morning, while I was waiting for the Fogo ferry, along came an old Chance Islander of long standing who knew Fred and Mary well and who had a different version of the death of Mary's long-lost lover.

Vernon Reed was the name of the man who, much to his surprise and to the surprise of many others, lost his life that day, aged forty-two. I didn't catch my new friend's name. Let's call him Psmith. For years Psmith ran a little business just around the bend from the ferry slip. He tried to salt money away for his retirement, but now he's retired, and all he has is his Canada pension cheque.

But he knew Mary and Vernon well. He knew Fred, too. He spoke frankly of Vernon and about the events of the final day. Without even trying, he made it sound like a perfect example of the Heraclitan notion of character and fate being one. His story was different than Mary's.

Both stories went in the same direction and at the same time, but not always hand in hand. I have no way of knowing which story was closer to the truth, and no desire to know really, but Mary's version would definitely be easier on the nerves.

A real sharp fellow, was how he described Vernon. And a real hard worker. He was a reliable carpenter and was often called upon to perform crucial boat repairs in a short time frame. But he didn't like going out in the boats. He wasn't a fisherman at all. And he would never have a gun.

But but but that was his shotgun, I exclaimed, and he was going to shoot a seal, then thought better of it. . . .

No no no, he said. It was the boys' gun. He let them have it. I never understood why, because he didn't have any time for guns. I don't know how those boys could live with themselves after that, he said.

Vernon was taking his boys to school in Seldom Come By, on Fogo Island. This was in the time before Scammell Academy was built. But he took those boys over to Fogo Island on the ferry, and when he got home he found the gun in the back seat of the car. He picked it up, and he pitched it onto a flat at the side of the house. As it landed, it discharged and caught him full blast.

My ear for the Newfoundland dialect was not yet perfectly attuned, and I had to strain to hear what he was saying. But he definitely repeated twice: I don't know how those boys live with themselves. If I'm interpreting rightly, his story was that the boys hounded Vernon till he caved in and bought them a gun, even though he loved them and hated firearms. But maybe they had bought one on their own, against his wishes, without telling him, accidentally leaving it in the car. And finding that gun was the final surprise in Vernon's sad life. Whatever, I bet his sons don't care for guns themselves today. . . .

Those wrecks decaying in the middle of the single Change Islands road, some of them look as if they've been sitting there since Vernon was a kid – old rusted-out ransacked wrecks. There's no speed limit posted on Change, and no police either, but anybody who speeds along this narrow, winding, hilly road can expect to come over a hill, smack into an old wreck, and become one more wreck himself.

But it's smart thinking not to tow the wrecks away. Where would you tow them to? So it would be a waste of energy. Also, you could think of those wrecks as super-effective speed bumps – you don't have to go to the trouble of putting up speed-limit signs or drive-carefully signs. There are even some wrecks of old buses lying around. They would be the Autobus Wrecks.

"We've got heaven on earth, we have, my son," Fred Fancy had told me. "On this island, compared to all the other islands in this world, we have heaven on earth." Unless of course you're eight years old and being horsewhipped. Or being a forty-two-year-old hater of firearms who gets splattered to bits by his sons' shotgun.

It must have been terribly hard for the sons to come to terms with what they had done. How often those boys must have wished it hadn't happened. How often and how painfully they must miss their dad, especially now, as they mature into middle age and find they are missing him more and more as they remember the old fellow, and things they do and things they say remind them, or each other, of what he used to be like.

It's well known that in Newfoundland almost everybody looks like someone just down the road a bit or in the next community. Vernon had a different look. But who knows, the boys may have done their dad a favour. It's necessary to live our lives as well and as long as we can, but the peace and totality of death is nothing to sneeze at when it comes. We cling to life like a lamprey eel clings to a Lake Huron whitefish. But sometimes I think we'd be better off if we just didn't suck so hard.

En route to Fogo Island the same would-be navy man (young Bobby Butt, as I later learned his name to be) was again working the tuck shop. There had been a change of fortune since I'd seen Bobby yesterday. Apparently I'd given him some positive reinforcement about the navy. He'd hardly been thinking about it till he brought it up yesterday in our chat. But since then, he'd been thinking about it non-stop. He'd decided he wanted to become a computer specialist in the navy.

"But computers change all the time," he worried.

"There's no problem to keep up when you have the basics."

He liked that, but he wanted a guarantee he'd never have to kill anyone. I told him he could probably get such a guarantee from the navy, though it may not stand up in a court martial.

He liked that as well. He was one smart kid. Did he ever read fiction? He said he was halfway through a really good book, but the other steward took it home for the weekend without even asking permission and lost it. It was about a kid growing up in the thirties in Toronto.

"Not Hugh Garner's *Cabbagetown?*"

"That's it!"

Already he's found out he can enlist either in Halifax on the Atlantic, or Victoria on the Pacific. So he's decided on Victoria. He wants to get as far from Fogo as feasible. He added that he wanted to get as far as feasible from any place that even looked like Fogo. He wasn't concerned when I told him the area around Victoria looked something like Fogo, except there's no snow, not even in the winter. Besides, he has some relatives out there, and they tell him it really is different. He figured Halifax would be too close to Fogo, not "radically different" enough for his exotic tastes.

The administrative centre for the entire island of Fogo is an interesting and progressive town called Fogo. Visitors will do well to remember that, when you mean the island, Fogo is pronounced FO-go, and when you're referring to the town it's Fo-GO. Or is it the other way around?

I was looking for information on the Flat Earth Society's notion that Fogo is one of the four corners of the biosphere. I said to the fellow behind the counter at the municipal office, "You're not the mayor are you?"

"No, I'm the town clerk-manager."

"I bet you get paid more than the mayor."

"Actually, he doesn't get paid – just a small remuneration."

"And whatever he gets under the table."

He laughed conspiratorially – friends forever. His assistant was a young lady with long blond hair and a pink mohair sweater. I was wordlessly wondering why it is that pretty blondes look even prettier in pink when he said to her, "Do we have anything on the Flat Earth Society?"

"De what?" She had never heard of such a thing.

He didn't pretend this was unusual. He said, "Where's the tourist file?" She began sighing impatiently and turning around in circles. Finally he found it himself.

He went through it and pulled out a single sheet of paper filled with narrow-margin single-spaced typing. The letterhead said "Town of Fogo Incorporated 1948."

He was mid-height and thin, with an athletic look in his stance and a philosophical look in his eye. I said, "How did you know I was going to ask about the Flat Earth Society?" I hadn't said a thing about it.

He said, "I don't know. It was just something about you."

I said, "Do you get a lot of requests for such information?"

"As far as I know, this is the first time ever."

"I'm certain I didn't say a word."

"That's right. You didn't."

"Do you have a bit of ESP perhaps?"

"It seems to be hit and miss."

He handed me the dope sheet. It looked like a rough draft for a lighthearted after-dinner speech. It suggests that the numerous oddly shaped hills on the way here from the ferry dock, and the giant igneous rocks with smaller black rocks perched on top of them, and the otherworldly shape of Brimstone Head, which could be seen from the front door of the office, altogether could cause someone to think he was at the world's end.

This caused me to imagine that at one time this entire island was afire, with Fogo deriving from the Basque word for fire, and Brimstone being closely associated.

"Amazing what people believe."

"You better believe it." He said the only thing about the Flat Earth Society that was of any interest to anyone he knew was that it caused people to be fractionally more aware of the existence of Fogo.

His dope sheet said that the other three corners were Papua New Guinea, the notorious Bermuda Triangle, and the Greek island of Hydra. It seemed strange that Hydra meant water and Fogo meant fire. I found it interesting that the Bermuda Triangle is where aircraft and ships vanish into thin air. And that Papua New Guinea is where the natives traditionally put earth (in the form of mud) on their faces and bodies. The sheet also contained two yawn-inducing quotes, one from G.K. Chesterton on the need to question all the dogmas of the age, the other from Somerset Maugham on how in his travels he sometimes felt the world was flat, though he knew it wasn't. A more scintillating quote, from the Reverend Brother Lee Harvey Oswald Smith, an American who bills himself on his Web site as "chairperson dei gratia" of the Flat Earth Society: "The earth is no longer flat, but it used to be, and may be again if all goes well." He believes the world was made round by a global conspiracy of television network executives. And he's a lousy speller.

The clerk-manager insisted I climb Brimstone Head. He said it was not as difficult as it looks from this angle, visible from every front step in town, and I might see some icebergs and some whales – not up there of course, but from that vantage point. He asked if I were "searching for the spiritual essence of the island."

"Yes, and maybe for a quiet little place to retire in."

"I envy you."

"But I don't have a lovely assistant like yours."

"Take her with you if you want."

"I wouldn't want to deprive you."

He laughed and presented me with a pin for my lapel, showing a tiny iceberg and a tinier boat. That would probably be the symbol for Fogo. Every island must have a symbol in this rickety card table of a planet, especially an island that has the distinction of being one of the four corners of said world.

I was beginning to think I wouldn't make it to the top of Brimstone Head, owing to my being a bit out of shape, when all of a sudden a portly couple appeared. They'd been to the top and were heading back down, and were very kind and encouraging. As soon as I reached the top, the sun disappeared behind the clouds, and the wind picked up. I thought I was going to be blown right off the edge.

But I hung on, and the view offered splendid wraparound views of the cold, cruel sea. Sure enough, I could see three large icebergs off to the east, and several long, skinny, rocky narrow treeless islands (miniature versions of the Change Islands) to the west, but no whales. "Here comes another travel writer, let's dive," they said, just before I reached the top. Good thing humans aren't that intelligent.

From here you get excellent views of the town, like a table-top town in a department-store window, with its three high-steepled churches, and low-slung office buildings, bars, stores, streets, houses. Everything is white except for the roofs, which are green, or red, or black. It's the perfect size for a town in which everybody knows everybody, or thinks they do, and from here it seems to be about half an inch above sea level.

At the foot of Brimstone Head is a weather-beaten old bandshell, which is about to get spruced up for the fifteenth annual Brimstone Head Festival of Folk Music. The bandshell faces a flat grassy field large enough to accommodate ten thousand folk-festival fans from the four corners of the earth, with three park benches, one of which bears an advert for Fogo Pharmacy, so that the folkies will know where to go to get their prescriptions filled. The festival isn't till August, so I'll have to miss it.

Brimstone Head looks even higher from the ground up than it did from the summit down. And here's somebody else coming down, which is strange, because I didn't see anybody else up there, and on the way down I didn't pass anybody on the way up. This is indeed a mystery. Was there some timid soul sharing the summit with me, hiding behind a rock and watching me scanning the horizon for whales?

An elderly granny, dressed in black trousers and white shirt, is hiking straight towards me. She stops. We chat. Turns out she had strolled up Brimstone the back way, a way I had no idea was climbable, even with picks and ropes.

"It's a nice walk," she says, shining with excellent muscle tone, "and this marks the thirtieth time I've done it." She's from Joe Batt's Arm, and whenever the spirit moves her, she walks the ten or twelve miles to Fogo, climbs up the formidable back of Brimstone Head, comes down the front, then walks home in time to make supper for her moribund husband. I offered to drive her, but she checked her wristwatch and said that wouldn't be necessary. She claimed to be seventy-five, and she still has red hair and, of course, a strong pair of legs. I wished her a long life as she strode away.

The Fogo pub is situated next door to the Fogo Gospel Hall, with its great billboard advising us that the Blood of Jesus Christ Cleanses Us ALL from Sin. On the other side of the pub sits the local church-yard, where rest eternally a grave number of members of the Coates and Shakes families. Strange that a pub would come between a church and its churchyard.

I recovered from my climb by drinking a Moosehead, playing a solo game of billiards, and doing a bit of self-analysis. For instance, I hate hypocrisy in others, but don't mind it in myself: if I see an older gentleman eyeballing a sexy young girl, I want to dial 9-1-1. But there were three sexy teenage girls playing darts in that pub and, no matter how hard I tried to avoid glancing at them, from time to time I found myself doing so. Especially when they would score a bull's eye and jump up and down, causing their miniskirts and pink mohair sweaters (ubiquitous on Fogo) to bounce brashly. I figured it was excusable, because I was only three times their age. Four times would be inexcusable, but three times was okay.

They really started bouncing up and down when somebody peeked out the window and cried, "Oh, Jerry's here!" In fact all three of them dropped their darts and bounced right out of that pub so fast I could hear that lonesome whistle blow.

"Do you wish you were a young guy like Jerry?" I said to the bartender.

He laughed. "Hell no, he's not young. Didn't you see him? He's about sixty."

"Sixty! The nerve! How come he's got all these young girls running after him?"

"I don't know," he said. "Probably he likes to buy them ice-cream cones or something."

Back on the Fogo to Farewell ferry, I offered a silent farewell to Fogo and wandered the decks watching for whales. The disturbing fight this morning was still bothersome. I may have misinterpreted, I may have misheard, I may be over-reacting, but I don't think so. They were talking loudly, almost as if they'd forgotten I was there. It was as if I were a dog listening to a human conversation. I didn't get most of the words, but I could smell what was going down emotionally. And if, as Clara Jean said so clearly, her mother lets her do it, I'm sure her mother was going to be having a serious chat with Fred and Mary, whatever the "it" may have referred to. No need to worry.

The splendour of spring is everywhere, as we ferry passengers step back on to the "Mainland," as the Fogo people refer to Newfoundland "proper." In Newfoundland, when spring springs, it springs fast. All the leaves are out on all the trees, and every single bird is singing for a mate.

Back at the Burnt Berry Lodge, strategically located in the middle of the island, halfway from everywhere, it was Brenda the bartender's night off, so the owner was discovering how simple the job was and will now probably cut her wages even further. The only problem was, he wasn't drawing the customers as well as she seemed to. The owner's name was Al Payne. He'd heard about my work-in-progress and with little enthusiasm said he supposed he'd have to do something really exciting to get a mention. It was as if he didn't want to be in the book, but it would be his duty, for business reasons, to publicize his lodge and other enterprises whenever possible.

Apparently Al was just another Newfoundland boy from the outports, but with special ambitions. He went out west and worked in the dirty, dangerous mines, brought back a bankroll, bought the motel and a tourist yacht, and entered the tourist business full-time. That's what I thought he said. I later found out he came back as broke as when he went.

I AIN'T BEEN NOWHERES

Burnt Berry • Robert's Arm • Pelley's Arm • Triton

Wednesday, May 30. From my window at the Burnt Berry I can see a grey satellite dish, a grey lake with heavily forested hills on the far side, a sky with the texture of a grey Nepalese sweater, and the outer walls of the motel, painted peach, with fresh orange-coloured vertical lines of dampness from the overnight rain, and a pink roof.

Oh, the rudeness of that woman last night in what was otherwise a typical rural Newfoundland convenience store – except that it was on the Trans-Canada Highway. May I use the phone? Would that be long distance? Yes, but I have my long-distance credit card. I showed it to her with the most innocent smile.

She said, "There's a public telephone outside." But it was raining buckets, and it was cold out there. Also there was no protection, as the phone was simply bolted to the side of the bare building. She just shrugged, then remained silent as I continued to look at her. Finally

I told her politely that I understood perfectly. I'd just drift off to a more convenient store.

Lying in bed at the Burnt Berry at five in the morning is almost like touring Newfoundland ("where the mountains and the valleys have been touched by God's grace"), because I've got the Newfoundland TV channel on! It's showing splendid scenic photos of interesting outports all around the island. An Irish tenor is singing sentimental Newfoundland ballads, with every kind of rhyme for every kind of place name anywhere around this fine land. He's calling the far-flung sons of Newfoundland back to these scenes of their blessed childhoods and/or trying to make them feel wretched for having left.

The songs are far too sentimental for popular consumption, and they're so predictable. "They bought a house in Dildo Bay / And they lived their life away" – the musical equivalent of Kentucky Fried Chicken, which I had last night and which is probably the reason I'm wide awake with a sick tummy and the jitters at five in the morning. The older we get the less tolerance we have for MSG.

A guy in a tux and a gal in a white gown with a diamond tiara are standing next to a rickety boathouse on a rickety dock, and the invisible tenor is singing: "From now on we will be as one. / We'll laugh together in the sun. / God gave us this day and we love him. / Our joy has only begun." This channel is available on Deluxe Starview 201. Just the thing for Dad on his birthday.

A few hours later I call Al Pittman out of the blue, tell him I'm a fan of his poetry, and I'd like to meet him when I'm next in Corner Brook, which would likely be tonight. We make arrangements, and he tells me that Burnt Berry is a ritual stop for him. Three or four times a year, motoring from Corner Brook to St. John's, he stops here overnight. One night he forgot his favourite cap, which had great sentimental value, because it was the last cap his mother knitted before she passed away. The next four times he stopped here, he forgot to ask for it. On the fifth stop, he remembered, and they whipped it out from behind the desk and handed it to him with a happy smile. He was so pleased.

What to have for breakfast after a night of unpleasant restlessness induced by Kentucky Fried Chicken? Two boiled eggs? Two pieces of dry toast? This is such a nice place, the cook came out to inspect the egg after I'd cracked it open. She thought it was a bit watery, but I declared it to be perfect. I even showed her my book of poems by Al Pittman. His picture was on the back cover. Do you recognize this guy? That's you, she said. Good heavens, we're both poets, we're born in the same year, we have the same taste in overnight lodging, at one time we were rivals for the affection of the same young woman (although we didn't get to meet at that time) – and now he even looks like me. So I'm really looking forward to meeting this prince of a chap, this iconic Newfoundland poet!

I told the waitress (who doubled as the cook) that the eggs tickled my tummy after that nasty bout with a big hunk of steaming Kentucky Fried Chicken last night. I told her what Vladimir Nabokov (in *Ada*) has to say about a boiled egg: "The most exquisite food in the world." And I suggested we should enter into a partnership and open a chain of restaurants to be called Nabokov Boiled Egg. No MSG. She stared at me with her mouth open and eyes a bit glazed. Had she ever been down to St. Alban's?

"Oh no, I ain't been nowheres."

"Nowheres? Surely you've been somewheres?"

"No way! I only been to St. John's once in my life."

"How did you like that?"

"I don't know," she said. "I took my fourteen-month-old daughter down dere to have a surgery, and it was all foggy. And I stayed de night in de hostel, and de next morning it was foggy, and den I left – so I didn't even get a chance to see St. John's, and so I've never even seen St. John's."

"What was the surgery for?"

"A cleft palate."

"When was this?"

"Hm . . . about 1984. She's eighteen now. They had to put her in a straitjacket, so's she wouldn't move around and ruin all de surgery." The girl now has to have more operations, because the doctor had transplanted some skin from her larynx onto her lip – and now the larynx hasn't grown properly. So they have to "do a couple of surgeries on her larynx now to get it to come alive again. But she's not fourteen months old now, so we don't have to worry so much."

I told her that I sympathized, which was true, and that I'm sure the doctors know exactly what they're doing, which was false. But everybody needs positive reinforcement whenever they can get it. Especially people who ain't been nowheres yet.

The beautiful and intelligent Elaine Payne ("Hey, that rhymes!" "I know!") is in charge this morning. She and her handsome husband, Al Payne (they look like a pair of movie stars), live in the motel year round for now. Al's big job these days is replacing the old doorknobs on the various rooms with new ultra-secure ones. But he's a smart cookie, he only replaces two each day. He replaced his two this morning, then said, "That's enough for today" – and took off up the peninsula to do some work on his boat. The engine needed a tune-up.

"Will he be doing it himself?"

"Oh, he does almost everything himself."

The boat is called *The Ancient Mariner*. It's a long, thin, aero-dynamic cabin cruiser from the twenties or thirties – you can imagine Scottie and Zelda zipping around in it – but it's been spruced up and fibreglassed for durability and looks handsome indeed in the framed photos on the office walls. It's had an ultra-modern radar system installed. Al takes tourists out on tours for fun and profit.

It turns out Elaine had followed Al out west years ago when he was working in the mines. She denied he made a bundle out there and came back and bought the motel and boat. "Oh no!" she adamantly cautioned, pricking the romantic bubbles of my fancy. "It's not that simple. All the money we made out west we spent out there. We came back with nothing." How did he get his hands on all this property then? Well, it seems that, somewhere along the line, he picked up the knack of impressing bank managers without even trying.

Both Mr. and Mrs. Payne are admirably laid back about their enterprises. Being an entrepreneur in Newfoundland perhaps isn't as scary a proposition as it might be elsewhere. Absolute ruthlessness is not a prerequisite. In Newfoundland there's a different bottom line: it's called compassion. And if you fail at business, there's no need to commit suicide. All your unemployed old friends will welcome you back into the fold.

If I want to get a close-up look at the heavily mortgaged boat, it's "down Robert's Arm. You goes across de causeway dere, den you looks to de left, and dere you sees the boat in de picture dere, and you'll probably see Al working on de boat, and you'll see a half-finished log cabin dere he's building for de boat, and dat's where we're going to live once he gets de roof on good and tight."

Just then a big fat man came in carrying an empty beaker. Al Pittman's book was on the counter backside up, and he flipped it over and said, "Oh, I know that book."

I said, "Do you know Al Pittman?"

He said, "No. But I read that book, and it's really good."

Mrs. Payne said to him, "I guess you want that sample, eh?"

He said, "Yup." Turns out he was the government water inspector and has to go around making sure nobody's going to get poisoned by drinking drainage from the pig farm down the road or whatever.

Mrs. Payne was saying they recently replaced the radar in the boat with a more up-to-date system, which they'd bought from a salesman who just happened to have been passing through and spent the night in the motel. She elbowed me in the ribs and whispered in my ear:

"See? We likes to make meaningful connections with de people who stops here." My face turned red. She giggled.

No sign of any cabin cruisers or half-finished log cabins in Robert's Arm, and I've checked on both sides of the causeway. The main thing about Robert's Arm is the ill-considered motto: WELCOME FAMILY AND FRIENDS. Kind of makes a paranoid fellow like me feel a bit left out and unwelcome to boot. No strangers allowed? Maybe they mean "friends" in the sense of anyone who looks at all friendly, and maybe they mean "family" in the sense of anyone who belongs to, or believes in, the Family of Man – or looks as if they may have at one time – rather than one who is actually related to someone who lives there. Maybe it's deliberately meant to discourage tax collectors and repo men from the Mainland.

In Pilley's Island, someone has scrawled the word GARB in front of a house. I thought maybe it was the family name, or maybe they sold cheap second-hand clothing there. But then I noticed it was on a garbage box. Soon I was all the way up to Triton (where the handsomest and most imposing building by far is the brown-brick Salvation Army Triton Corps – it positively dwarfs the Brian Peckford Elementary School), across numerous causeways (each a bit longer than the previous), with no sign of Al Payne, or his boat, or his roofless log cabin. I told Mrs. Payne that, if I spotted him messing with any other women, I'd be sure to tell her. She seemed to like that one, and the look on her face indicated she wouldn't mind if he would fool around with other women, because then she'd feel more comfortable fooling around with other men. But that was just her look. She was so crazy about Al, even after all these years, she couldn't admit it to anybody.

Many grizzled old former fishermen are wandering and waddling along the muddy, rainy roads leading north to Notre Dame Bay, scanning the stagnant ditches for empty bottles to cash in, trying to raise the price of a bottle of Canadian Club, and it occurred to me you could choose a dozen of them at random, give them a haircut, a shower, a shave, and a new suit of clothes, and they'd be indistinguishable from any number of Liberal cabinet ministers or bank presidents. Except they would probably be better educated and more polite. What a world!

These are the dispossessed. They didn't bother studying hard at school, because all they wanted to be was fishermen like their daddies, and that's all their daddies wanted them to be. Nobody ever told them the cod were going to disappear. In fact they still find it hard to believe.

So now they collect bottles, shoot the odd rabbit, plant a few turnips, and spread capelin around the garden for fertilizer. And, when they can, buy a case of Moosehead and a bottle of CC to help them forget the miseries of living dirt poor in the outports of Canada's paradoxically oldest and newest province.

One of these guys flags me down and wants a ride down to the beer store. He seems to have been on a monumental bender and needs more supplies to continue, because sobering up is just too painful a proposition to bear.

He has a patch over one eye, and says he's a Queen's Man. What's a Queen's Man? I'm a Britisher by descent, he slurs, and proud of it.

He claims to be forty-eight, but he doesn't like the older women. He prefers them between sixteen and eighteen. I say you can get in trouble that way. He smiles and says he knows that, he loves to get in trouble. "I get into a lot of it." He says he's been in jail twenty years in toto – but not all in one stretch.

What's the worst thing you ever did?

"The worst thing I ever did? Drink beer."

And gave yourself a lot of tattoos.

"That was because of the beer."

The second worst thing he ever did was kill someone, but that was also because of the beer.

Who did you kill?

"I don't even know who it was. It was in Ontario. I hit him, he fell down, he was dead, and I didn't stick around to find out who he was."

Why did you hit him?

"He stole my beer."

You killed him for a beer?

"A beer? No way. It was a whole case of twenty-four."

He said he'd been drinking beer ever since he got up this morning at three o'clock. He always likes to get up early. He wouldn't tell me how many drinks he'd had since getting up and would only say that he drinks "with discretion." But he must have been drinking more than just beer; you can't get that hammered on beer unless you're really determined. He claims to have been "turned down" by the doctor, because he drinks too much – "and I mean turned down. I'm not even supposed to be drinking beer, but I drink anyway, because I do a lot of things I'm not supposed to do, and I don't give one holy damn about my ulcers and my seizures." And his philosophy of life was an admirable one: "You have to help yourself before you can help others."

He said he broke three shovels last winter shovelling himself out of his cabin after snowfalls.

And he said his mother taught him good.

Did she teach you to drink?

"No, she never taught me that. I taught myself that."

Lloyd Buttenham was his name. Curly blond hair, bright blue eyes, well-shaped oval face, perfect nose, nice moustache, a wispy goatee, and he was clean and well-groomed, dressed in blue jeans and jacket, and had the sweetest and most endearing smile. A really good-looking guy for a drunk of almost fifty. If he sobered up, he could be a pretty sharp confidence man. In fact, he told me an elaborate story about how he cheated his own brother out of $775.37, but he made it seem as if he had no other choice, he had to do it, it wasn't his fault, it was his fate.

His other philosophy of life was, if you drink, hitchhike. He said, even if he had a car, he'd never drive it while drunk, because you could have a seizure and hurt someone. And that person might be your daughter, or your friend, or anything like that, right?

At the beer store, he just wanted to sit and talk, perhaps hoping I'd split with him on the beer. But I finally got him out of the car by telling him my wife was waiting for me up at the highway. He got out fast then. He didn't want to tangle with anybody's angry wife. I told him I knew he was a drunken homicidal maniac, but he was a real nice guy anyway. He liked that a lot. It would have made his day, if he'd been able to remember it that long.

"I know I'm drunk, but take care of yourself," he said. "Thank you very much."

There was no wife waiting for me at the highway, so I stopped in a convenience store for a six-pack and the lady behind the counter said I could get it myself in the walk-in cooler. Ooh, was it ever cold in there. It was amazing the beer wasn't frozen.

"Yep, dey don't linger long in dere," said the old babe. "Dey just gets der beer and gets out real fast."

I told her I was going to take a day off, watch TV, drink beer, and read a book.

"Read a book, eh? Sounds wonderful. Wish I could do dat."

I wasn't sure if she wished she could read, or could take a day off to read, but something in her tone aroused my sympathies. So I said, jokingly, she could join me if she wanted. For a moment I panicked, because sometimes jokes misfire and are taken seriously, and then you're forced to follow through. Imagine having to read Michael Ondaatje's *Anil's Ghost* to this nice lady all day. But she simply blushed and said, "No, I have to work all day long . . . till nine o'clock tonight."

Back at the Burnt Berry for a lazy afternoon, the NTV channel isn't all Irish tenors singing schmaltzy songs about the outports. Just now they're running really interesting old documentaries and newsreels from the provincial archives – with up-to-date analytic comments and insights. There were plenty of shots of fiery young socialist Joey Smallwood, back in the days before he ran for office. Shots of old wobbly fishing boats coming in with tons of codfish gasping for air. Shots of brand-new fishing boats being launched amid glowing optimism. Soldiers marching off on a free tour of Europe and a cruel date with miserable bloody death, face-down in the cold muddy trenches. Really good stuff.

FIRST MOOSE IN
NEWFOUNDLAND

Burnt Berry • Coffee Cove • Springdale • Howley

Thursday, May 31. Why would a driver leave his truck running in front of the Burnt Berry while he goes in to play the slots all morning? Surely any money he would possibly win would be eaten up by the fuel he's lost, at a dollar a litre. "Oh, they just don't know any better," says Al Payne. "They're in such a hurry they haven't got time to switch off the ignition, and they don't want to take the time to switch it back on when they go back out."

Al Payne is a sweet guy and has a charmingly simple ambition in life. He has a bar-restaurant-motel, a wife who's there for him all the time, a boat for taking tourists out to visit whales and icebergs, a log house he's building – and when he has his bills all paid off, his biggest ambition in life is to take his boat and sail all the way around Newfoundland. Just like the Beothuk boy in *Beothuk Saga*, by the late Bernard Assiniwi, a francophone Cree novelist/anthropologist. In the idyllic days prior to European contact, which brought about the destruction of the Beothuk culture and the extinction of the

Beothuk, the boy canoes all the way around the island to prove his theory that the island is in fact an island, as Columbus proved the world was round. Al Payne hadn't read Assiniwi's book or even heard of it. But such ideas spring eternal.

Al says his boat was built in 1958, though from the picture it looked like the twenties to me. It was all wood, but he's put three layers of fibreglass on it. He also said he couldn't figure out how I could have missed his boat yesterday. It could be seen clearly from the causeway. . . .

Al rakes in a lot of money from his little bank of slot machines, but he is no propagandist for their use. It's true, he said, that sometimes, occasionally, someone will come in with a loonie, play for two minutes, and leave with twenty dollars. One time a woman came in with $350, played the slots for four hours, and managed to leave with $275. But she told everyone, including herself, that she had actually *won* the $275. He said if people were more forthright about how much they lost, pretty soon the slots would lose their appeal.

Last night at the bar my favourite, besides bartender Al Payne, was Donna Boyles (rhymes with "dials"), close to six feet, with big fuzzy hair and a long, slender face. She has a son fourteen and a little girl two, and she was shooting pool and playing all the Rolling Stones songs on the jukebox. She had just split up with her husband who, over their fifteen-year marriage, repeatedly – I repeat, repeatedly – tried to strangle her, and even came close to killing her a few times. And only by her own strength and size was she successful each time in fending him off.

The last time it happened, her brother happened to be in the house. He was horrified, he had no idea, he got her out of there real fast and ordered her never to return. Then he went back in and got the kids out of the house. That was all she needed. She had remained silent all those years when he was abusing her, beating her, strangling her. And now her brother knew. And the more people he told, the stronger became her resolve never to return to the sadistic savagery of her spouse. She had the air of the newly liberated about her and seemed to be breathing freely for the first time in a decade.

I told Al about the interesting drunk yesterday, and how he kept saying that he never tells a lie, and he would tell me about that murder, even if he knew I was a cop. But after he told me that he was born in Newfoundland, and both his parents were too, he mentioned that his mother was from Springhill. Aha, I thought. A lie! Springhill is in Nova Scotia.

But Al Payne right away set me straight. He said the drunk was probably slurringly referring to the big town of Springdale. Even when the speaker is sober, in fact, Springhill is basically the local pronunciation of Springdale, which is just a few miles down the Trans-Canada. I felt badly for misbelieving that honest drunk. Wherever you are, Lloyd Buttenham, I salute your honesty. And may you never run out of beer, teenage girls, or luck.

Today I'm on my way back to Corner Brook, but there's no rush, so I'm exploring all the side roads off the Trans-Canada Highway that look inviting. In the convenience store in the ironically named village of Coffee Cove, I sleepily asked if it would be possible to get a coffee to go. "Oh, we don't have no coffee, me love," said the stout little lady behind the counter.

"No place in Coffee Cove to get a cup of coffee?"

"No, I's afraid not."

"But I'm falling asleep on the road!" I pleaded.

"Dat's no good," she said.

"Couldn't sleep a wink last night owing to being poisoned by the Colonel."

"I've had dat; it's de pits."

"Do you have any wake-up pills?"

"None of dem neither."

"Rats!"

"But we have Seltzer!"

"My stomach's okay now. I just need a coffee."

"What if de problem hits you again?"

"No way. It's Mary Brown from now on."

"I likes her best too."

This area, just north of the Trans-Canada Highway and a bay or two west of where Al Payne claims to have his *Ancient Mariner* moored, marks a return to Afro-American Lawn Art. But here's a refreshing change: a homemade, full-sized, nicely painted moose is standing there, as if pulling an actual little wagon full of firewood. And next to it is the Green Bay Wholesaler Warehouse with a sign saying DAY OLD HENS. No indication if you get them for half-price, like day-old bagels.

It's been raining heavily since late yesterday afternoon. It's still only 11 degrees in St. John's, but a bit warmer here. Rolling low cloud and fog, only serves to emphasize the greenery, ever more lush as spring advances.

Springdale is indeed a largish town scattered along the west shore of Hall's Bay – a polite and friendly-looking place, not overly tidy, not too messy, just right. No wrecked cars on the road or anything like that. Housewives, like Amsterdam hookers, are leaning out their windows and smoking cigarettes. They have a Kingdom Hall for the Jehovah's Witnesses, if any should happen by. Some houses are for sale, some have been sold. Some people are moving in, some are liquidating. There's a liquidation sale sign in the window of the Girl Guide headquarters.

The Salvation Army Citadel is a bright, newish building with only one car in the spacious parking lot, a rusted-out Chevrolet from the early sixties that hasn't been stripped yet. Out front, an enormously fat man is chatting with a tiny one-legged lady, who is supporting herself with a single crutch that seems far too short for her.

Across the street the Living Waters Ministries Pentecostal Church seems fairly busy, with some scowling people getting out of their cars and going in for a bout of holy rolling. I went into a little bakery for the coffee I so badly needed. The grouchiest lady served me. It was embarrassing. I was presentable, in clean jeans and a Newfoundland T-shirt, greeted her with a friendly hello, and asked politely for a coffee and a raisin scone.

The bakery/coffee shop was called Momma's, so in the most polite manner imaginable, I innocently asked if she was "Momma." She snarlingly told me that "I am a momma, but no, I'm not . . . Momma."

Sounds ridiculous, but she sighed irritably and slammed the plate and cup down on the counter. Did everything she could to make me feel as if it was a terrible mistake I hadn't been born on another planet. Then she really looked glum and let out some bitter sighs and rolling of eyes when I asked if I might use the washroom.

When I left, I gave her a cheery goodbye and received cold, stony silence in reply. But it was just probably a bad day she was having, she couldn't possibly have been that rude and boorish on a full-time basis – and readers should not let this stop them from popping in to Momma's Café and Bakery on the Main Street of Springdale, Newfoundland.

There were some other ladies in there, sitting in booths, drinking coffee, eating scones, and they noticed her rudeness and seemed a bit embarrassed also. They in fact cheerily called out goodbye as I left, and then no doubt asked "momma but not . . . Momma" why she'd been so abusive to that poor little man.

Maybe it was because I had the very well written and edited *Downhomer* magazine under my arm, and Newfoundlanders in this area tend to be suspicious of people who are serious readers, or maybe *Downhomer* had rejected one of her stories. Maybe this café was considered suitable only for women – and, when men come in, it's for all the wrong reasons. Maybe she felt real men didn't eat scones. Maybe she didn't like it that I pronounced "scone" correctly – to rhyme with John, instead of Joan or June. (I later found out that the word "scone" isn't generally used in Newfoundland. "Tea biscuit" is the term. Perhaps "scone" seemed pretentious to her ear.)

But the most probable source of her irritation could have been the T-shirt I was wearing: it bore a frightening picture of a bear knocking over an outhouse, and a guy running away from the outhouse with his pants down. Maybe she felt her café was too high class for a guy with such a T-shirt – even though I bought it at Riff's.

Farther west, a short road leading south from the Trans-Canada Highway enters an unpopulated area of high hills, still topped with big fat patches of snow crusty enough to support a full-grown man, as long as he didn't try jumping up and down to test the crust's thickness. Heavy forests too, even more virginal than the snow. Powerful rivers. Cold lakes full of fish.

In the middle of it all appeared a true wilderness town – like the kind of remote and snow-bound towns in the extreme north of Russia that pop up in the travel essays of Ryszard Kapuscinski. It's called Howley, and no way could anyone guess at a glance what it was famous for. But don't worry, I'm here so you don't have to guess: it's famous for the first moose in Newfoundland having been dropped off at this spot, a former stop on the "Newfie Bullet." The moose was brought to this mooseless (but not useless) wilderness, in 1904, by train and ferry, from some part of the moose-thronged Mainland where a moose wouldn't be missed.

So I couldn't miss the opportunity to buy, in the Trapper's Lounge of the Howley Pub and Motel, for twenty bucks, a white sweatshirt commemorating that event. I told the lady behind the counter that I'd be making a big fashion statement this summer, strutting along Yonge Street in this sweatshirt featuring a monstrous moose with a tiny train in the background. She said, "Yes. Especially if that's all you're wearing." She pointed out the sign saying THIS IS A CASUAL BAR . . . CLOTHING OPTIONAL.

The good-humoured lady was itching to tell me about her goofy son. When he was seventeen, he quit school and applied to join the army. When he didn't hear back for several months, he got a job driving a truck, married his local sweetheart, they had two babies, then bought a mobile home and set it up on a vacant lot. . . .

His mother told him not to do it, just rent, don't buy, because the army still might call. But he said no way, he didn't want to throw away any more rent money, he wanted to accumulate some equity in his heavily mortgaged mobile home, before it was too late. And just two weeks after they forked over their down payment on the trailer, the army did in fact call. So he quit his job, sold his little home at a big loss, and moved his little family down to Upper Canada, where he is serving at Camp Borden, driving trucks, managing heavy equipment for the army, and patiently waiting again, this time to get into the ever-popular computer course.

The way he's going, he'll be a five-star general in ten years, said I, causing her to laugh hysterically. Upon recovering she told me I'd laugh too if I knew her son. He is definitely not officer material. Thanks, Mom.

How could such a remote, isolated village be so neat and tidy? Well, it was just this winter they got a directive from the government that they had to get rid of all the wrecked cars on the road or face a fine. So all the old wrecks got dumped over the cliff into the cold fishy waters of Grand Lake, which is four times larger than its companion to the north, Deer Lake, but is not as famous because it's not visible from the Trans-Canada Highway, and it doesn't have large communities hugging its shores as the towns of Deer Lake and Pasadena hug the shores of Deer Lake. All it has is tiny perfect Howley. For Pete's sake, Grand Lake has an island in it, called Glover Island, which is larger than the entire lake of Deer Lake. As if size matters.

As far as is known, there had always been lots of caribou, but there had never been a moose in all of Newfoundland until 1904, when the train stopped at Howley and a moose stepped out. Where did that first moose come from? She thought really hard, then called out the cook, a cute, shy nineteen-year-old girl, and the cook thought really hard too, and then both their husbands came in and they thought really hard – but damned if they could remember where that moose came from. Then a smart little kid about ten years old came in and, without even thinking hard, said he thought it might have been from down somewhere Nova Scotia way.

The following year some bright soul came up with the idea of importing a female moose, and pretty soon there were moose all over the place. The silence of the woods was broken by continual gunfire and cries of agony from dying moose of both sexes and all ages. This caused a sad look to pass over my face.

"Cheer up," she said. "After all, you are the first tourist of the season." Then she started rattling off all the places they had tourists from last year. There was a lady from Miami, for instance, just driving around in her cream-coloured Cadillac. And a family of Pakistanis from Toronto came through and stopped over. She said, "Boy, did we ever have a hard time understanding their accent." I started laughing.

"It wasn't funny," she said. "It was really confusing." She added, musingly, that the Pakistanis didn't seem to have any trouble under-standing the Newfoundland accent, but it didn't go both ways. I suggested they have sweatshirts printed up with a picture of a Pakistani on it, saying First Pakistani in Newfoundland – 2001. This brought on another bout of giggling.

Shall I spend the night here? Probably not, for it's only an hour to Corner Brook, and I'm beginning to miss the buzz of urbanity. In the outports, you get lots of chit-chat, lots of laughter, but you can't get a newspaper worth reading, or magazines, and the people, through no fault of their own, aren't well informed – with notable exceptions, such as the young Salvation Army minister on the ferry. Besides, Al

Pittman was expecting me. And I might never get another chance to meet him.

The town of Howley was named after James P. Howley (1847–1918), author of *The Beothucks, or Red Indians*, which was published in 1915. It's a highly regarded, sympathetic, and very moving book, the source of much fascinating and sometimes quirky information about the vanished race. He speaks of the "sorrow that so peculiar and so superior a people should have disappeared from the earth like a shadow."

In his long-term capacity as geological surveyor, Howley had been an early explorer of what was then the mysterious interior of Newfoundland. He met large numbers of Micmacs, fairly recently arrived from the mainland, but no Beothuks. His travels clearly inspired his fascination with the Beothuk nation, but the last of the Beothuks, Shanawdithit (also known as Nancy), had died of consumption in 1829, at the age of twenty-eight, eighteen years before Howley was born. After a funeral to which no one came, she was given her final resting place in a Protestant cemetery in a suburb of St. John's, a cemetery that was unceremoniously paved over by the Trans-Canada Highway in the following century.

AL PITTMAN'S
ANCIENT FRACTURE

Corner Brook

Friday, June 1. The Hotel Corner Brook is a fat old whore with a happy heart – and she'll only charge you half the going rate. Go around the corner to the Holiday Inn (also showing its age), your room will be twice the price – and it won't have as much graffiti on the walls.

Like a cookie cutter, when a Holiday Inn gets old it gets dull. But with a uniquely atmospheric place like the Hotel Corner Brook, the older it gets the more interesting it becomes. There's even a Take Off Pounds Sensibly (TOPS) convention here. The heaviest, happiest, and funniest women from all over Newfoundland have taken over the hotel, and extra-strength cables have been installed in the one skinny little elevator. I managed to get a last-minute cancellation. Let's hope some poor thing's husband didn't decide she couldn't go.

It's fun to mingle among this grand multitude of fast-food addicts making merry, so happy they are to be on a holiday. They've even been heard referring to their organization as "Take Off Panties,

Stupid." Are they serious about regaining their long-lost svelteness? Haw haw! No way. What for? Weight loss is just their cover story. They're here for a good time, not a skinny time. They're drinking Pepsi and eating potato chips for the most part, it seems. And they always use the elevator, forcing me to run up and down to and from the third floor, which is good for my heart but not theirs. There's one elevator, and three of these well-packed women can squeeze in at a time. They gigglingly insist there's room for a little lad like me, but no way. Not to be at all unkind, but I'd feel like a field mouse in a herd of elephants.

These women are dressed in their best freshly laundered clothes, and they smell soapy clean as they chugalug their Pepsis and tell hilarious ribald outport jokes with their mouths full of pretzels and potato chips. We're all Canadians, and I for one am proud of them. Some of them were really young and looked old, while others were really old and looked young.

One was sipping a Black Horse at the bar and keeping the bartender busy refilling her pretzel dish. She was so fat I had to sit three barstools away, but she looked so young I asked what grade she was in. "What grade? My son, I've got six grandchildren and more coming all the time." Yes, the outport women, the daughters of the ancient fisherfolk, do tend to age slowly and gracefully in the face, but they certainly get a huge head start in putting on the pounds. The pounds are like grandchildren, more keep coming all the time.

History is a big factor. Newfoundlanders over the centuries have had to survive frequent long periods of starvation, when the sea inexplicably refused to yield its fish. Now their descendants have to learn how to survive in a sea of low-cost fast-food joints.

In other words, if you're descended from people who survived in spite of an unreliable food supply, and you now live in an area where fast-food chains abound, you're going to be burdened with huge parcels of fat – unless you're eternally vigilant. If you have hard-time genes, you can't turn them off during good times. The only way to stay at all slim is to starve yourself, stay away from the fast-food franchises, and speed-walk five miles a day.

But if the food supply ever fails, and famine stalks the land, the people with hard-time genes will have more potential for survival than the skinny people with the good-time genes.

So keep in shape and live a lovely long life, ladies! We love ya!

Most of my day was spent watching television out of one eye. A well-regarded U.S. congressman, Joe Moakley, had died, and live funeral-of-the-century coverage was being presented from St. Brigid Church in South Boston. Someone was eulogizing Moakley for his concern for the disadvantaged, and the clever cameraman swivelled and focused close-up on President George W. Bush. He looked mean, bored, and uncomfortable, as if someone had tricked him into being there, the only Republican in a sea of high-profile Democrats.

I was also getting organized and had a wide assortment of absolute necessities spread all over the bed, the coffee table, and the floor. It was an awful mess. I answered a knock at the door and three happy TOPS ladies, each with a toilet roll in her hand, sang out in unison, "Do you need any toilet paper?" Then they looked wide-eyed at the mess of the room, before focusing on me wearing one sock and a pair of boxer shorts. They apologized for bothering me. They apparently thought every room would have a TOPS conventioneer in it.

I phoned Jim Baird in St. John's to tell him I'd found a key of his in my bag, and I'd be dropping it in the mail. No big deal, but I also mentioned I was meeting with Al Pittman tonight, and he seriously warned me that Al had a huge problem with alcohol. This was the first I'd heard about it. Al had sounded perfectly bright and sober when I phoned him early yesterday. Al did tell me he has his own special stool, which no one else can use, at the bar of Casual Jack's

Roadhouse, and his favourite drink is the Newfoundland Libre – Screech and Cola. But surely they wouldn't dedicate a barstool to a serious alcoholic.

I asked the desk clerk why it is that, when a pedestrian looks as if he wants to cross the street, even if it's far from a crosswalk or an intersection, all traffic comes to a halt for him. He said, "Oh, we're polite in Corner Brook."

I said, "I wish we could import some of that to Toronto."

He said, "Ah, they'll never get polite over there. They're too far gone for recovery."

The Roadhouse was halfway between glitzy and barn-like. It was on a tree-lined street, with the trees on each side bending towards each other and bearing butterfly-green leaves. This gave Corner Brook an aura of tropical elegance, except that there were no snake-like vines hanging from the branches, and everybody was wearing heavy clothes and had faces white as snow.

Casual Jack's was a magnet for academic drunks, slap-happy misfits, Englishmen in exile, male nurses, and the occasional teenage poet hoping to get a kind word and a bit of advice from the great Al Pittman. It was a pleasure meeting Al, but I was alarmed at the state of his health. Because of an ancient fracture that hadn't healed, he walked with a cane, and only with great pain and difficulty. It was whispered around that, for several years now, he'd been drinking much more than he thought anyone knew. He claimed that the first round of Newfoundland Libres we shared was his first of the day, but the others told me in confidence it was more likely his twenty-first, and they wouldn't lie about something like that.

The conversation between Al and me, in the corner of the bar, next to the south wall, was bright at first but rapidly degenerated into nothing more than poetry gossip – news about this and that poet, stories of past indiscretions and stupidities involving other poets. His speech was dead slow and getting slower, whisky-deep, Screech-slurred, and he would offer nothing about himself or his work. He preferred to pepper me with familiar tales about dead Canadian poets such as Al Purdy, Milton Acorn, Gwendolyn MacEwen, and his favourite, Alden Nowlan. "The conversation, though congenial, is incoherent," as Al Pittman says in one of his poems.

He was well regarded and admired by the others in the bar, however, probably both as a human being and a poetry icon, and everyone seemed to have sympathy for his condition. After an hour or two, someone offered to drive him home. I felt terrible, and in my mind blamed the drinking on the continuing leg pains, and the leg pains on the nameless quack who mangled the fracture. I'm empty of details, but full of suspicions, and it's a cruel world that always seeks to kill off its best and brightest poets.

With Al gone, I began conversing with a short fellow to my right. He was so round and so little you'd almost want to bounce him like a basketball. He was clean-shaven, with a little tuft of hair under his lower lip.

This fellow drinks, smokes, and claims to be the only male nurse in all of Newfoundland. When he was in high school, he took an aptitude test, which said he should be a nurse, because he had a natural sense of caring for people. He had a choice: either study to become a nurse, or try to toughen up and become more macho. So he chose to be a nurse, and I congratulated him on his courage. I was sure he'd done the right thing.

He also wanted me to know he was heterosexual. He said most people figure he's gay when they find out he's a nurse. I told him I couldn't think of a better job for a hot-blooded young male heterosexual than being a nurse, surrounded by so many loving, caring females.

He brightened considerably and told me I understood perfectly.

Another fellow at the bar I seemed to hit it off with was Randy McTwist, a short, comical, rowdy Irishman with a Yorkshire accent, having grown up in Sheffield, but with Irish mannerisms. He taught an introductory physics course at the local college and was going up to visit Clyde Rose, the publisher of Breakwater Books, with Al Pittman, the next day. He wanted me to come along. He'd phoned Clyde, and I'd be most welcome. Clyde was staying at his Breakwater chalet, on the south shore of Bonne Bay (sounds like Bombay), in Gros Morne National Park. I'd follow in my car, so that Randy and Al could return to Corner Brook in Randy's car, and I could continue my tour up the west coast to L'Anse aux Meadows at the northern tip. It sounded perfect, especially since Breakwater had always been Al Pittman's publisher, and I'd heard great things about Clyde.

A bit later I got into an interesting chat with the bartender, who was complaining about how scary and fraught with difficulty it was to be a lesbian in a Newfoundland of dwindling birth rate and population. She wanted me to tape her on the subject. So I got out my tape recorder. But a nasty drunk immediately noticed and yelled out across the room insulting accusations that I wanted to tape all the "stupid Newfies," then play the tapes for my "intellectual friends up in Toronto," so they could laugh themselves silly. Apparently he was the son of an old Englishman who taught at the local college, and the young fellow was having problems figuring out what he wanted to do with his life.

False accusations were nothing new to me, and I knew that it would be prudent to leave. Besides, there was a grain of truth in what he said, and it made me terribly depressed, for I grew up in a working-class neighbourhood in a working-class town and was born ultra-sensitive to issues involving unfair class distinctions, gender stereotypes, racial prejudices, and socio-economic generalities.

He was a tall, mean-looking Englishman, probably quite handsome when sober, in his late twenties, a dangerous age, and I found him a bit menacing. I'd hate to have to knock out his two front teeth with a sucker punch. So I went home. The lesbian bartender followed me to the door, apologized for the fellow's rudeness, and gave me a big hug and the sweetest little kiss.

GOOD OLD VALENTINE

Corner Brook • Pasadena • Deer Lake
Gros Morne National Park • Woody Point

Saturday, June 2. Randy McTwist was at Casual Jack's early today. So was the Englishman who had been angry about the tape recorder last night. He apologized for his bad manners. He blamed it on the booze. He said he was drunker than he'd ever been in his life. So that was nice. When I saw him my heart fell, and I wanted to clear out again, but his apology was rather graceful and won me over.

But to blame it on the booze seemed wrong, for the booze simply allows the ugliness to come out. The ugliness has to be there in the first place. Also, why would he be there so early the next day, already starting on a new day's replenishment of this vital fluid? Who would he be bullying tonight? Certainly not me. I'd been so depressed when I got back to my room, I wanted to call the trip off and crawl home. I lost all sense of the value of the material I'd already accumulated. I was certain I lacked the ability to put it together into a readable book. Sometimes innocence isn't enough. It was one of those sudden trauma-depressions that can strike a body blow with no warning.

The only thing that got me over it was the sort of inertia that makes one continue with a plan of action even though it seems futile and bound to end badly, like the Newfoundland Regiment's attack on the Germans at Beaumont–Hamel.

But the countryside today was full of spring colour and sunlight, and I followed Randy east on the Trans-Canada Highway through Pasadena and Deer Lake, then north. Al Pittman wasn't coming with us after all. He had been so drunk last night it took three close friends a considerable amount of time to get him into the car, then just as long to get him out of the car and up to his lonely apartment. Randy went over to Al's this morning to help him get ready, but it was impossible. Al had to do this, and had to do that, and had to buy some new clothes. . . .

So after an hour of Al listing, relisting, revising, and relating all the things he had to do before he could go, and not making a move to do any of them, Randy decided to take off and leave him sitting there. Randy decided that only a "small part" of Al's psyche wanted to come up with us, the rest of him just wanted to hole up by himself and stare at the walls, get drunk to dull the pain in his leg, and work on his poems. There's a lot of metal in that leg (as well as in the poems), and it just hadn't healed properly. He may have been a drunk before the fracture, I don't know, but the fracture didn't help. It hadn't healed the way it should have, and it was killing him. (Sadly he would die a few months later.)

Our first stop was a remote and solitudinous log cabin, where Randy picked up his dog, who was being cared for temporarily by a friend.

Randy McTwist has a cute red face and a full salt-and-pepper beard. He's a spontaneous and enthusiastic fellow, a fast talker with a perennially blissful look on his face. He's incapable of silence when others are around. He says what's on his mind, often before he knows it's on his mind, and it's usually fairly entertaining stuff, if surprisingly disjointed at times. He specializes in the wildest non sequiturs.

Randy's dog, Katie, has a long bushing tail that wags so vigorously the whole rear end of her body wags right along with it.

Randy's friend, Shelley, who had been taking care of Katie, was a pleasant lawyer in her mid-thirties. Randy obviously has good taste in dogs and in women.

Because of her love of solitude and her lack of avarice, Shelley has managed to cut her office hours to the point where she only has to go into Corner Brook three days a week. She spends the rest of the time in solitary splendour in a newly built log cabin, beautifully furnished with antiques, in a wooded area on the shore of a small lake. She often goes across to St. John's for meetings, and friends come up here to visit. She seems to be discovering an idyllic life for herself. With us she was animated, with flashing eyes and a satirical sense of fun. She and Randy are obviously old friends and share lots of affectionate secrets.

Shelley says when she opens her eyes in the morning she can't believe her luck to be living in such a place. She says she knows Corner Brook is a fairly quiet town as towns go, but the noise had started to bother her. The only neighbours she wanted were frogs and the occasional curious moose. She just may have been the brightest of all the bright people I'd met so far in Newfoundland.

Shelley couldn't come with us, but soon I was again following Randy's car, this time with Katie seatbelted into the front passenger seat, and keeping her eye open for ducks and other dogs as we drove north past tarpaper shacks with muddy old rusty motorcycles out front and piles of old lumber and firewood, and the whole scene covered by a sky so blue it was like a dream remembered from infancy. Each little house, well separated from the others, had a little garden fenced off, but was surrounded by forest on three sides, and in the gaps between the houses the forest came right down to the road. Thick forests gradually and then precipitously rose to the top of a whole series of steep rounded hills around nine hundred feet high on the horizon. Behind the hills were the long, pale blue, distant, ribbon-like Long

Range Mountains, treeless, and with a glacier-like patch of snow or two on top.

My heart felt pangs of pleasure whenever I caught sight of those transparent, blue, flat-topped mountains floating over distant horizons. I didn't feel pleasure about leaving Al at home, but Randy insisted he'd done all he could, and he obviously knew the situation better than I.

Clyde Rose is a big man with tremendous magnetic appeal. He looks like a cross between Ken Kesey and Anthony Quinn. He is the sort of fellow who attracts butterflies. He could tame a fox with a glance. Good luck and hummingbirds follow him wherever he goes. He could do whatever he wants and raise any sum of money for whatever project he wanted, he's that sort of guy.

We had only just arrived at the Breakwater chalet, when who should pop in for a quick howdy-do but Mrs. Wigglebum and her two kids. Mr. Wigglebum is working up in Ontario, but that doesn't slow down Mrs. Wigglebum one little bit. She was at a dance at the Canadian Legion, and a little old lady said to her, "My dear, I just wants ye to know my husband likes to see ye jiggle. He says when you dance you jiggle all over."

I said, "Was she laughing when she said it?"

"No, she was dead serious!"

"Was she being critical?"

"No, she was being complimentary, but in a serious manner."

Clyde had given her the name Mrs. Wigglebum. She loves it.

Clyde's friend Ulrike was a psychotherapist on a brief visit from Switzerland. She and Clyde were our hosts at the chalet, near Woody Point, with a great view over Bonne Bay. We were treated to a Bulgarian salad that had all of us whimpering with pleasure. I forgot to get the recipe, which Ulrike had acquired from a famous Czech violinist named Valentine. She was disappointed that none of us had heard of him. She kept saying, "Good old Valentine!" The two huge bowls she'd prepared went in a flash. At one point, out of the blue, Randy looked up from his plate and said, with a wacky look on his face, "I'm computer illiterate!"

After dinner and cleanup, Clyde and Ulrike spent the evening singing beautiful Irish, Newfoundlandish, and German folk songs, with Clyde on accordion. It was amazing that he had taught her so many songs in such a short time and she had taught him so many German songs as well. "Curragh of Kildare" was terrific, but the most enchanting was their version of the dark and tragic "Long Black Veil," the verses of which they sang at a pace so slow it gave a different spin to the first word of the title. But it was as if I'd never heard it before, and that made it all the more exquisitely tragic and frightening.

At one point I mistakenly referred to the accordion as a squeeze-box, because that's what I thought small accordions without piano-like keyboards were called. But Clyde corrected me, and rightly so. He found the term squeeze-box almost as offensive as a "Newfie" joke. This is an accordion, he said. The big ones with the keyboards are piano-accordions.

Clyde sang one long song on his own, with about eighty-five stanzas, and he kept squeezing away on the accordion. It had been a long day, and his lids were beginning to droop, but he was determined to finish the song without messing up a single stanza. He was sitting on a hardbacked chair, and as he sang, Ulrike had her left hand on his right shoulder, and her right hand on his chest, and was gazing at him adoringly. When his lids would droop, she'd take her hand off his chest and run her fingers through his hair, and then his eyes would pop open again. She knew when it was the final stanza, and she sang the last line with him, then reached down and gave him a hug.

After Clyde climbed the stairs to bed with a book on the history of Dublin under his arm, sweetly soft-spoken Ulrike and I managed to have a rather serious conversation, even though Randy, who had drunk too much, kept interrupting us with silly remarks at sensitive moments. She was telling me how she had "untied a knot" in her psychology years ago simply by concentrating on it over a long period. "That's highly unlikely," said Randy.

Each night her dreams would become gradually more vivid and more related to the central psychic problem she was struggling to solve. Finally she triumphed, the riddle was solved, the dreams became increasingly rich and vivid, and one night they just opened up and presented her with the solution.

She told the story without revealing intimate details of the nature of the problem or the solution, but it was obviously a deep dark one, and the solution was miraculous.

Did she subscribe to the notion that the unconscious mind has a way of killing off people who don't pay attention to it?

She did subscribe to that theory and spoke of how in many cultures ancient traditions are still current in which people afflicted with excessive grief after the death of a loved one are placed in solitary confinement for several weeks, with all their meals brought to them and all their needs taken care of.

Ulrike complained that she had received her academic training at a university where everything revolved around Sigmund Freud. They had no time for any of the other theorists of the unconscious and were particularly opposed to anything that smacked of Jungianism. As a result, when she got her degree and went to work in a psychiatric hospital, she knew everything about Freud but couldn't connect his theories to what was going on in the minds of her patients.

"There I was, having finished my studies," she said, "and now I had to deal with human beings. "I tried what I learned, but I failed, and none of my theories helped me because of the phenomena I was seeing." Her eyes were filling with tears. "So I tried desperately to find some way to gain some understanding." She was just about to explain how she solved this problem, when Randy broke in with some comment that broke her thread of thought.

She went on to speak of her interest in the theories of Gershen Kaufman and Leon Wurmser, both of whom had written books in the early eighties on the subject of shame, which they termed the "ignored emotion." Their theories were apparently the ones that gave her insight into the problems her patients were facing.

At that point, Randy demanded to know what was the thing in our lives that has most bothered us. I knew, but I didn't feel like talking about it with such recent acquaintances, no matter how nice they were, and Ulrike heartily agreed. So finally I shut him up by saying the thing that most bugged me was the size of my weeny. Ulrike looked shocked and whispered to me, "You don't worry about that any more, do you?" I assured her it was a joke.

As Ulrike went to her room, Randy called out after her, "I've already told Clyde that if you're not up by nine o'clock cooking us a big breakfast I'm leaving."

Then he turned to me and said, in the most scornful Yorkshire tones, that there are no mental-health problems that three months in Fiji wouldn't sort out – guaranteed! I suggested he book a flight immediately.

I was tickling Katie behind the ears and marvelling at her intensely soulful eye contact. I remembered a saying by Gurdjieff: "Practise love on animals; they are more sensitive and respond better." And as I continued stroking her, I spoke to her adoringly, then kept staring into her eyes as I touched different parts of her body and described them to Randy. Katie was hanging on my every word, she knew exactly what I was saying: "She has a long bushy tail like a fox, and is slender and svelte, curvaceous really, with a large chest and a narrow waist. And look at these big fat paws and just a little snout. . . ."

Randy was silent throughout all this, until I asked what she was. "She's a Nova Scotian duck tolling retriever," he said in a moment of lucidity. I said that Katie really seemed to be offering living proof that dogs have a soul. Randy said that many have remarked on how well Katie interacts with human beings, and it was suggested once that he take Katie to visit the patients in the psychiatric ward – but he refused because they weren't going to pay him for it.

Undaunted, I told him that my friend April English used to take her dog, Ben – on a volunteer basis – to help promote healing on the psychiatric ward. Unfortunately, on one such trip Ben bit a patient, and April was told not to bring him back. Randy started laughing so uncontrollably I was afraid he was going to choke to death.

It turns out the Nova Scotia duck toller is a rare breed of hunting dog, born with an instinctive bag of tricks for enticing ducks into narrow inlets where they can be captured with nets. In fact these dogs are so intelligent they have been known to give their owners a look of disgust when they miss an easy shot.

Now that things had quietened down I began looking at the pictures on the wall. There was a beautiful photo of Clyde at age seventeen. He was lying on his side in a grassy springtime meadow and smiling at the camera, while sucking on the stem of a buttercup. He's wearing jeans and a T-shirt and is propping his head up on his hand, with the most adorable smile on his face. All the joy of being seventeen was in his eyes. It reminded me of the famous photo of the poet Allen Ginsberg at about the same age, barefooted, bare-chested, in rolled-up jeans and standing way up on a limb of a cherry tree in blossom, and with the happiest, most radiant look.

The first photo must have been taken almost fifty years ago, but it was instantly recognizable as Clyde. I didn't realize it at the time, but Clyde is not only a publisher but a poet. In 1999 he published a book of verse called *Christ in the Pizza Place*.

There was another photo, this time a group family portrait, with Clyde's parents and what seemed to be about fourteen children. They grew up in the isolated community of Fox Island Harbour on the south shore. Clyde looked about twenty-one this time. His Zorba-the-Greek good looks would have stood out from the crowd – even if he hadn't been wearing an ascot! It's a remarkably handsome family, but if a thousand people were shown this photo and asked to select the person who would later become a great success as a professor at Memorial University, a naval diving officer, a published poet, and a leading national figure in his field (literary and educational publishing, in both book and software format), I'd predict that most would immediately point to Clyde.

THREE COD AND
THREE MACKEREL

Woody Point • Lobster Cove • Cow Head
Parson's Pond • Port au Choix

Sunday, June 3. Clyde and Ulrike have taken off in their boat. We rolled it out of the boathouse on a homemade boat carrier, then launched it and pulled it up to the dock at a spot immediately below the chalet. I asked who made the carrier, and a little old fisherman, who had been standing there watching us, put up his hand like a schoolboy. He said it took him about half a day. It was made out of four-by-four rough-hewn spruce timbers, bolted together in a most pleasing manner, then an axle and a couple of wheels from an old tractor were bolted into place.

"You certainly saved a lot of money." The old fisherman just smiled. "If you wanted to buy a trailer like this new, it'd cost you what? A thousand? Two thousand?"

"Fourteen hundred dollars," said the fisherman.

"And it cost you . . .?"

"Oh, no more than twenty dollars."

"Did that include the beer?"

"No, that was a little extra."

We held the boat close to the dock, and Clyde and Ulrike daintily stepped in with their picnic basket. Clyde gave a good solid yank on the engine, and after about ten such yanks – with everybody on the shore shouting encouragement ("Let 'er warm up, b'y, let 'er warm up" and "Give her a good strong pull, b'y") – the engine kicked in with an explosive bang that echoed off the distant hills, and off they went backwards out of the shallow water, rather than bothering to turn around and go frontwards.

"Does that boat go forwards too?" I said.

The old fisherman squinched his eyes and giggled.

It was a thirty-six-horsepower outboard motor, and quite a big boat for such a small engine, especially when this was the first time it had been fired up since last fall. But they got the boat straightened out and off they went, frontwards, with many a backward wave as they headed toward a little island up the bay where they planned to spend a lazy afternoon birdwatching, eating lobster, drinking champagne, singing songs, and reading romantic poetry to each other.

The fisherman gave his age as sixty-seven. He'd fished all his life; he was born right here on Bonne Bay, in Gros Morne National Park, on the west coast of Newfoundland, and had always lived here. Had he made much money at fishing? "Oh yeah, there was tons of money in it till ten years ago." But you've spent it all now, right? "Oh no, b'y," he said, with another big laugh. "I've still got some of it salted away." He said living is really cheap here, there's no mortgage on his house, and he was obviously as happy as could be. For this old fisherman the cod moratorium has not been a tragedy – not on a personal level at any rate.

He only fly-fishes now. He has a cap with a fishing fly on it, and he takes it off and shows it to me, and says, "That's what we use. We put about six flies on it and we throw it out, b'y. And we might get six cod, or we might get six mackerel, or we might get three cod and three mackerel."

He told me a long story about lobsters, only part of which I could follow. But there are hardly any small lobsters any more, he maintained. They can only get the big ones. The lobsters have stopped reproducing. If that's true, who can blame them? Why bother reproducing when the humans along the shore will steal your babies and plunge them into boiling water? Maybe they're in telepathic contact. I read somewhere that lobsters moult at different times, and when one has shed its shell, it is a tempting morsel indeed. So its mate, and sometimes other lobsters, will hover over it and protect it from sneaky predators until its new shell has hardened (like those long-ago summers on Lake Erie when Dad would hold up the beach blanket so that Mom could change into her bathing suit without being ogled).

Like everyone else so far, he agrees with the seal hunt, but doesn't agree with skinning the little guys alive. He says it's just like winging a moose then skinning it alive while it's still bleeding. You just don't do that; it's not civilized behaviour. You make sure your moose is dead first, he said. Why don't they do that with the seals too?

He insisted the seal had to take its share of blame for the dwindling cod and lobster stocks. I said the fisheries department people claim the seals don't eat significant amounts of either. He looked disgusted. "What d'they eat then, b'y? Turnips and cabbages?" Then he started laughing with glee.

He also said that, if the seals don't eat salmon, as many so-called experts say, why do so many seals go up the salmon streams at this time of year when the salmon are coming up to spawn? Maybe they just enjoy watching, I offered. He started giggling again.

What about the winters? "Oh, they're not so bad around here on the west coast." What do you do to amuse yourself? He said he shoots rabbits. He sometimes gets two, or he can come back with a dozen if his freezer is getting low. But the rabbits are going down too, he says.

There was a fairly high and steep hill back from where we were standing, and the old fisherman was telling me that, in the winter, the younger fellows in their snowmobiles like to go up to the top along a gradual trail that leads up from the south side, which isn't steep at all. Then they get to the treeless top, shoot a few rabbits, and they come flying like the wind down the steep side of the hill. They follow the creek beds so they can get down real fast without trees getting in the way. It's dangerous. They screech their heads off all the way down – with their engine off and the brakes on. It must be quite a scary, thrilling ride, but I don't think it'll ever qualify as an Olympic sport.

No wonder the rabbit numbers are down. They're not dying off. With all that noise, they're just relocating deeper in the forest, beyond the snowmobile trails.

With the field glasses I can make out Newfoundland and Canadian flags flying in little villages on the far side of Bonne Bay. Each little settlement has its own low-slung vinyl-sided church, with a short, squat steeple and a red or blue roof. And each has its cemetery. And there are some chalets, surrounded by decks, in natural stained wood.

Everything seems to sparkle, pure and pristine, with no sign of environmental degradations. Even the roads that come winding along the shore of the bay seem to have been cut with care. To the northwest, way off in the distance, is the peculiarly flat-topped Gros Morne (722 metres). And on the almost-vertical side facing us, three great snow patches formed good approximations of T 7 F. They were approximate enough for me – and even Randy, who considered himself a "hard-nosed scientist," could see it. No idea what message the mountain was sending out, but I took T 7 F, whatever it stands for, to be a lucky omen.

A neighbour not far off is busily hammering away on his shingles, but that doesn't bother the birds or the waves, which continue chirping or lapping the shore. Randy and Katie are inside the house laughing and barking. Clyde and Ulrike are off having their picnic, and over in the distance the mountains look as if they have been shaved off at the top on a perfectly level basis by some kind of a huge laser beam. There are numerous mountains, but they all come to the same height, at which point they are flattened off at the top, indiscriminately, by some jealously democratic god who didn't think it fair that some mountains should be higher than others. What mighty force did that? The *Canadian Encyclopedia* claims it was the action of the retreating glaciers. If so, why didn't they do that to other mountains at the same latitude? To my amateur eye, these mountains had flat tops long before the last ice age. But whenever and however the flat tops came to be, these are interesting and likeable tabletop mountains, as they're called locally, or sometimes just flat-tops. They look like aircraft carriers.

A little white house down the shore a bit has a large sign out front, with large black block letters on white, saying "JIMS" – and an identical sign, except slightly smaller, obviously by the same hand, on the side of the house, saying "JIM's." Maybe the fellow wasn't sure if it looked better with or without the apostrophe. That would be him, slouched over sound asleep on a chair on the porch, with a cat snoozing on his lap.

Here's what I think. A friend was asked to make the sign, to return a favour, and was thoughtful enough to ask Jim if he wanted it with or without an apostrophe. He said, "I don't know. Could I have one of each?"

I shook paws with Randy and Katie and hit the road to the extreme north, with my mind all by itself busy trying to organize impressions and experiences of the past three weeks.

A highway sign gives the number of moose in accidents with cars this year: 6. Number of caribou: 5. So it's 6 to 5 for the moose! The visitors are beating the home team!

Sometimes you'll be driving along, there'll be a moose on the side of the road, and you'll be looking at him so intently that you won't notice his mate right in front of you until you almost smack into her. A heavy forest comes right down to the side of the road, and sometimes there will even be a beaver dam right in the middle of the road. So it's best not to speed. I can't actually remember seeing a beaver dam in the middle of the road, but according to my notes, there was one. So what shall I trust, my memory or my notes?

But there are so few roads in Newfoundland. Who knows what is hidden in the great stretches of wilderness? There could be UFO launching pads for all we know, or clandestine uranium mines, or networks of towers beaming out mind-control messages all over the world, and distracting our little minds from more important things by projecting fake flying saucers in the sky, or imprinting ingenious crop circles in wheat fields.

Somewhere north of Lobster Cove, I'm walking along the beach and gazing out at a level calm sea, with little ripples of delight moving northwards. It's the kind of sea familiar from the work of the Newfoundland painter Christopher Pratt. Heavy, low-lying clouds leave little holes for shots of light to blast through here and there, and off in the distance is a lovely spilling of pink light.

But the highway keeps taking me north, with the sea on the left and the bog on the right. The bog disappears into forests and the forests disappear halfway up a range of high old mountains – some flat-tops, some more rugged, but none with the traditional pointy peaks. There are a lot of old cars with Newfoundland plates travelling along slowly, with the passengers and sometimes even the driver gawking at the scenery. These are probably Newfoundlanders who have been meaning to get up to Gros Morne for decades and are finally doing it.

I'd give the scenery five stars; it reminds me of the old road between Banff and Lake Louise, although this road is just five feet above sea level rather than five thousand. But as my old pal the Montreal poet Artie Gold used to say, "It's not how high you are, it's hi, how are you?"

My friend Ellen Jaffe said her parents took her to Newfoundland for a holiday when she was a child, and all she can remember is visiting a village called Cow Head, where everybody looked alike. So now here I am in Cow Head, eager to see if the people still look alike. There's Our Lady of the Coast Church, the Cow Head Variety, and the P&B Open Fruit Market, with a board nailed over the word fruit, although the board doesn't completely cover the word. I guess they don't have any fruit and they're tired of having to tell people. The closest thing they can offer is Tang frozen orange juice and Juicy Fruit chewing gum. I haven't knowingly seen any fruit in this province, except in the supermarkets in the larger centres, but luckily I have a half-bushel of Nova Scotia apples, which I bought in New Brunswick – and I've been eating two a day all along, in order to keep two doctors away.

Our Lady of the Coast Church is doing extremely well, with the parking lot full of parked cars, the occupants of which are all presumably inside pestering the Blessed Virgin Mary for boons. The only people out in the open are a woman and her daughter and her son, and all three of them look alike. Then I saw another woman, and she looked like the first woman. Then I saw a third woman, and she looked like the second one. Then I saw a woman on a bicycle who looked like the first woman's son. Then I saw a man leaning against a car, and he didn't look like any of them. Then I saw a man with a full beard and he seemed to be an out-of-towner. And all the time I was looking at those people, none of them was looking at me. So I think that Ellen Jaffe's observations, from so many years ago, were probably correct, but since that time there has been some outbreeding.

La mer, grey and immense, is serene this evening. Petrels in pairs are skimming the surface, the tips of their wings making little rings. The fabled sense of cosmic unity, that oneness with the universe, is a great privilege to feel on a night like this; at 7:13 p.m., I'm the only person on the entire beach, with long, thin, multicoloured ribbons stretched out on the horizon, and with air so clean, so fragrant, so easy to breathe. An emphysema patient could throw his oxygen tank into the sea on a night like this.

It's also such a privilege to be out of Toronto, where I've been wheezing asthmatically off and on all winter, and doing crazy things like making ironic comments to perfect strangers, and sticking my hat out on a busy street to see how long it would take for someone to put a loonie in, then giving the loonie to a real panhandler. So I had to get out of town, and suddenly I'm sane again! Soon I'll be so sane I'll have to scamper back to the big city to get reacquainted with my neuroses.

A little graveyard overlooking the beach is full of Whites, Caines, Parsons, and Clarks. Next to it is a shallow lake with a sign saying Parson's Pond. There's a bit of sporadic oil drilling going on in the vicinity, and it's said natural oil seeps into the pond. In fact, it's said Old Man Parson in days of yore thought nothing of getting naked and having a good swim in the pond to ease the pains of his rheumatism. And his hair would be slicked back like Rudolph Valentino's for days after.

Once out of Gros Morne National Park the highway becomes full of rough potholes, and the traffic, paradoxically, speeds up alarmingly. The cars, trucks, and buses swoosh by so furiously I can hardly hang on. They've been gawking at the scenery long enough, now they have to make up for it.

Late evening is a good time for misreading highway signs, such as "Caution – Metaphysical Entry," or "Jesus Died for Your Brother Jack," or "Slow – Two Strangers." The winter storms sweep in off the sea around here with such force all the mature spruce trees are permanently bent over like Olympic gymnasts, with their pointy crowns almost touching the ground.

A few miles farther north is the Arches, a much-photographed but still sublime natural rock formation rising out of a sandy beach right at the edge of the high tide. It's a whale-backed kind of erratic, worn smooth with time. The sea over the ages has bored four dream-like arches through the base of the rock, forming a hollowed-out cavern with eight entrances. It resembles a low-slung, thin bear, walking along with its nose to the ground, or a human hand with fingers pressing firmly on a tabletop and the hand curving above the fingers. Picasso would have painted it. Henry Moore spent a lifetime trying to carve a stone into a shape this sublime but never came close. It'd be wonderful to be here during a storm. I wonder how much the Newfoundland government would ask for it. It'd look terrific sitting in the middle of Queen's Park in Toronto.

The photographs one sees of the Arches, for instance on page 41 of my wildflower book, don't give any sense of it at all. The photos make it seem trite. It's not a spot you would go out of your way to visit. But once you've visited it, it will stick with you, and you will not wish to see any photos of it.

Meanwhile, the sea sits there as flat as morning-after champagne. And it's just not fair, I can't see one whale. I may as well be searching for the Loch Ness monster. Perhaps one must stop wanting to see them before they'll appear.

I've also been unable so far to discover any unknown Viking settlements. But, in Port au Choix, I found a motel, where I could sleep and snore like a weary wanderer, but not before a little stroll down the beach, inspecting the numerous whale-backed patches of crusty ice that are still sitting on the fine sand on this warm evening in June.

TWELVE ANGRY
FISHERMEN

*Port aux Choix • Gargamelle • Bartletts Harbour
Deadmans Cove • L'Anse aux Meadows*

Monday, June 4. One picture shows a dock with an outhouse at the far end. A sign says OUTHOUSE CLOSED. So the fisherman is standing on the roof, with his back to the viewer, and he is peeing into the sea, with the sun setting in the distance. Why is the fellow standing on top of the outhouse rather than just on the dock? That's for the viewer to figure out. Whether you succeed isn't all that important. Unfortunately, by the way the dockside flag of Newfoundland is blowing, the fellow must be peeing into the wind – which is not recommended. Fortunately, he does have his sou'wester on.

Ben J. Ploughman uses real thread to represent the ropes on the flagpole, and a natural knothole to represent the setting sun.

Another piece is called "Sailing Home" and shows a big boat and a little boat sailing in tandem past a tall lighthouse next to a short, dark house.

These two works hang in the dining room of the Port au Choix Motel, where I savoured a breakfast of clam chowder and two coffees while gazing with fascination at Ploughman's paintings. I'd earlier admired one hanging in the Burnt Berry dining room.

Studio Gargamelle, in the village of Gargamelle, on the Viking Trail, a short walk southeast of Port au Choix, is the place to go if you want to get a load of Ben J. Ploughman. He's a homespun guy from this area, studied geology at Memorial University, and worked for Hibernia. But there was something missing.

His relaxed, easy-to-miss studio is housed in a large one-storey warehouse a step or two back from the highway. It's partitioned into three: a studio for his art, a studio for his museum, and the museum, which isn't ready to open yet.

In studio one, he has a set of cupboards, with shallow drawers in which he stores bits and pieces of painted wood. Perfectly organized for quick access are painted and variously sized seagulls, codfish, moose, caribou, fishermen, boats, trees, hills, islands, rocks, docks, ducks, fishing huts, lobster traps, lobsters, houses, churches, smiling politicians with excellent haircuts, scowling bureaucrats with clipboards, clouds, skies, suns, moons, stars, galaxies, tourists with skis atop their SUVs, filling stations, convenience stores, whales, seals, dogs, cats, wolves, rabbits, moose, icebergs, flags of different nations, and so on.

Ben often will do the same subject twice, or more, depending on how popular it has been, with slight changes and improvements with each variation to keep it interesting for himself.

He whips open the iceberg drawer for my inspection, and I'm almost blinded by a jumble of hundreds of little gleaming icebergs in all sorts of icebergy shapes.

"Twelve Angry Fishermen" shows the backs of twelve fishermen in a row, standing on the dock and peeing into the sea. To me that's a great work of the imagination, before beginning to think of the cod moratorium, or even without taking into consideration that the piece is similar in shape and composition to Leonardo's *Last Supper*, though not as large. Ben's a practising Catholic.

In studio two, a forty-six-foot sperm-whale skeleton in progress hangs from the ceiling. Detailed plans for the skeleton are tacked to the wall like Michelangelo's plans for the Sistine Chapel. Each piece is hanging from a plastic string from the ceiling, so that it sits exactly where it's supposed to sit. This is a huge project. Ben's pleased with the tail hanging from the ceiling. "Dere's no bones in de tail, right? Only cartilage. So we made a fibreglass tail to go on 'im. We made dat last winter. It's made out of plywood wi' de fibreglass over it, same as de technique what dey do on de boats, right? Dis is an ongoing project for a year or two, right?"

He's treating me to a sneak preview of the whale in progress, because we're in a similar situation: I'm trying to string together the skeleton of a whale of a book. He shows me a handful of teeth from a sperm whale. "Here's de real ones. I didn't have all of 'em, I only had about half. De whale was dead, de teeth were missing, but I managed to get half, right? So I put a casting on over 'em an' made de moulds." So some of the teeth will be real and some homemade.

He says, "People, they come in here, and they don't even know there are two kinds of whales: the ones with the teeth and the ones without the teeth. So at least they leave here knowing that."

"I knew that," I said, smilingly.

"Shore ye did," he says.

He would hear of a whale that had been hit by a boat, or got tangled up in the nets, and the corpse had washed up on shore. He'd go down to inspect the remains. He'd cut the corpse up, take out all the bones. He had a fifty-gallon boiler steaming away in a shed out back of the studio, and he'd throw all the bones in and boil them down until they were clean as a whistle.

He'd stack the bones up, according to type, on long tables in studio two. Now he doesn't have to make any more trips to the beach; all the material he needs is on hand. If any piece is missing, he'll be able to figure out a way to fashion it himself. He's also planning to start local talent shows in his studio, on Tuesday and

Thursday evenings, just to get people in to see what he's doing. There'll be musicians, singers, recitations.

"We get visits from a polar bear now and den, and when de sea is calm dey come off de iceberg and chase de seals."

Do they kill many seals?

"We might only see one polar bear per year, but we see hundreds of thousands of seals."

Huge issue, right?

"Oh yes, it's on everybody's mind in Newfoundland. We know we're in a mess. We had a mass migration of our young people. We got a brain drain in Newfoundland. All of our brains are gone."

When I saw the small work by Ben J. Ploughman in the Burnt Berry dining room, I asked Al Payne why the fisherman was smiling. He said because he was going on pogey. Ben said Mr. Payne was dead right on that.

It's a joy to visit an artist's studio when he's on top of things, working every day, full of enthusiasm and optimism. Ben has a large piece showing the *Titanic*, with its four smokestacks, sailing straight toward the iceberg. Another shows the *Titanic* breaking up and going down, with tiny people jumping into lifeboats or leaping madly into the sea.

He also has a series of champagne bottles from 1912, labelled "Last Note from the Titanic" – each containing a note forged on a telegraph form from that era.

He also has "The Fisherman's Mona Lisa," a portrait of a bearded old fisherman with his pipe and sou'wester, and he's looking out at the viewer with a perfect little Mona Lisa smile on his face.

Ben was the first Newfoundlander I heard express the sealers' side of the seal-skinning story. He said the sealers would bop a seal three times on the head with a club, and then skin it, because they were in a hurry. The reason they were in a hurry was (1) because it was so cold out, (2) because the coats were only pure white for a short time and after that the price drops, (3) if they shot them first, they had to spend more time patching up the bullet holes, and (4) they'd never make a profit, because the people who buy sealskins were such cheapskates when it came to paying the sealers for their time and energy.

So it's one vicious circle, with the rich skinning the poor alive, just as sure as the poor skin the seals alive to try to stay alive themselves.

But, he added, it's been a good winter for seals, with 285,000 seals being taken, and a fairly good price being offered – $28 apiece – so lots of sealers are feeling fairly prosperous this spring.

On the way back to Port au Choix, I have an encounter with a caribou stag, with a splendid rack of antlers, and for a split second I want to pick him up and slide him into a drawer, or get out the pot of glue and paste him up on the sky. Unfortunately, this caribou is in danger of being shot, for he is standing with his snout in someone's vegetable garden and is pulling up all the carrots and onions, while munching away at cabbages and cucumbers. When the people get home, they'll likely just start planting again. I should chase him away, but sometimes it's not all that wise to interfere with nature: what if I shouted at him and he became frightened and leaped through the front window of the convenience store?

But when I went to drive away, he leaped in front of the car, causing me to swerve around him and accelerate. He seemed to be out to perpetuate his genetic material, and because I was moving slowly (and had a hot tailpipe), he might have mistaken me for a likely female.

When the warm weather comes, it doesn't take the Newfoundlanders long to plant their gardens, either in their own yards or in a staked-out plot in long ribbons of such plots running along both sides of the highway for miles on either side of every town – in addition to the gardens in their front and back yards.

At Bartletts Harbour, I run in for a package of Brazil nuts and a bottle of spring water at a little store painted with vertical stripes of pink and white. When I say, "Nice place you have here," Effie Scanlan, proprietress, gives me an odd look as if to say, "You must be out of your mind. This is a dump." She places my purchases in a paper bag.

As I leave the store, a very obese lady is coming in. She is looking at my little bag with X-ray eyes, as if she is trying to determine what's in there. So I slip to one side in order to hear the conversation through the open door. Sure enough, she's saying to Effie, "What'd that guy get who was just in here? What's in that guy's bag? What did he buy?"

Effie tells her.

"Okay then, that's what I'll have," she says, "except make the mineral water a Pepsi."

So I sat on the step and ate the Brazil nuts, and the large lady came out with her little bag and disappeared down the road; then Effie came out. I asked Effie how to get to the museum.

She said, "You see that post office over there? You turn there, then you go down there as far as you can till you get to the doll's house, then turn right. See that doll's house over there?"

I couldn't see any doll's house, but I didn't want to be uncooperative, so I said, "Yes?"

She tricked me. She said, "No you can't. You can't see it from here."

You shoulda seen me blush!

The "doll's house" turns out to be an imposing and un-Newfoundlandish brick house with artificial Elizabethan half-timbers. It looks as if it was built around 1973. Strange that such a place would be called the doll's house, but such is down-home humour. The museum, which was farther on along the beach, was closed, as are most of the museums in the tourist areas of Newfoundland this early in the season.

The dark grey cliffs of Labrador loom across the shimmering waters of the Strait of Belle Isle. A small iceberg hugs the shore. It has two big ears and looks like Mickey Mouse swimming, with his hind end sticking up out of the water in such a way you can't see the tail. When a wave hits an iceberg that is stuck on the bottom, the wave jumps back as if it has smashed into a rock. When a wave hits one that is floating free, it's the iceberg that jumps back.

An iceberg is something that is pure – it has a purity of texture, form, and content. It contains no sodium or salt, no fluorocarbons, no sulphuric acid. Not the slightest trace of human, animal, or industrial wastes. No carcinogens. No DDT. No oil spills or artificial colouring. No old periscope covers off submarines. Just pure, distilled water from precipitations that fell from the sky ten thousand years ago. The iceberg level of purity is far beyond even the purity of the ice caps on those Labrador cliffs across the strait. It's a wonder everyone isn't constantly guzzling Newfoundland iceberg vodka.

"Grief is heavier than the sea," says a line in an Al Pittman poem, and at Deadmans Cove, someone has died. The casket is sitting in the sun. The six pallbearers wear black leather jackets, black leather caps, black jeans, black boots. The corpse seems badly in need of burial, because the gravediggers are working furiously, and a handful of mourners are staring speechlessly at each other, and they are continually shifting their weight from one leg to the other in a manner that speaks of acute discomfort and impatience beyond grief. One of the diggers stops for a beat to wipe his brow, and a pallbearer jumps in, grabs the shovel from him, and goes to work.

A few miles farther north, I'm watching a kid on a ladder scraping and sanding the side of a house. It looks as if he's getting the walls prepared for vinyl siding, or maybe the siding has been removed and he's getting the walls ready for paint. A green SUV pulls up and a tiny old fellow about seventy-five gets out. He's dressed in a maroon T-shirt and green shorts. He looks like the writer Farley Mowat. He goes to the foot of the ladder and says to the kid: "You've got your work cut out for you on such a hot day." Just the sort of friendly thing

Farley would say. Then he walks back to his SUV. He sees me gaping at him and gives me a friendly smile. So I say, "You must be distantly related to Farley Mowat, you look so much like him." His mouth drops. Nobody ever told him that before.

"I wouldn't mind looking like Farley Mowat if I could write half as good as he does."

"You like his books?"

"Oh yeah, I've read them all. The ones he wrote about Newfoundland, I've read them twice."

At the northern tip of the Northern Peninsula, L'Anse aux Meadows, there's a restaurant with a plain atmosphere, a clean place with simple decor, and an excellent little bookstore, featuring Newfoundland titles, behind the dining room. One enters the restaurant through the side door and walks through the bookstore into the dining room.

"That couple over there, they're from Toronto too," says the young locally born and raised proprietress. She seats me at a large table at the large front window overlooking the sea. I'm too far away from the Toronto couple to eavesdrop on their conversation without straining, but watching the shrimp boats bobbing in the waves makes up for it. The couple is at a smaller table at the side window, overlooking the road and the driveway. I fantasize they're planning to buy the restaurant and install three or four of those fake marble rearing horses favoured by the pricier Italian restaurants in Toronto. The village is quiet, no traffic, but in a month it'll be choking with tourists, who are notorious for never leaving tips, looking anyone in the eye, or smiling. The proprietress hands me a well-thumbed copy of *Where to Eat in Canada*. This restaurant has an enthusiastic write-up. There's a wonderful line in the book's preface: "Nobody can pay to be mentioned in this book, and nobody can pay not to be mentioned." I should adopt it for this book. To be perfectly honest, I might change "Nobody can pay" to "Nobody *would* pay." This is my sixth travel book, and no one has yet dared to offer me a bribe.

I had the seafood chowder, with Viking-size chunks of lobster and cod. I didn't need a main course, but the young proprietress was so enthusiastic and chatty I couldn't resist asking her what she was most proud of on her menu. She said the baked codfish, which was done with an exclusive mixture of Dijon mustard and garlic. She also pointed out a little fishing hut across the road.

She said the lucky fisherman over there is one of only twenty-six in the Northern Peninsula who are allowed to ignore the cod moratorium. And this is part of a government study of the cod stocks. The twenty-six were chosen by lottery. She assures me it's perfectly open and legal: the fisherman phones when he's coming in with fish, she goes over and buys all she needs, and he takes the rest to the government depot. So that's why the fish is so unutterably fresh. Everybody's going to want to move to Newfoundland when they read this book.

She had no trace of the Newfoundland twang. Her father died shortly after she was born, and she was raised by her mother, who had opinions about the English language and always corrected her as a child when she made an "error" in pronunciation. So now she has a perfect mainstream CBC accent. And if such an accent seems out of place in L'Anse aux Meadows, it doesn't seem to bother her one little bit.

For sure I took my time at the Norseman Café, run by Gina Hodge, then drove out to the Valhalla guest home, run by her mother, Bella Hodge. Bella hadn't entirely shaken off her own Newfoundland twang. But as for Gina's, it seems that, when a mother is determined about something, and the daughter is similarly determined, nothing can stop it from happening. It's inevitable.

Bella owns the Valhalla, as well as a house in St. Anthony. She was miffed when I slipped an "s" on the end of the name of the town. "Please don't say St. Anthony's," she said in polite-but-distressed tones. "It's St. Anthony." I apologized profusely. I was still back in St. John's, St. Vincent's, St. Shotts, St. Alban's, etc.

Bella was hosting her sister and her sister's friend. They were both nurses at the Shalom Retirement Village in Hamilton, Ontario, and were on vacation. From the dining room there was an amazing view. We were perched atop a heavily forested hill, and the view took in the entire downward slope to the sea, and, out in the sea, icebergs the size of outports. Only thing wrong, we were socked in. We had the view, but it was currently unavailable on account of dense fog. So Bella got out her copy of the *Ancient Mysteries* videotape and inserted it into her VCR. It was a special instalment devoted to the area around L'Anse aux Meadows. The tape played for a while, then she freeze-framed it and exclaimed: "There, there's the view from my place." And sure enough, there it was, but with the sun rising and clear focus. "The cameraman was standing exactly where you're standing," she said. I was standing right in front of the socked-in window, but within view of the TV. I had to laugh, for it was an interesting experience, and a definite first for me.

Bella seems to have the knack of attracting interesting people who can help promote her business enterprises. That cameraman from *Ancient Mysteries* brought her a lot of business when he got back to New York. Annie Proulx spent two weeks at the Valhalla guest home writing the first draft of her famous novel *The Shipping News*, the film version of which was at that moment being shot a few peninsulas to the east of here. Bella again corrects me: I shouldn't say first draft. It was the entire book, from gestation to final draft, that was written in two weeks while staying here. Nobody said anything, but I had the feeling Bella may have actually given Annie the inspiration, the title, the idea, the opening scene, the ending, and so on.

So Bella and Annie are the greatest friends. Bella is as keen on literary stuff as is Annie. Bella's dining-room bookshelf attests to that: it bulges and sags with the most wonderful ancient tomes, mostly dealing with life in Newfoundland and other themes of local and regional interest, both historical and contemporary. It's the finest example of Newfoundlandia you could assemble in about twenty feet of shelf space.

Bella Hodge said she had a call from London last September, from a writer from the *Sunday Times*. He was writing an article about the author of *The Shipping News*, so he wanted to come and see Bella, to see the exact place where she (Annie) conceived of and wrote the book. Could he come in November? No, said Bella, she'd be closed in November. Could he come in October? No, she'd be closed then. Could he come this month? Well, I'm going to close in about a week. He said I'll be on a plane right away.

And he came. He spent two weeks there. But she wouldn't tell him anything. Nothing whatsoever about Annie Proulx, the author, for that would be a violation of their friendship. Bella is nothing if not loyal. He'd underestimated the integrity of the Newfoundlanders. But he stayed anyway, and he ended up writing his whole article about the guest home in which Annie stayed while writing her book. I didn't ask to see the article, for I believed Bella.

So there I was in the candlelit dining room of a house enshrouded with fog, in the company of three middle-aged women, who just happened to be wearing pyjamas that glowed in the dark. This was definitely another first for me – two firsts in one hour! But I was so interested in "Ancient Mysteries," they chatted among themselves and left me to watch TV.

The moment the tape was over, Bella brought in a cauldron brimming with clam chowder, five bowls, a loaf, and a bottle of Australian Shiraz. The only light was from the pyjamas and two candles. Ghostly illuminated spirits waited for me to pull out their chairs before sitting down. Through the window you could sense the fog quietly observing us.

LEIF ERICSSON
SLEPT HERE

L'Anse aux Meadows • St. Anthony • Goose Cove

Tuesday, June 5. Loretta Decker was the woman who took me on the tour today. She didn't need much encouragement to tell me she was the granddaughter of George Decker, for it meant a lot to her. George Decker was a fisherman – born and bred in L'Anse aux Meadows, as were his forebears. He knew the sea, but he'd also been conscious of the landscape from childhood. Two archaeologists from Norway had been going all over the peninsula for years, armed with an educated hunch, stopping in every hamlet, asking if people knew of any interesting ruins, anything that might be the remains of a Viking cairn or whatever. They'd been having no luck whatsoever, but then one day they stopped George Decker and asked him the question they'd asked everybody else. Imagine the joy of those Norwegians when George Decker instantly understood what they wanted and took them to what are now the world-famous Viking ruins.

"Yeah, I know where there are some old ruins," said George, as if he'd been practising the lines all his life. "Follow me." He might have added, "What took you so long?"

George didn't know it was a Viking site. Nobody did. This was about 1960. Bella Hodge grew up in this area and said they always referred to the ruins as "Indian huts." Loretta confirmed that's what everyone called them a few years back. Some might still, she said sardonically.

The discovery became the archaeological event of the year worldwide and the news story of the year in all the Canadian papers. But George did more than just lead the Norwegians to the site. To his everlasting credit, something clicked in his brain, and he got interested, and he got involved. The whole family did. Loretta grew up with it. It's still her life.

Loretta's job is to take people on long tours along the boardwalk over the bog, through the reconstructed houses and around the ruins, and talk, and to be able to answer the most difficult questions, although most of the questions are far too elementary for her taste. She has a mind, therefore likes to be challenged.

When not guiding tours, she's fielding questions inside the tourist office/museum (architecturally similar to the Tuck Centre at St. Mary's Bay), while standing by the counter. She's devoting her life to the study and care of what used to be called the Indian huts. She attends all the lectures in St. John's about early Viking history and Viking interactions with the peoples of the world. She's studying ethnic migrations and economic patterns from A.D. 1000. She's reaching for the big picture.

I was scheduled to get another woman as a guide, but it was her first day on the job, fresh out of school, and she was a little nervous, so Loretta kindly relieved her. Not to put the others down in the slightest, but Loretta seemed to be the best and the brightest. Enthusiasm and dedication are hard to beat, but it's only the icing on the cake of actually being George Decker's granddaughter. It'd be hard to get a woman like Loretta off the Rock. Not that I'm about to try, but I bet many have, and failed bitterly.

On my way to Bella's from Gina's last night, I'd hopped the rear fence at L'Anse aux Meadows, after everyone had gone home, and spent two hours touring the place on my own, in the long shadows of sunset. ("I thought it was fogged in," notes my very sharp editor, but Bella's place was farther inland, and higher up in the hills.) My clandestine little visit was one of those experiences one might be forgiven for calling unforgettable. I had general knowledge of the site, but I'd done no serious research, so it was strange, especially when my mind would go blank after giving up trying to figure out what everything was and why it was there. Loretta, without knowing about last night, set me straight without making me feel like a fool. Some of my interpretations, though amateurish, were fundamentally correct, but some were so far off the mark I later forgot ever having made them.

Loretta maintained that everything had been excavated thoroughly. Even areas that look as if they have not seen a shovel in a thousand years have actually been scientifically sifted in living memory. It hadn't occurred to me last night that this had been a steel mill, but it turns out the Vikings used local bog iron ore to make steel. And they had a good smithy there, and a good open hearth for instant cooling of the reddest, hottest ingot. This thousand-year-old open hearth can still be seen, covered with vegetation, on the bank of a clear, winding stream. It looks like a massive green chair, big enough to serve as a throne for a prehistoric giant thirty feet tall.

So the reconstructed longhouses, tall, heavily timbered, topped with thatch, which I had thought last night had been built on the site of the original ruins, with the original fence posts and all that, had not actually been. That would have been too destructive of the beauty of the ruins. Lucky another spot for the reconstructions was right at hand. The main embarrassment was my marvelling at Viking wisdom in building these houses where they actually had not in fact built them. The original site was in the valley below, and, as it turns out, still retains more charm and interest than the noble and impressive reconstructions overlooking the harbour.

It's almost positively known that this was Leif Ericsson's stronghold. And there were women there, though last night I had the sense there hadn't been. How can they tell? By some of the stuff that was left behind.

"Either women or effeminate men," said Loretta.

"What sort of stuff?"

"Knitting needles." I laughed. The Viking stay, she added, was very short in duration, and "there is absolutely no evidence of anyone being born or dying here."

The notion used to be strongly held that the settlement was abandoned prematurely because of the large numbers of hostile indigenous people surrounding them, handing them their eviction notice over and over again, each one slightly more strongly worded. But it turns out the evidence for this does not exist. They would have left because of that, naturally, if it had happened. But they didn't, because it hadn't. In fact, it appears Newfoundland was otherwise uninhabited at the time of the Viking settlement. The Maritime Archaic people had died out and/or moved north, and the Proto-Beothuk hadn't arrived yet.

Loretta said that there were three major documentaries dealing with L'Anse aux Meadows. Unfortunately the first two proudly trumpet the now-outdated and disproved notion that the natives made an offer the Vikings couldn't refuse. She wasn't calling for the films to be suppressed, because "they're in circulation and you can't recall them like an automobile with a faulty airbag." Only the third one has the correct conclusion of the facts as they are now known to intersect. It was trouble at home that caused the Vikings to abandon the entire vast uninhabited island of Newfoundland. Nothing to do with the natives, non-existent or not. It was change of trade balances in Europe.

In time of trouble people go home?

"Not always," she said, "but in this case yes."

Who, before 1960, would have dreamt this would become Viking country, and there would be a Snorri Motel in the Viking Mall of St. Anthony? There's a relaxed, retired feel to the town. Comical signs abound, for instance, "Drive Through Haircuts – Convertibles Only." The town has a bright whiteness to it, but it has the aura of faded grandeur, as have all of the outports – but not all in the same way. St. Anthony should have some money spent on it, for conservation rather than development.

St. Anthony is famous for the Grenfell Mission. Wilfred Grenfell was a holistic pioneer in the medical field, whose vision was driven by compassion for the courageous suffering of the fisherfolk of Newfoundland and Labrador, although he was also resented somewhat in certain quarters for being a bit too much of a "missionary to the natives." His account of being adrift on an ice floe with his pack dogs overnight, on Hare Bay, just a few miles straight out from St. Anthony, is one of the great little classics of world literature. Photographs of him are anything but impressive, even the one where he's surrounded by adoring Newfoundland dogs. But he was a powerful and courageous man. There are little Grenfell Appreciation Societies here and there in the larger world, I understand. Somebody told me there was a study group in Tasmania, even.

At the St. Anthony lighthouse, overlooking the northern tip of Iceberg Alley, there's a cute and charmingly designed octagonal white restaurant on stilts.

"Do you ever see whales from here?"

"Oh yes, when you least expect it. You never know when whales are going to show up," the waitress said. "Sometimes they come up so close to the shore you can stand out there on the rock and look down into their mouths," she added. "But you never know when it's going to happen. I've been here seven years, and I'll look out and I'll see a whale and I'll still get all excited and I'll yell out, 'Whale! Whale!' and everybody will clear the restaurant. Leave their meals and go running down to the shore."

"In a Mr. Bean movie, he'd stay behind and eat all the meals."

"You're right. I can see him doing it."

My window overlooks the best iceberg I've seen. It's a beast of a berg, but it's beached. The tail end of it, the end sticking out farthest from the shore, is continually being smacked by waves heading in to shore. Each wave that hits the iceberg curves up and away from it, forming an inward curve. Or does the inward curve cause the wave to curve up and away?

So the wave action creates an inwardly curving ledge that gradually has made its way all the way around the iceberg, and this ledge curves up and down in the most harmonious manner. The up-and-down curve resembles the flounce of a skirt, and its lineaments depend on how high the waves had been when the iceberg was pointing in the direction to receive the striking of the waves on that particular side. So it's all random and chaotic, and yet it produces such harmonics!

The reason this iceberg was in so close to shore was that it didn't have much height to it. When an iceberg loses height, it loses depth – not because it's shrinking all over, but because anything that melts off the top causes the bottom to lift up. From the highest point to the lowest point, this one was maybe seventy-five feet. It just sat there rocking in the surf like a downed, frozen UFO. Horizontally, the diameter would have been about two hundred feet.

A white Triton "sports utility vehicle" has just pulled in beside me where I'm now standing meditating on the death of a once-proud iceberg. It's got Utah licence plates, with the cheesy slogan "The

Greatest Snow on Earth: Utah!" Even U.S. snow is superior to other snow. What a special country!

The waitress had a strong way of aspirating her i's. She would say High C, when she meant I see. No matter how short it was, an iceberg would always be a high-sberg. She wouldn't wear anything high-vory because of the elephants, she high-dolizes Joey Smallwood, and Tennyson's famous poem was High Dills of the King. Other than that little quirk, her English was flawless, as if she too had been raised by Bella Hodge.

"You look out there in the winter and you can see seals on the highce," she informed me.

She said of the whales, "We saw one yesterday, we'll probably see one tomorrow, but we haven't seen one today yet."

If I were on the committee, and if nobody had offered me a bribe to vote otherwise, one sufficiently large for a man of my integrity, I'd nominate Goose Cove for the Tidy Town award. For one thing, the town doesn't have a motto, one of those fake homilies on the road sign welcoming you to town. Few of these mottoes are fun, most of them are open for serious misinterpretation, and a town would be tidier without one. Not only is Goose Cove free of mottoes, garbage, and wrecked cars, but also, in the middle of the well-protected cove, there is a flat-topped rock sticking a few feet out of the water at high tide. Somebody has rowed out there and lovingly placed on this rock a giant flowerpot full of red geraniums. It's a charming sight for a pair of weary eyes, and a gentle sign of civilization. An old fellow sitting on a bench was looking out at the rock. I inquired as to what the name of that rock would be. "That's Geranium Rock," he said. I laughed. "At least it is now," he added.

And what a lovely town to stroll around on a sunny day! The Anastasia McDonald Memorial Hall is one of Goose Cove's many attractive buildings. Several people stopped and chatted, and to everybody I put the question: Who was Anastasia McDonald? They would look at me blankly, then take a quick look at the hall, and then say, oh yes, Anastasia McDonald. Oh, oh, oh . . . I used to know but I forgot. . . .

So Newfoundland is definitely part of North American society, a society in which few of us can remember anything. Gore Vidal's bitter denunciation of the U.S.A. as the United States of Amnesia could perhaps apply to a lot of Canada as well.

In old maps of this area, the Northern Peninsula was called Promontorius, for it was thought to be attached to Labrador farther south. The Strait of Belle Isle would have been thought of as a bay. Early mapmakers presumed that, once they'd sailed so far southwards in the strait, they wouldn't be able to sail any farther, but they were wrong.

Back on the west side of Promontorius, the Strait of Belle Isle has retained, in my absence, its shiny, silky, plastic moonlit calmness. There was a ferocious storm in the Long Range Mountains, on the road over the hump from Goose Cove. But here everything's quiet and calm. As a child, poring over maps, I imagined the Strait of Belle Isle was never calm, that it was like the Straits of Magellan, with constant storms tossing battleships around like the nests of those birds that lay their eggs on the sea. The storm up in the Long Range Mountains must have been too high to cause a ripple in the strait. It was on a night like this (in 1912) that the *Titanic* went down, but off the southeast coast of Newfoundland, rather than here, the northwest coast.

The grassy cliffs above the sandy shore of the Strait of Belle Isle are flooded with bird's-eye primrose. These are five-petalled blue flowers with bright yellow centres, each petal bearing such a distinct indentation it seems like a ten-petal flower. They resemble banks of violets in the moonlight. The alpine chickweeds, short-lived flowers, blossom on a gravel slope leading down to the sandy beach, where I sat contemplating the awesome power hiding in all that oceanic serenity.

In climbing back up from the beach, I said aloud, "Hey, I didn't leave my headlights on, did I?" A step or two farther up, and a stupendous sight appeared low in the eastern sky – a vibrantly orange moon, as full as full can be without bursting, and almost blood red in hue, rising out of the Atlantic Ocean and shining over the Long Range Mountains of Promontorius.

LONG AND
WINDING ROAD

Promontorius • Wendell's Place • Stephenville
Port au Port Peninsula • Piccadilly • Lourdes
Mainland • Corner Brook

Wednesday, June 6. It's a silent, glistening morning, misty by the sea, foggy in the hills. On this day in 1925, a "battlefield park" in France was dedicated by Earl Haig to the memory of the courageous soldiers of the Newfoundland Regiment who got wiped out in the first day of the Battle of the Somme.

At first I thought I was the first person up on the entire Promontorius, but out there, in the Strait of Belle Isle, are eight boats, the fellows in them yawning, rubbing their eyes, drinking coffee out of giant Thermoses, and checking their lobster traps. The strait is shining again, but with a touch of bright choppy eagerness, as opposed to the flat serenity of night.

I've slept the entire night in a tiny car, but I feel fine. Back at the highway, a serious-looking nun, who also seems to have been sleeping in her car, is taking a photograph of a clever new road sign, the one showing a perfectly healthy moose looking down at a wrecked car that has just ploughed into it.

❖

You go down the road till you get to the Ultramar, and right next to it is Wendell's Place. Wendell is a tall man about fifty with a broad smile. He keeps humming "It's a Long and Winding Road." He brews an excellent country coffee and scrambles up a couple of farm-fresh eggs with chopped green onions. "Oh yisss, I could do that for ye," he enthuses. Toast? "Oh yiss, I could do that for ye too," he says, jauntily, and with happy eyes.

Who should stumble in but a grumpy little guy who looked like the premier of Alberta, Ralph Klein, with a hangover. He wore a grumpy little outfit – a navy-blue, tight-necked sweatshirt and tailored navy-blue jeans, freshly laundered and ironed. He looked around silently, unsmilingly, sat at a table next to mine, then looked straight at me and said, out of the corner of his mouth, "Ever been to Las Vegas?"

"What's it to you?" I said.

He jumped back a bit and looked out the window. I laughed. When you see a nasty guy, it's best to be nasty to him right off. Especially if he looks like Ralph Klein.

So then he got all nice and said he was from Windsor, Ontario, but he had to leave because of the gambling. Gambling is ruining the place. It's driving prices up, including real estate, and nobody has any money any more, so he had to sell up and move to Newfoundland.

And besides, said Ralph, it draws too many Afro-Americans over from Detroit (he actually used the ugly n-word). He was one of those old guys who has to repeat everything he says three times, but each time he said the n-word he would whisper it, as if he didn't want to offend anyone but me. "I mean, it'd be okay if there was just a few niggers but there's too many niggers, and they come over here – I mean over to Windsor – because of the low dollar."

The low dollar. That'll do it. They used to like watermelons, but now it's low dollars. This guy should read a book or two on African-American history. That would smarten him up.

But Ralph was down in Biloxi, Mississippi, the other day, and boy they have good gambling down there. They've got the coin-operated gambling down there, and they're happy about it. It's built up their real estate and lowered their taxes. He had a great time down there.

Wendell is listening from the kitchen. He's still smiling, but he's rolling his eyes like Mr. Bojangles.

"Oh yeah, and there's that there Tulica down there in Tennessee. They got gambling. Oh, that's a fine place for gambling down there."

Ralph's eyes aren't overly excited. He seems calm and rational. No signs of craziness in anything but the weird way his mind seems not to be working.

"There's all kinds of little places," he says, "where you can find gambling going on."

To be truthful, I feared this fellow. But I screwed up my courage and asked him a question.

"What about Newfoundland? Isn't the gambling here good enough for a high-class low-tax guy like you?"

"Ech," he uttered. "I don't care for that. That's not gambling as far as I'm concerned."

"Why not?"

"Well, they don't pay off the way they should."

Did he mean they didn't pay off as well? No, it would appear that he does not like the fact that, when you win, you just get a slip of paper, rather than the money. And then you have to take the slip to the bar to get your payout.

"What's the problem with that?"

"It's just not the same," he said, with a reassuring air. "I like it when all the money comes out at once."

Let's face it, we know Ralph has a gambling fetish with a strong psychotic element. He's probably under strict orders not to gamble. He might even be on some new experimental drug therapy to cure gambling fever forever.

"I like it when the bells and whistles go off, and the girls come running in their little miniskirts, and the money comes rolling out right in front of you. Now that's what I call gambling."

His eyes reminded me of the Manchurian Candidate. It was also strange that, out of all the bar-restaurants in Newfoundland, he would have shown up in this one, which just happens to have no slot machines. Maybe any place with slots is off-limits for him.

I said to Wendell, while the man from Windsor ruminated about his obsessions, "Those eggs were terrific. Extend my compliments to the hens that laid them."

"If I do that, I'm going to have to go all the way back to Cormack."

This grumbling, grouchy gambler was here, as it turns out, to borrow Wendell's tractor. But the tractor was all booked up for today. He had some time on his hands, so he ordered the all-day bacon-and-egg special.

"Aw," he said, "it's too wet to do the job today anyway, so I'm just as happy."

I told him, insincerely, that I'd had him pegged for a fairly happy person.

"I take life as it comes," he said.

I paid up and said next time I'm in here, I'm gonna have the Mooseburger. There was a sign on the wall: Mooseburger $4.85. "Are they any good?"

"Haw haw," chuckled Wendell, pointing at Ralph. "Just ask him."

"Are they any good?" I said to Ralph.

"They're okay, I guess."

Wendell laughed. "He comes in for one almost every day."

"Oh, those Mooseburgs. Yes, they're good those Mooseburgs," said Ralph.

"Better than gambling in Biloxi?"

"Almost."

They're getting ready for a June 19 by-election in Corner Brook. June Alteen is running for the Liberals. Her radio commercial comes on every half-hour, with someone saying that Alteen is the best person for the job, because she is "a characteristic person." If anyone can decipher that, please drop me a line. I decide against phoning up her constituency office and suggesting a catchier slogan: "Vote June Alteen on June Nineteen." They've probably already thought of it and turned it down.

It's Wednesday, and people in shorts and rubber boots are hanging their laundry out to dry and mowing the lawns. Lawn care is split along gender lines. In Stephenville, it's the women who cut the lawn, the men who water the lawn and trim the roses. It used to be the opposite before power mowers.

Now here's my chance to tour the Port au Port Peninsula, and I'm glad I did, because of the fascinating villages, churches, graveyards, spring meadows cluttered with wildflowers, cliff-top views out over the sea – and it must be the world's capital for Lawn Art. Along the north shore is a row of low-density communities – Piccadilly, Lourdes, and Mainland – which are so close they seem to be one. A fellow has taken great sheets of plywood and cut out a whole team of life-sized horses, then painted them brown. He has them propped up all around his house. Each seems to commemorate a real horse, probably now dead. He also has a couple of cows, painted black and white. Perhaps these are to remind him of the old days when he was a gentleman farmer. He doesn't seem to have any livestock around these days.

Two guys farther on have built a whole series of hip-high cairns all over their dual front lawns. All the rocks are lipstick red, all the plaster is cocaine white – and these two wild and crazy guys have built little pyramids with a lot of white plaster supporting a relatively small number of red stones, something like big fat cherries in a vanilla cake that comes to a point at the top. Excellent workmanship on both the cairns and the livestock. These "folk artists" knew they were trying to build something unique – Lawn Art with an emphasis on the word "art." They wanted to be able to say, "No, I didn't see it in a book or anything like that. I came up with the idea all by myself."

And his partner would say, "Yeah, so did I. I bet him I could make some Lawn Art totally never done before but still interesting."

"Who won the bet?"

"Nobody. We couldn't get nobody to judge us. Which one do you like best?"

"Geez, I don't know."

"See?"

By the time I got off the Port au Port, it was getting late, so I was happy to book into the Hotel Corner Brook again, hoping to take the road down to Burgeo the next day. The TOPS ladies had gone home, the place was quiet, so at about ten o'clock I popped into a noisy pub next door called Cheers. I was watching the guys play darts, and then, on my way back to the bar, I came around a corner just as a girl who was playing the slot machine struck it rich. She had two girls watching her. By girls I mean in their twenties, black lipstick, purple hair sort of thing. So she had a royal flush and won a tremendous amount of money the moment I walked by. The machine was going crazy, and so was she.

She instantly leapt to her feet, threw her arms around me, gave me a huge sloppy French kiss, and said, when she came up for air, "You brought me luck. I'm buying you a drink." Soon a hush had settled over the pub as she dragged me by the ear to the bar, and everyone stared at the stranger who goes around bringing people luck. Her girlfriends were trying to touch me, but she was pushing them away.

She asked my name, then introduced me to the bartender. A tall, grizzly old guy who had been sitting at a barstool bent his head down and whispered in my ear, "You be good to this woman. She's an old friend of mine and I love her dearly, so you be good to her tonight." He seemed to be fighting back the tears. I guess he figured I'd won her heart and would soon be gearing up for a heavy night of lovemaking. He didn't actually say, "You be nice to her, or I'll beat your head in," but there was that tone in his voice, as well as a tone that said that he was in great pain because of his unrequited love.

So I waited till the coast was clear, then tiptoed out. Back in my room, it dawned on me that maybe she just wanted me as protection against the smothering advances of that old sentimental lecher, and I almost went back down to rescue her from him.

But first I'd have a little nap.

The next thing I knew it was morning.

I'm not the man I used to be.

Thank God.

FOR
NEWFOUNDLANDERS
ONLY

Corner Brook • Caribou Trail • Peter Stride's Lake • Burgeo

Thursday, June 7. For sure it's the Hotel Corner Brook, but is it the same room I had before? I open the drawer of the night table, and the graffiti is different. Someone with the thoroughly respectable name of Dave wrote "Dave Was Here!", with a wavy arrow going to the front of the drawer, where he'd written "Apr. 9/6:30pm/1981." Next to it, in a saucy imitation, eighteen years later, someone had written "Clayton Was To!", and a similar wavy arrow, followed by "Feb. 14/10:02pm/1999." It still seems like the same room. Maybe somebody from TOPS sat on the previous night table and it had to be replaced.

Also Gerard and Tammy wrote they were here on Feb. 13, 1990, but wish them luck, because they had no money and were going to try climbing out the window.

Well rested and relaxed, I phoned my friend Bernice Hopcraft in Toronto. She was an expatriate New York Catholic with a fondness for Newfoundland and had told me about a convent she loved so much she'd been fantasizing about spending her later years there. I thought she might have told me it was in Burgeo, but she informed me it wasn't Burgeo, it was Brigus. Not Brigus South, but the other Brigus, which is up north but which is not to be called Brigus North. "Don't call it Brigus North, whatever you do," she said.

Bernice gave me several phone numbers and hot tips about life on the Rock, and the name of the guest home she stays in while in St. John's. And so on. She cheered me up by reminding me how pleased she was I was writing a book about her favourite island.

"Welcome to the Caribou Trail," says what appears to be the largest highway sign in Newfoundland, near Stephenville, just off the Trans-Canada Highway, where the Caribou Trail begins. I'm heading down to Burgeo on the south shore. It feels like an adventure. The Trail is 146 klicks straight north and south, with Stephenville on the north end and Burgeo, on the south shore, at the south end. To be more accurate, the Trail goes straight east from Stephenville for about thirty klicks, then starts going due south for the remainder. There are no crossroads of any sort. This is a road cut through wilderness.

One could take that huge sign down and build a house on it big enough for a small family. Diego Rivera could paint the entire history of Mexico on it. But for now, all that's painted on it, besides verbal information about the lack of filling stations and various advisories about wildlife, logging trucks, interesting geological facts, is an oversized caribou drinking from a reflecting pool and standing on a moss-covered rock with a beach in the background. This is Route 480. Farley Mowat lived in Burgeo while writing *A Whale for the Killing* and *The Boat That Wouldn't Float*.

What do the moose think of the caribou and vice versa? They must have developed some form of cooperative reciprocation when it comes to fundamental things like food sources, vegetable gardens, forest fires, danger from hunters, and so on. Do the caribou look down at the moose for being arrivistes? Do the moose look down on the caribou for being mere low-life natives?

Nestled around the marge of Peter Stride's Pond, halfway to Burgeo and named after a renowned Micmac guide, is a good-sized community of trailers and campers. In Young's Country Diner there's a large dining room, with clean tablecloths, china, silverware. Nice to find such a classy joint in the barrens where the "gravel bed campers" congregate, people who pull up in their camper vans and spend the spring, summer, and fall there, fishing, hunting, drinking beer, playing cribbage, listening to the radio, swatting flies. . . .

On the counter at Young's is a model of St. Peter's Basilica.

"St. Peter's! Who made that?"

"My son did."

"How old's he?"

"Nineteen. I buys it for myself, y'see. But my son has it put together before I gets a chance to."

She, her son, and her husband live here and run the diner from May till November, then they go up to Marble Mountain for the winter, then they come back here and get the restaurant ready for another year of it in the spring. Marble Mountain is a new ski area and winter tourist-processing zone on the Trans-Canada Highway. This little family runs a similar restaurant up there for winter skiers.

"I thought you'd be spending your winters in Palm Beach."

"Not us."

Her husband came out from the back room. Without a word she disappeared into the back. He looked at me and said, "All by yerself?"

He was short and plump, with a fuzzy moustache. He may have been suppressing resentment about me chatting with his wife as if she were a real human being. Maybe he thought I'd cause her to become discontented, because they couldn't go to Palm Beach. But mainly he took over because he thought he'd have a better chance of selling me something.

"How's the fishing?" I said.

"A picture's worth a thousand words." He pointed to a photo of a large fish on the wall.

"You catch that?"

"Caught it and took the picture both!"

All around this lonely little restaurant is a wilderness of lakes, rivers, waterfalls, forests, barrens, hills, valleys, mountains. The sky sat over it all, like a giant skullcap of ever-changing colours. It'd be the perfect place for a Zen monastery.

He wanted me to book a twenty-five-dollar fishing cabin for the night. I could start fishing immediately and fish till dinnertime, then continue fishing after dinner. Or he'd pack me a lunch and I could fish straight through till bedtime. He'd throw in the boat, the hip waders, bait, gear, tackle, map. Everything except a guide; his guide had a ruptured appendix and wouldn't be back till tomorrow.

"Sounds like a good deal all right, and ordinarily I'd jump at the chance, but I just don't feel like it today."

He looked at me sadly, as if he couldn't imagine a man who would not bite at the chance to go fishing.

"Besides, if I go fishing, I won't catch anything, and if you came with me you wouldn't catch anything either."

"Ah, you're a jinx, are you?" He seemed happier now, because I had such a good excuse.

"Since birth, my friend. But only when it comes to huntin' an' fishin'."

He said, "Did you see any caribou on the way down?"

"No."

"The guy before you, he saw a moose."

I didn't see a moose or a caribou. I paid him for the coffee.

"Drive careful now. Just because you didn't see one yet, there could be one on the road just waiting to jump out in front of you. And you'd probably spill your coffee all over your nice new T-shirt."

I laughed and looked down. It was a Black Horse Lager T-shirt, and it said on it: FOR NEWFOUNDLANDERS ONLY.

"I'll go real slow now for sure. But I'm so much of a jinx, I couldn't hit a moose if it was having a power nap in the centre lane."

"I knew a fellow a bit like that once. . . ."

A bit farther south, the road runs out of forest. It's all fantastic rock outcroppings, like a landscape out of *Krazy Kat*, boulder-strewn landscapes in all directions, surrealistic house-sized erratics split in two, or sometimes three, by extremes of temperature, an intricately tangled web of streams and ponds sparkling in the sun, one lake sitting up on a ledge and joined to its lower-down twin in the valley by the silvery scarf of a waterfall, and the occasional un-inhabited cabin way off in the distance, slowly decomposing with the years.

Farther south was Man Rock Lake. There was only one rock in that little lake, and sure enough it looked like a man, standing still as a stone up to its shoulders in the water: he had a man's face and was wearing a pointed hat, and he was just staring northwards, serenely, as if waiting for the return of the Vikings. But from another angle he looked like Joey Smallwood waiting for the election returns.

And now, it's the end of the line, sooner than expected, Burgeo, with the cold grey sea winking and blinking in the distance. It was a surprise. I came over a hill and there was a little collection of giant vinyl-sided warehouses, surrounded by a serious Frost fence twelve feet high. And an old Blue Line bus from 1949 that looked as if it was just dying to have someone climb behind the wheel and drive away. There's Rick's Reliable Auto Parts, with a few of the usual suspects hanging around outside. And a couple of sneaky police cruisers hiding around a curve behind a speed-limit sign. They heard me coming from a long way off and were hoping I wouldn't slow down for the "Slow Down" sign, but I did.

The outskirts of Burgeo are the same as everywhere: people living in trailers, filling up at Irving's Gas Bar, shopping at Irving's Foodland, eating at Irving's Diner, and squadrons of high-school kids walking along the centre of the main road as though silently asserting the existential value of the individual human being over the individual rental car being driven by some jerk who doesn't even belong here.

People are working on scaffolds. They can see little lakes and ponds all around, cupped in various-sized depressions in the rock. Somebody's chimney is all wrapped in pink plastic. On Shorts Lane everybody is wearing long pants. Joy's Place has a giant ice-cream cone out front painted blue and white, with a giant ball on top painted strawberry. There's a Sandbanks Provincial Park sign pointing along Inspiration Road. . . .

Also there's a delicate smell of cod-liver oil in the air, and there are no kids walking along School Road. People are industrious around here, you can sense the high-energy buzz in the air, and a deep pleasure taken in hard work. Even the West Muddy Hole Road has been freshly paved. People are whitewashing their doorknobs, shingling their sheds, painting their trim, getting their hair trimmed.

So it would appear that layabouts are not highly regarded here. Even Farley Mowat was energized by his eight-year stay. In his *A Whale for the Killing*, he energetically portrayed some of the Burgeo residents abusing a whale that had become trapped in a tidal pool. But that was a long time ago, and although I remember there having been some negative reactions to the portrayal, I can't recall if Mowat left town before the book came out or after.

Maybe they're not literary around here, and maybe they can't even spell – the local convenience store is called the Quik Shoppe – but a group of three women last year raised six thousand dollars (with the largest portion from the Bank of Nova Scotia) to buy books for the Burgeo Public Library. After all, the nearest bookstore is 150 klicks away. And it seems like a happy community, and maybe a bit zany in a nice way. For instance, one fellow has painted both chimneys on his house lipstick red. Another fellow has taken his trousers off, as well as his socks and shoes, and has both legs sticking out of a third-storey window of the St. John's Central High School.

In Newfoundland, every town has something distinctive about it, and in Burgeo it's this: they paint cartoon characters on their satellite dishes. There's the Road Runner on one, Bugs Bunny, Elmer Fudd, Sylvester and Tweety. And the Islandview Café actually has a view of an island.

The people here seem to have forgotten the indignities of Farley Mowat's portrayal (more than thirty years ago), because everybody's smiling, if not laughing. Twenty men mill around outside the Strickland Variety, and every one of them is laughing. The Strickland Monument in the centre of town is having an ornamental fence erected around it, and the workmen are all laughing, as are the people who are watching them work.

A dozen men and women, who are busy chainsawing trees felled by a late winter storm, are all laughing with the joy of being alive at the end of winter, and having all this firewood for next winter. A fellow cutting his lawn is laughing. A mother and daughter are walking along the street, and the daughter is laughing, but the mother is intent on looking at people out of the side of her head with a general air of disapproval. Of two people gossiping in the parking lot of Foodland, where you can get a four-kilogram keg of salt beef for $6.99, one seems about to stop laughing and the other seems about to start.

In 1864 five fishermen named Strickland were listed in the Burgeo directory, and today there are still numerous Stricklands around town. The handsome Strickland Monument, which seems to do double duty as a Masonic and War Memorial, had recently been erected by Hubert Strickland to commemorate his fifty years in the Masons.

The Burgeo Public Wharf and Ferry Terminal is the jumping-off spot for visiting such lonely but merry seaside settlements as Cape Le Hune, François, Mosquito, and Ramea. I missed the two o'clock sailing to Ramea, and that's it for today. My instincts told me not to wait for the next sailing tomorrow morning. The people of the south shore like to call themselves puffins, but over the past decade the populations have dwindled alarmingly, and I didn't feel that old pull toward the unknown that I need to feel before plunging into it.

But there is a contemplative view of the sea and islands from this wharf – and the islands are medium grey as they lift up out of the light grey sea, and the thick forests on each island are dark grey under the pale grey sky.

But first, there's Sandbanks Provincial Park to check out. One thing the people of Burgeo don't take to, apparently, is late-night picnics. Here's a sign saying Picnic Area: Closed 10 p.m. If anyone tried to close my picnic down at such an early hour, I'd just offer them a Moosehead and a plate heaping with cod cheeks and tongues.

Anyway this must be a paradise for kids, for who could be bored here with tall rocks sticking straight up out of the sand, lots and lots of sand, and the sea, giant spruce trees, boardwalks. . . .

On the way back out, a raging river hops down from the hills, racing to catch the tide. I've been hopping from rock to rock for the fun of it and am now sitting on a flat, dry stone in the middle of the river. I'm all caught up in the music of that river, in its amazing rush to reach the sea – as if every molecule of H_2O were trying to get ahead of all the other little molecules.

The Beothuk painted red ochre on everything, we're told. It was their sacred taboo symbol, their trademark, their logo. It was their way of saying that they were here first. Even today, when a grave is discovered in the forest, and there's a trace of red ochre on it, it's straightaway thought to be from the Beothuk era. The Beothuk on sacred occasions painted themselves red, inspiring the term "Red Indian," which came to mean all Indians who were not from the land of elephants and maharajahs.

There's a lot of red oxide in the rocks around here, and red oxide was the principal ingredient used in the manufacture of red ochre, but how the Beothuks got the oxide out of the rock is a mystery to me.

The Man Rock in Man Rock Lake looks different than it did earlier today, from a different angle. He has quite the overhung brow now and seems angry about being stuck in this cold lake forever, while everybody else can have picnics and drink beer.

Also in these parts there is little litter. Cars go by full of people; they wave at you, but litter they save for later. Not even a match do they toss. The only litter is left by logging trucks.

Clyde Rose, as mentioned before, is from Fox Island Harbour, which isn't far from Burgeo, though the ferry schedules make no reference to it, and there is no road connection. As also mentioned, he is an Anthony Quinn/Zorba the Greek sort of guy – tough, gentle, supremely attractive, all that kind of thing. During my visit, Clyde was at one point complaining a bit about problems of aging, so I gave him Zorba's last words, not from the movie version, but from Nikos Kazantzakis's 1946 novel, *Zorba the Greek*: "Men like me ought to live a thousand years. Good night!"

Clyde's eyes, which had been sleepy, opened wide and a smile flickered across his face. You could tell he liked those last words. For a moment he seemed to believe that he actually was at the least a member of the lost tribe of Zorba.

And today, strange coincidence, I find out that, on the day I was visiting Clyde, Anthony Quinn died, in a Boston hospital. I later tried to find out what Quinn's last words were, but all I could find was what he said when he first found out he was finished. He said he'd like to come back as a butterfly.

LIGHTNING
AT MIDNIGHT

Corner Brook • Deer Lake • Burnt Berry

Friday, June 8. At breakfast, in the dining room of the Hotel Corner Brook, the waitress, a pleasantly unpainted and pretty young woman, about twenty-one, was getting curious about me, since I'd been there last week as well. She wanted to know what I was doing. I told her I was gathering impressions for a book about Newfoundland. She wanted to know the title. I told her *Naked Newfoundland*, forgetting to mention it was just one of several titles I was considering. She smiled pleasantly, then as I watched, a blush started in her cheeks and grew until her whole face was bright red. "Sounds interesting," she stuttered, then hurried away to let me eat my grilled capelin in peace.

You never know when an innocent joke will be hurtful. If only I'd asked her what her favourite TV show was, or what her favourite movie of all time was. Or if she could have suggested a less embarrassing title.

In Newfoundland friendships last forever. Statistics back up the impression of low divorce rates. The Newfoundland rate is half what it is in Canada as a whole, and one-third what it is in certain parts of Canada such as Yukon. People rely on each other more than on big banks and big government. If I were to paint your house or give your car a major tune-up, you might present me with a winter's supply of firewood, carrots, and moose meat. "Your call is important to us" is more than an empty, mocking, tape-recorded message.

I've bypassed the town of Deer Lake several times without actually popping in to say hello. First impressions: it's got sidewalks, paved streets, and two or three maple trees that would predate Canadian Confederation in 1867, rather than Newfoundland's (un)fortunately belated entry into same. There's the Driftwood Arms, which would date back to the driftwood craze of the late fifties, when sunbaked and shellacked pieces of grotesquely twisted driftwood were the ultimate in coffee-table ornamentation, and pubs all over North America took the name Driftwood Arms. People would phone up and say, "Come on over and see my new piece of driftwood." Friends would stop to chat on the street and ask each other if they had their driftwood yet.

Deer Lake has a Jungle Jim's Eatery, a Hair Shack, and a Best of Billiards Lounge, which boasts two signs: one saying "Every Friday night D.J. Jeff," and the other saying "We Wash Work Clothes."

It's early evening in Deer Lake, and the streets are quiet. Has everybody gone to Corner Brook for the weekend? Even the billiard lounge is empty. The bartender appears to be weeping. There is a feeling of universal sadness in the air.

One would expect a town with a name like Deer Lake to be pretty, but it needs a little pothole repair here and there. Weeds grow in cracks in the road. Joan is in the doorway of her store, with a sign saying Joan's Video Convenience – Rent 2 Pay for 3 – Cold Beer.

"Does anyone fall for that Rent 2 Pay for 3 deal?"

"You'd be amazed what they fall for around here, mister."

They've even got a Chinese restaurant. That does it. They say one should never eat Chinese in a city of less than a million. But I'm going to prove them wrong. And if I fail, I'll have died a hero's death. . . .

It's called Tai Lee's Garden Restaurant – Chinese and Canadian Food and, like the Driftwood Arms, it has a strong aura of the fifties about it. Mom and Pop come out to look at me, then Pop returns to the kitchen to watch TV and wait for the order. The signs on the jukebox say "Please Make Sure the Juke Box Is Plugged in Before Inserting Your Coins" and "Please Don't Sit on Juke Box." The magazine rack has a whole mess of Sears catalogues and *TV Guide* magazines going back to 1952.

Pop tilts back on his hardback chair as he watches TV in the kitchen, occasionally bursting into laughter. Mom is the waitress. She doesn't seem like the laughing type. I ask for tea and get a cup of Salada, with a big 350-millilitre can of Nestlé's Carnation 2-per-cent, rich-and-creamy, evaporated, partly skimmed milk – 80 per cent more calcium than the same amount of regular milk. But when she brings out my order, the *specialité de la maison* – a steaming plate of almonds and broccoli on rice – I know I've come to the right place.

A man and woman and their kid came in and sat in the next booth to mine, even though there were several booths and tables to choose from. The man was heavy and kept pushing against me with his back. He ordered spare ribs, but the kid just wanted rice. "Rice . . . Rice . . . Rice . . ." he chanted, as if it were a football cheer.

"You gotta have more than rice," said Dad, who finally ordered pineapple chicken balls and rice for the kid. Mama had chicken chow mein. I couldn't resist turning my head now and then for a quick look.

Then the kid wanted a drink.

"What kind of a drink?"

"Just a drink . . . I just wanna drink . . . a drink drink . . . I wanna drink."

"Do you want Coke, do you want Pepsi, do you want 7-Up, do you want what?"

"Drink drink drink drink drink," said the kid.

I'm not sure what he finally got to drink, but when his meal came he ate only the rice. In fact, he started impaling the pineapple chicken balls one at a time on his chopstick, bending it way back, then letting it fly. He aimed for the jukebox and hit it, then he aimed straight at me, but it curved and hit his dad in the face. Dad didn't say a thing, but mother said, "Tell your father you're sorry."

"Sorry, Dad."

A car pulled up on the other side of the street with three teens about eighteen in it – a girl driver, a girl passenger, and young Tai Lee Junior in the back seat. He got out of the car in a flash and ran through the restaurant. He exchanged a few mumbled words with his mother. Then he ran upstairs to his room and came running down with a sweater in his hand, pulling it over his T-shirt as he dashed out and hopped back in the car. And they drove off.

When I paid my bill, I gave Mom a perfectly ordinary tip of a loonie. Maybe it was a fraction more than the normal 15 per cent, but her face started beaming with pleasure, and it sounded as if she might cry with joy. You'd think it was their first tip of the year and their largest of all time. So, if you ever dine at Tai Lee's in Deer Lake, don't leave more than fifty cents.

Mom said they'd been twenty-nine years in Canada – fifteen years in Deer Lake, twelve years running a similar diner in Grand Falls, and before that two years somewhere on the Mainland, but she didn't remember where. They were originally from Hong Kong.

She was a worried little lady, with a pageboy haircut, and slim in Chinese silk pyjamas with reddish-orange dragons on pale yellow. Her husband seemed like a merry old Taoist wizard back there. I couldn't see much of him, but he looked anything but worried. And he kept laughing out loud at *The Simpsons*.

As for the boy, he was bright and had a lot of affection for his parents, but seemed to wish they were more Canadian, and that they were more fluent in English, so they could have a wider circle of friends – and maybe join the bowling league.

Thick fog levels the landscape, hiding the highlands, veiling the valleys. Even the summits are socked in. I pretend to myself that I have no idea what the fog is hiding. It could be anything! Beothuk pyramids, perhaps! I could have stayed at the guest home in Deer Lake, but Burnt Berry beckoned, and it would be only an hour's drive.

There's a good crowd for a change, and I don't recognize anyone but blond Brenda the Burnt Berry bartender from my first visit. She's smiling at an old picture-packed copy of *American Bowler Magazine*, with the words "Memory Lanes Glow in the Dark Bowling Alley" on the cover.

She sees me, pours my drink, then gasps and stage-whispers: "Oh, here comes Bruce, my husband." He doesn't live up to my expectations. For instance, he's about a foot shorter than the six-foot-seven she claimed for him. And rather corpulent. And although Brenda thinks he worships her like a goddess, I get the feeling he worships the young woman he's with every bit as much, if not more. Brenda doesn't seem to notice her.

He's in his mid-thirties, a bit younger than Brenda, and he wouldn't look so pudgy if he hadn't been wearing a suit of powder-blue denim, which was tight on him. Even the Jack Daniel's T-shirt he wore under the suit was too tight for words! He was strong and silent, and even though he did come in with an attractive young woman, Brenda didn't look at all concerned, not even when Bruce and Nancy began to shoot a game of pool. They played well. He made some wonderful bank shots, which indicated he was a student of the game. Nancy made some confident and suspenseful long shots, and when the ball went into the pocket after such a shot, she never seemed surprised.

After the game, Bruce took Brenda aside and had a private chat with her. No matter how hard I strained, I couldn't hear a thing, and their faces gave nothing away. Neither seemed to be annoyed; it appeared to be merely an exchange of routine private information. He then ordered a Jack Daniel's and Cola, to match his T-shirt. And Nancy went over to the sound system on the wall behind the pool table and put on her Rod Stewart tapes, which caused my eyes to flash.

"He's my favourite," I said.

"Ah, he's great!" she exclaimed. "Nobody sings those love songs like Rod Stewart."

All his top hits were gushing out of a pair of giant speakers in this strangely over-large, dream-like barroom, big enough for a square dance with live band, and such a small bar, only five stools, and one full-sized pool table, and over on the far side, just by the door leading into the lobby, a set of sullen, silent slot zombies. Brenda tells me they go for so many hours without taking a break, she'd swear they must have catheters installed.

So Bruce went over there to get rid of ten or twenty dollars' worth of change in a hurry, leaving Nancy and me to swap Rod Stewart stories, and to see how similar our tastes were in other ways as well. Brenda, with her shoulder-length tightly curled golden Botticelli locks, sat motionless on her high stool behind the bar, smiling her eternal smile.

Brenda thought the barter system might have been more established twenty years ago. "Things have been falling apart pretty much in Newfoundland for the past twenty years, you know."

"Not just the ten years since the cod moratorium?"

"Oh no, for about ten years before then," butted in Old Bill, who had joined us at the bar, "and with no stop in sight." Old Bill was a smart-looking fellow, well dressed, lived alone in a cabin down the road a bit, and Heath his name was, with a silent h, pronounced Heat, as in Old Bill Heat.

"How long have you been living alone?"

"About twenty years."

"Didn't you ever hear that old saying, man was not meant to live alone?"

"I prefers the one about loving thy neighbour as thyself."

Everything became a bit fuzzy until, at the stroke of midnight, there was a brilliant flash of lightning, a deafening clap of thunder, the two big doors burst open, and in walked a little Willy Loman with a big sample case. Everyone in the pub, including the slot zombies, turned to look at this apparition. There was a pause. He filled it with an electrifying "Good day!" that caused a red billiard ball, which was sitting on the lip of the far pocket, to tumble in with a loud echo.

Brenda bought a shoulder bag from him for fifteen dollars – a black plastic bag that would fall apart if you tried to carry a bottle of Screech any distance in it. She also bought a little foamy covering for a cell phone for five dollars.

"You paid twenty dollars for those two things?"

"This is for my brother-in-law. He has a cell phone. Now, if he drops it, it won't break."

"If I ever get a sister-in-law, I hope she'll be just like you."

"I've always been this way," she said. "I just loves to buy little gifts for people."

To me it seemed a shame she had to make up twenty dollars' worth of tips just to pay for that junk. But I'm undoubtedly applying my mercenary Mainlander mentality to a different set of attitudes here on the island. There's not as much division between work and non-work in Newfoundland. There's a lot of play in work and a lot of work in play. Everything one does is part of staying alive and keeping on good terms with everyone, no matter what.

She also claimed she's seen plastic bags like that in stores for thirty-five dollars. She was certain about this, even though I was saying No Way!

"Go ahead, feel it. It's tougher than it looks."

She was right. It looked like cheap plastic, but it felt almost like real leather.

"You're right, I apologize."

This young Willie Loman was busy selling stuff right and left. Everyone was buying except me. He said he was going to be head of his company some day.

"Who's the head now?"

"Mr. Sam Loman," he said.

"Where is he?"

"He's sound asleep in the back of the car."

"Your dad?"

"How did you guess?"

"I'm not as dumb as I look."

"Thank God for that."

"Ouch! Why don't you and your dad take a room for the night?"

"We'd have to boost our prices."

Meanwhile Brenda's husband's girlfriend, Nancy, was taken with young Willie Loman. She was ten years older than he, but she wouldn't mind hitching her star to the wagon of all this energy and wildness and ambition. His career was just taking off, and she visualized herself taking off with him. "Oh, you're so wonderful, you're such a darling," and all this kind of stuff, she kept saying, bending down and kissing him on the forehead, flicking little flecks of last summer's birdshit off his lapels, etc. The atmosphere was so electrifying, I decided to retire for the night.

MICMAC MYSTERIES

Burnt Berry • *Bishop's Falls* • *St. Alban's*
Conne River • *St. Jacques*

Saturday, June 9. The same waitress who said "I ain't been nowheres" came out with her pencil and said, "Good morning." I have a wallpaper face, changeable and easily forgotten. Had she forgotten me? Or was she wondering if I'd forgotten her?

"What would you like?" she said.

"How's about the same as last time?"

"Whole-wheat toast," she said, unerringly, "two soft-boiled eggs," and so on.

"How can you remember so well? Haven't had many customers?"

"None that ordered soft-boiled eggs."

I laughed. She stuck the tip of her tongue out, twisted her torso shyly, and looked at me with the cutest little-girl-with-pigtails look. My poor little heart wanted to take her somewhere.

"And then you had tea."

"I recall distinctly ordering coffee."

"You did have a cup of coffee, but you said it was too strong, so you asked for some tea."

That didn't sound like me, but what the heck. "You're right, I'm wrong. For a minute there I thought you must have me mixed up with some other old codger, but. . . ."

"You're not old."

At the forty-five-klick mark south from the Trans-Canada Highway, on the long, straight road to St. Alban's, deep inky-blue patches are forming in the western sky. A large one looked like a dory, but now it's dissolved. The tourism people call this road the Coast of Bays Passage.

April had insisted I visit St. Alban's. She hadn't visited herself, but had been told the scenery surpasses even the Gros Morne area. I've pulled off the road for a restful stroll. Moose droppings are everywhere, the size of walnuts, but a rich dark chocolate-brown colour. They're fairly dry, with a lot of solid form to them. If you step on one it resists for a crunchy moment, and then it squashes out nicely with a rather pleasant smell, because moose are vegetarians (and it's sad for them we're not).

At a spot farther in, roughly signposted "Rolling Pond," appeared a flat, triangular, pale-grey, almost-white granite stone standing on edge four feet high. On the flat side of the stone, facing away from the path, someone had painted a graceful but comical moose, quite Picassoesque. It seemed to have been painted by one of those natural draughtsmen who are incapable of drawing an imperfect line. It had a big fat snout, a whisker of a smile, two quick little twists of paint for antlers, and so on. But why was it painted on the side of the rock facing away from the rain-puddled path and towards nothing but thick woods? The chances of me having seen this moose were astronomical, for you can't see the rock from the road, and you can't see the moose from the path. From the path, I saw what seemed to be merely a chunk of granite that had been pulled upright. For some reason, I was drawn to examine it from the other side, and what a surprise!

The paint is a red-purplish colour, identical to that of the orchid-like wildflowers on either side of the path, so it looks as if the paint came from their juice. The flowers are at about knee level and tend to point in the same direction on their stems, as if they're all staring at the painted moose. This modest but exquisite painting may have been intended to impress the spirits in the invisible world, and the spirits of the animals, flowers, and forests of the visible.

It also may have been an attempt to attract a real moose from a distance. But maybe it was simply painted so that the flowers will be able to come up each spring and stare for a while at the merry prancing moose made from their blood.

At the eighty-five-klick mark, a bit off the right side of the road and hidden from the road by trees, there are nine interesting wooden structures with something of the same shamanistic quality as the moose. My favourite is the first one, which happens to be the simplest in design and execution. The construction comprises nine untrimmed and slender spruce logs, about two inches in diameter. The longest are the four uprights, each five feet high. There are four shorter lengths linking the uprights together at the top. Some of the logs are nailed together, others are tied with bits of twine.

The eight others stretch in a curved line about two hundred feet long. Each is progressively more complex, but they all use the same thin spruce logs and emanate from the same mind or group mind. They're wonderful to look at, to speculate about, but tedious to describe. They're all strangely symmetrical, and each is a variation on a theme, and none of them tries to overwhelm the viewer or each other. I'm sure they have a metaphysical function and purpose – something involving design, mystery, beauty, philosophical pleasure . . .

I didn't check all the rough unmarked roads leading off the main highway, but every time I checked one, I had luck. The next time I stopped, ten minutes south of the pole-art, I beheld a spectacular Christian cross. Six or eight stones formed each of the sides of the square base. A slender, unpainted spruce pole rose seven feet high, along with a crossbar in proportions relative to the traditional Christian cross. But to transform this ordinary cross into the "interesting zone," attached to the crossbars were similarly slender vertical poles that formed two lesser crosses while still being an integral part of the first cross.

So what we have is three crosses sharing one crossbar – certainly a beautiful and original variation on an ancient theme. In one leap the artist has destroyed that gulf between Jesus and the two thieves who shared his fate. Jesus and the thieves have become united, in another kind of trinity that this artist may have been the first to give expression to. It's an abstraction that provides an extra metaphysical dimension for those who like to meditate on that scene on Calvary. To me it's proof there's somehow a climate conducive to radical Christian thinking in this area – and it's contagious.

The moment I entered the pub in St. Alban's a great silence descended. Everyone had their eyes on the music channel, pretending they were doing that when I came in. All of them? With the sound off? No way!

There were four people at the bar – a woman about twenty-five, a guy about thirty-five, a rosy-cheeked fellow about nineteen, and the male bartender about forty. They were extremely shy. You could tell they were locals and had been having a conversation about floating a loan for the new streets, or what to do about dogs chewing the tires off the police cruisers (a story about the latter problem had been on the radio earlier).

On the screen was a guy dressed all in white and silently playing a white piano, while people threw blood at him. So I made a little speech, to announce to these shy folks that there's no harm in being friendly to strangers, because look at how friendly I am, even though all of you are strangers to me. So being friendly to strangers isn't harming me any to speak of.

Complete silence.

So I confessed that the same thing always happens to me. Every time I get dressed up in my white tuxedo and sit down to play my white baby grand, somebody throws a bucket of blood at me.

Complete silence. Then a titter or two. Then everyone started laughing. Even the five slot-machine people, who hadn't heard what I'd said, stopped playing for a minute and looked our way and laughed.

When the laughter died down the young fellow said, "Yeah, but dat weren't no real blood."

"What was it den, Mr. Smarty?" said his uncle Bob.

"It were just yer blood-coloured paint is what it probably must have been," said the thoughtful young feller.

After the blood had all been splattered and there was no white left, the song ended (but still no sound). Then there was a cut, and a guy came out playing a silent guitar.

"Isn't that the same guy?" I said.

"Yeah yeah yeah," everybody said. "It's de same guy. Dat's right. Looks different but it's de same guy."

The guy's name came on. It was Garth Brooks.

"Oh, dat's Garth Brooks. He look different," said someone.

Then the girl said, "Yeah dat's Garth Brooks. He looks really young. I didn't know he looked dat young. Dat's weird, cuz last time I saw him he looked really old and now here he is looking really young."

Nobody offered any explanation. They were all scratching their heads and trying to figure out this great mystery of the ages.

"Maybe where he looked so young, dat was just aye old film from when he really was young," said the same fellow who said that wasn't really blood.

"Maybe."

"Yeah. Dat sounds right."
"Oh yeah, dat's de answer."
"Dat's gotta be it."
"Sure, dat's it."

The lady in the Loony Toony store is wearing a pink smock. I'd visited a church down the road a bit and had forgotten the name of it already. She reminded me it was St. Ignatius Church, and she said it was "the closest thing you can get to a real cathedral made entirely from wood." I'd gone in to light a candle for each of two sisters of my acquaintance, one recently deceased and the other grieving.

She says it's the church she belongs to. "The priest is a black man. He's from South America somewhere. Everybody's welcomed him with open arms around here. But he's a shy man. That's why he didn't come out of his office to see you."

I said I noticed someone stirring in the office as if about to come out, but then they seemed to have noticed me and decided against coming out.

"That'd be him," she said. "That's what he's like."

"Was he the first black man in town?"

"Yes, he was. Far as I know."

"Was anyone miffed because he was black?"

"No, not one person dropped out of church. But some people complain they can't understand what he says, because he's got such a bad accent."

"That can be distressing," I said, comfortingly. "But at least it's not Latin."

"No, and it seems to be improving."

"But not his shyness."

"No, that's a constant."

Anyway, this woman seemed to be obsessed with marriage. "How's your wife doing today?" were her first words when I walked in.

"You've got the wrong guy," I said.

Then another guy came in and started looking at plastic champagne glasses. So she tiptoed over to him and asked if he was getting married. "No," he said, "I've been married twenty years already."

St. Alban's is just one of a whole series of small communities clustered around this area on the south shore. They will probably be amalgamated into one big town some day. On the dock at one such community, there's a red truck with four men getting out of it. The dwarf is the only one doing any work. He's got short bow legs, and he's pulling in line after line. The other guys are fairly short too – in the five-seven range, a foot taller than he, maybe more – but they're just standing watching him. The wind is causing their unbuttoned shirts to flap like flags. The dwarf has the long green cord all nicely looped on the dock now. And he's picking the whole pile of it up, holding it in his arms like Mary holding Christ and taking it over to the pickup truck. By standing on tippy-toe he finally manages to get it up and over into the truck box, while the three taller guys just stand and watch. Nobody helped that little person one little bit, and it was a lot of work, and they easily could have helped. How strange. Can you dig it? I can't. A fish-farm cage was tied to the wharf with the same green cord.

Every lawn around here is being mowed. A tall teenage boy and a short teenage girl go speed-walking by, with their elbows up around their shoulders, and chatting with each other as they zip along. Six guys, I imagine, have pooled their money and bought for a song a derelict old house with peeling paint. At first glance it looks as if it's been ruined in a winter storm and they're rebuilding it. But it turns out they're simply adding a second floor to what was a one-floor house. It's going to be a jewel when they're finished.

A bridge has been destroyed in a not-so-recent storm. On the road to Conne River, the trees along the sides of the road haven't been trimmed in so long that a two-lane highway has become a one-way tunnel, which suddenly stops at a large mound of earth intended to warn people the bridge is out and to stop people from driving into the river.

St. Jacques has wide streets, a large filling station, a large Canadian flag blowing in the breeze, and a spring jacket airing on the line. Steps have been built into the waterfall to give the salmon a helping hand. There's an unhappy schoolgirl standing all alone outside an empty school bus.

But old-timers may recall the fifteen minutes of terror St. Jacques experienced on the afternoon of October 19, 1936, when a series of giant fireballs appeared in the sky, along with powerful explosions. Some reports said innumerable great balls of fire exploded and fell into the sea, others said spherical objects exploded and turned into fireballs and then fell into the sea – or into distant forested areas, causing fires to break out briefly. This is in Jack Fitzgerald's *Amazing Newfoundland Stories*, and on the cover there's a terrific watercolour by Maurice Fitzgerald depicting the event. Similar fireballs were seen in other parts of Newfoundland that day. "The sightings caused all sorts of speculation," writes Fitzgerald, a retired journalist of wide experience as a reporter, feature writer, political columnist, editor, and public-relations administrator with the Smallwood government. "But the official explanation given was that Newfoundland had passed through the strange astronomical event known as 'a shower of meteors.'"

A really cute little girl I took to be about twelve came flying down the street on her bicycle. But she was not an innocent twelve. She flashed me the sexiest smile as she sailed by, and only then did I notice she had a little baby strapped to her back, with its head in a little helmet not much bigger than a softball.

I was so touched by the combination of innocence and experience in her dear face, I found myself sending her a silly little prayer, wishing her a long sweet life and the freedom to do all the things she wants to do and to refuse to do all the things she doesn't want to do.

Just think, when she's thirty-two her daughter will be twenty already. And her daughter will show her this book. And she will say, "Could that have been us?"

The night crept up on me, and I had no idea where I was going to stay, as usual. I pulled into a filling station somewhere north of St. Alban's at the moment the lights were being turned off. "We're just locking up," said the Micmac lady, "but if there's anything we can do to help you. . . ."

"Am I too late for a tank of gas?"

"Absolutely not. All I have to do is flick the switch on. Anyone who tells you that you can't get gas after a certain time because the pumps are off, they don't know what they're talking about. All I have to do is flick this switch. And the pumps come right back on like a light bulb. Anyone who wouldn't help someone low on gas late at night shouldn't be in the business."

I was spellbound. I knew I wasn't in Ontario. I followed her and the kids inside to pay the bill and she said, "Are you hungry? Coffee? Sandwich?"

I said yes to all three and am glad I did. She was Micmac, her husband was from the Six Nations, and his mother was a Tuscarora. What does he do? He's an antler carver. And she pointed to one of his works. It was a pair of antlers, all right, but it was carved so that it looked like the wings of a fantastic bird. It was mysterious and made you think of the interconnectedness of life.

She said he was in New York City visiting his ailing mother and father who lived there. Her little girl was nine years old, but small for her age. She had a slightly short body and a slightly large head. She had a perfect heart-shaped face, with sparkling intelligent eyes. She'd be the same height as the dwarf on the wharf, but she's still young enough for growth spurts.

I thanked the mother for her kindness, told her I admired her philosophy. She said it was this: "If you wake up in the morning and you're on the green side of the sod, that means things are okay." It had a shamanistic tone to it, as if it's axiomatic that this world is better than the other, with its hungry ghosts and smooth-talking demons.

Given that her husband was a professional artist, I was disappointed that she knew so little about the works of art I'd seen along the road.

She said, "Oh, this is a country where people put rocks on top of other rocks, and they wander around, and they move things around, and they do rock paintings and things like that."

Was she referring to the Micmac people?

She said, "No, to everybody. It's that kind of island." She didn't seem to want to talk about the moose painting facing into the woods and away from the path. Or the spruce-pole sculptures. As soon as I tried to explain what I found so remarkable about them, I sensed her defocusing.

She suggested the reasons may have been something quite practical that I, being from the Mainland, might not understand. But she didn't seem to understand either.

"Watch out for the caribou and the moose," said Madame Micmac.

ONE OF OUR
PILOTS IS SAFE

Gander • Gambo • Glovertown • Traytown

Sunday, June 10. Silent Witness Memorial is on a hill overlooking Gander Lake and the forests beyond. This is the spot where the entire 248-man U.S. 101st Airborne Division was wiped out, along with a six-person flight crew, when their plane crashed under strange circumstances on takeoff from Gander on the last leg of its way home to Fort Campbell, Kentucky, on the night of December 11, 1985.

The plane was a DC8 operated by a private carrier called Arrow Airlines, and the flight originated in Cairo. The soldiers had been on a peacekeeping mission in the Sinai Desert.

A few hours after the crash, an anonymous caller telephoned a French international news agency in Beirut, stating that the Islamic Jihad, the Shiite Moslem extremist group, had planted a bomb on board the aircraft and was claiming responsibility. According to a report of the Union of Canadian Transport Employees, dismissals came instantly from the Pentagon, the White House, the RCMP, and the Canadian government.

The majority report of the Canadian Aviation Safety Board (CASB), which was published almost three years later, on October 28, 1988, stated the cause of the plane stalling then crashing could not be determined, though icing was considered a likely factor.

A minority "dissenting" report, published by four members of the CASB a few weeks after the majority report, said that several witnesses, including the crew of a nearby airplane, stated that they had seen spectacular explosions and extremely bright flame as the plane continued to lift off over the Trans-Canada Highway.

This report seems to have been largely ignored, at least in any official way. But after all these years, the cause of the crash is still controversial, and there are some intriguing theories published on the Internet, with one retired U.S. colonel maintaining that the Screaming Eagles, as the 101st Airborne Division was called, were done in by Russian "over-the-horizon radars" with "infolded Whittaker bidirectional EM wave structures to provide distance-independent holography and dispersion-free phase conjugate shooting."

The good people of Gander and surrounding communities threw their spare change together to build a memorial. The Masonic Lodge of Newfoundland organized the construction of the site. The monument was designed by a St. John's artist and executed by an artist from Kentucky. The local Masonic lodge still maintains a collection box at the site to take contributions for the upkeep of the memorial. There's a very touching statue of a larger-than-life unarmed U.S. soldier, holding hands with two little children, both bearing olive branches.

The Americans built their own memorial, in Hopkinsville, Kentucky, and it was much different in tone. It shows a lone soldier, with no little children at his side, and no olive branches. The soldier is fully armed, and there is no reference to his "peacekeeper" status.

Also, in Hopkinsville, there is a little copse of 248 trees, one for each of the military people killed, but no trees for the civilian crew members.

Closer to the airport, on the north side of the Trans-Canada Highway, is a large graveyard run by the Commonwealth Graves Commission, adjacent to the major runway at Gander International Airport. This is the final resting place for many who died here during the Second World War. Mostly RCAF. Some RAF, some Australians. Most of the deaths would have involved plane crashes during training flights.

Gravestones abound for a few large and many small groups of young men, all of whom died on the same day. Crashes killing two or three men seemed to be almost routine. Most of them were in their early twenties.

"This was a proud extravagance of giving" is inscribed under the name of RCAF Squadron Leader Richard L. Lee, who died, along with numerous others, in a crash on October 2, 1943. RAF Pilot Officer David J. Owen, who died in a crash in February of the same year, has "One of our pilots is safe" inscribed below his name.

The cemetery took its first body in 1936 and now contains a hundred graves of Commonwealth servicemen, ninety-four of them airmen and six army, from the following countries: Canada (eighty), the United Kingdom (eighteen), Australia (two).

Giovanni's Café seems to be the most with-it, most postmodern place in Gander. It's where all the hepcats hang out. The walls are covered with cool black-and-white beatnik posters of great jazz musicians of the forties and fifties – Monk, Charlie, Miles, the Count, the Duke, Lester, Billie. And they have an authentic beatnik espresso machine, but I didn't see any beatnik cigarette holders or fake beards for sale. I had a raisin tea biscuit with my East Coast Dark coffee. It was either that or Colombian, and I was feeling adventurous. As for the raisin tea biscuit, it looked like a raisin scone, it tasted like a raisin scone, but the young lady behind the counter had never heard it called that. It appears that the scone era is dead. This is the new, improved tea-biscuit era.

I came in at the wrong time, just when a huge line was forming. A whole ragged family from Change Islands was demanding immediate attention on account of their numbers. A woman about fifty had brought her mother and her whole extended family, and they'd never been in a coffee shop before, except for Tim Hortons. It's hard to describe the scene, but it was interesting to see that these people were not at all embarrassed by their confusion and indecision, and by the fact that they were holding up a large line of people gasping for coffee. They were determined they weren't going to order anything until they knew exactly what it was and how much it would cost. Nobody was going to cheat them. They were suspicious and didn't try to hide it. I suspected the posters of jazz musicians were making them nervous. In their eyes there was something atheistic about this place, if I read their eyes right.

Newfoundland friendliness is always put to the test and passes with flying colours when someone has had an accident, no matter how minor, or has experienced some petty embarrassment. Giovanni's Café was in a mall, and when I pulled in to my parking spot, I pulled in too far and hit the high curb with an awful crunch. I hopped out of the car just as an elderly lady walked by and gave me a sympathetic smile. I got down to look for damage as a big cheerful bearded man getting into his car yelled over, "I've done that!" – and a young woman putting her car in gear rolled the window down and yelled out, "So have I."

They were so sweet. They figured I'd be terribly embarrassed, so they tried to make me feel better. Greatly appreciated.

In the Gander airport museum, a high-school girl has produced a collage composed of cut-out colour pictures of all the famous movie stars who have ever stopped over in Gander. Until 1965 or so, if you flew the north Atlantic, you had to stop over in Gander for refuelling.

But now the airport's struggling. In the collage, front and centre, was a young Woody Allen, unknowingly surrounded by Humphrey Bogart, Lauren Bacall, Laurence Olivier, Yul Brynner, the Beatles – but not the Rolling Stones – and dozens more.

The Tickleview Restaurant in nearby Gambo has a big hand-painted sign saying Home-Cooked Eals. That'd make a good meel. A peal and a peel are somewhat different, a heal and a heel are different (though a heel can be healed), but an eal and an eel are the same thing.

I made some purchases of intimate apparel at Riff's in Glovertown. What a bargain! A pair of sandals, four pairs of boxer shorts, and three pairs of socks for thirty bucks. The fellow who waited on me, you could tell he wasn't the average outport fellow, because his jeans fit him properly, they weren't the baggy and droopy style the locals feel comfy in. Also he had a good haircut and his moustache was nicely trimmed. I'd seen Riff's all over the island. "Yes, I believe there are about forty-three on the island," he said.

And the Cohen's Furniture Stores, would there be as many of them?

"Oh, uh, ah," he said, wondering if it would be right to say anything. "You know, I'll give you a little tip on that one. I'm pretty sure there's going to be a merger soon between Riff's and Cohen's. Yes, they're good buddies apparently. And they're just talking about throwing their money in together. And expanding."

"As long as it makes for lower prices and more jobs."

"Yes, yes. Indeed!"

Lisa is the bright lady who is working at a fishing resort in Traytown, on the northern border of Terra Nova National Park. It has about twenty-five very spiffy holiday cabins, and a bar and dining room currently being expanded and renovated. It's Lisa's first day on the job, but you'd never know it, for it's amazing how she has everything figured out. She really knows how to take charge. She and her husband and two kids spent a year and a half in Toronto. But they had to leave; they couldn't stand it any longer. Toronto's loss, for sure.

She insisted her biggest problem was her complete inability to get her mind around the fact that you had to pay to park. Also, she hated it that her kids used to get in trouble simply for going into other people's backyards to play with the other kids' toys without asking permission or waiting to be invited. "My kids were so naive, they thought Toronto was just like Newfoundland. They soon found out they couldn't get away with that sort of thing. So they're happy to be home."

Newfoundland is more civilized than Toronto?

"Hah! Definitely. Our kids will think that till their dying day."

They were lonelier in the big city than they could ever be back home?

"Definitely. They'll never go back."

Things are so much cheaper in Newfoundland, she said, that if you make twenty dollars an hour in Toronto, that's the same as eight dollars an hour back home. But people seem more well off here, even if their income is low. Her husband's not making quite as much money here in construction as he was in Toronto, but he's much happier. He's busy building a new wing on the hospital in Gander right now.

She said one evening they had tickets to a hockey game at Maple Leaf Gardens, which was smack dab in the middle of Toronto's gay ghetto. A tall transvestite took a fancy to her husband and engaged him in conversation all the way down Church Street from Wellesley, then tried to kiss him right there on the northwest corner of Church and Carlton. . . .

She also said that, if you see someone all bruised and battered on Yonge Street, you naturally want to do something about it. But as soon as you try, their pimp shows up and tells you to get lost. So that is an unusual situation for a Newfoundlander to be in – to be ordered not to help an ailing human being.

In Newfoundland, if you see someone who looks a bit unusual, a little different, she said, people will stare, they steal glances. They try not to, but they can't help it. But in Toronto you can't do that or you get in trouble.

It was a great pleasure talking to Lisa, and I told her that she, along with many others, was writing my book for me.

Lisa put me in ultra-spacious and luxurious Pine Cabin 17 – two large bedrooms with double beds and a large living/dining area.

This is a friendly place. There's a guy who has just moved in a few cabins down, and he's already got his fishing gear out and is standing in the pouring rain practising his casting, seeing how close he can get that plug to the road at the end of the lawn.

Somebody came around the corner at the far end and said, "Hey, you're not going to catch anything there, you have to go down to the pond." The owner of the place, Joan, who was technically Lisa's boss, was cleaning out the cabin next to mine and yelled out, "I just got finished saying that myself." "It's true, she did," said the fisherman.

This spot isn't far from Cape Freels, and April English returned my call. She's been having trouble with her car and had to rent one in Gander. She wants to come down tomorrow and take me to visit some friends in Eastport.

Tsk! When I got back to the lodge for dinner, bad news was waiting. The renovations had created such chaos in the dining room that Joan "didn't bother" to replenish major food supplies. "It's a waste of time looking at the menu," said Lisa. "I can give you onion rings, and I can give you a chicken sandwich with fresh tomato."

So while Lisa fed me at the bar, we had another chat. She knew how to deliver her bright opinions in a most amusing manner. I still preferred the term Newfoundlanders, because it has an aura of respect to it, and there's no race of people I respect more than the Newfoundlanders. I've heard the term "Newfie," or "goofy Newfie," uttered disparagingly or condescendingly too often for my taste. And I too hated all those goofy Newfie jokes. I would feel disrespectful if I called anyone a Newfie, even if they didn't mind. I told her about Minny Lorry, whose choice is to be called a "Newf." But Lisa didn't care for that and gave me official sanction to use the term Newfies all I wanted.

What I liked about Lisa was that she came on at noon, it was her first day, and by seven o'clock she had mastered every aspect of the job, even to figuring out the switchboard. She was relaxed, leaning against the counter, barking out orders to lesser people, she seemed to have lots of time to chat, and she was impressive on the phone, taking fishing-party bookings from all over North America.

With great authority she phoned Joan, because she couldn't understand a certain marking in the reservations book. Five hours on the job and she was already in total command, taking full responsibility, even for the boss's errors.

Her son was fifteen now, all grown up, a big "Newfie" (I cringed), who loved to fish and hunt every chance he got. She took it seriously when I asked what she liked about Toronto, what she missed most. She thought hard, then said the rapid transit was just wonderful. You didn't always have to be driving, you could just get out of your car and hop on a streetcar, and it would take you to the subway, and the subway would take you to the GO Train or Via Rail or to the airport bus – or, in a pinch, even the bus to St. John's. In Newfoundland you have to rely on your car for everything.

"Were there any special people up there you really miss?"

"Sometimes I'll phone them or they'll phone us for little chats, just to say hello, but basically you don't really get to know the people in Toronto much."

I said, "It must have been a huge thing for you to have suddenly upped and moved your family down to Toronto."

"You would think so," she said, "but everything went remarkably easy. And it was really easy to come home, too. It was scary going to Toronto, but it was just joy coming home."

Back in my cabin, I had my tape recorder standing on end on the dining-room table, and it suddenly without warning toppled over and killed a lone ant on a long walk. But no, I picked the recorder up and the ant was dazed but still alive. It just sat there staring at me for half a minute, then took off as good as new. He was down for the count but he's all right now. When he gets home his spouse will say, "Where have you been all this time?"

"You won't believe this but I got crushed by a bloody tape recorder."

"Oh, that's the best one yet."

Wait a minute, something strange is happening. The ant has come back, and he goes right up to the spot where he was crushed by the tape recorder and resumes his immobile position. Even his antennae have stopped twitching. He's lying still. Is this some kind of religious ritual? Or does he hope the tape recorder will fall again because he's tired of life? The things you don't find out in science class.

Maybe other ants are watching from cracks in the walls, and he's showing them, at great danger to himself, exactly where it happened, so they can avoid the same painful mishap.

Maybe his friends in the cracks were curious and asked if he'd give them an exact replay of what happened. So everything happened the same except the tape recorder didn't fall on him this time.

I'm sitting invisible on the porch of a dark cabin listening to the midnight breezes whispering through the willows and birch trees, like vast schools of fish shimmering in the night as they pass. There's little doubt in my mind that Sam French will be happy to find that April and I are friends once more, because then he and I will be able to be buddies again.

CHAPTER 25

POND-ITCH ALERT!

Traytown • Eastport

Monday, June 11. I'm drinking coffee on the front porch and breathing in the fresh vegetative smell of a rainy spring morning. A little Newfoundlander is getting amazing speed out of his tricycle. He's splashing through puddles, getting soaked and mud-splattered, darting between the cabins, then coming around from where you least expect him. He's having fun, and he's also looking forward to catching a big fish with Daddy.

Without being asked, Lisa brought over the biggest pot of hot coffee to kick-start my day. She also had a new telephone tucked under her arm, because she knew mine was a bit unreliable. And she brought over a lovely selection of shampoos in all different kinds of fruity flavours, such as orange marmalade and rhubarb pie. She brought me a stopper for the tub, because she had me down for the sort of guy who'd rather soak than shower.

I said, "This kid's having more fun with his ten-dollar tricycle than we could have with a ten-million-dollar lottery win."

"Aye, but it's sad," she said. "The family came up yesterday, but the fishing didn't pan out, so they're going home today. He doesn't know it yet."

"But I thought this was a fisherman's paradise. They couldn't be very good fishermen."

"Oh no, sometimes these ponds are like that. Depends on the winds and the currents. There's lots of fish in there, but sometimes they just go for a week or two without a nibble."

"Was that his dad who was casting on the lawn yesterday?"

"Yes. It was. And there was another couple leaving. They come for the fishing, so they leave if they're not biting."

So I had a good soak, and it's true that the water was sedimentary, as at the Fancy home and elsewhere, but it wasn't as sedimentary as it would be when I got out of it an hour later. I decided to try the orange-marmalade shampoo. It seemed awfully sticky. Turned out it *was* orange marmalade, period. All the others were real shampoo, and the jam was soon washed right out of my hair. I'm lying low till two-thirty, when April will be arriving to take me to visit her friend over at Eastport. I seem to be as agreeable in Newfoundland as I am disagreeable in Toronto.

April has a good eye for traditional Newfoundland building techniques. When she arrives, she notes that the floor of my cabin appears to have once been part of a dock. But she's relaxed, like the old days. Stuff from my bag is all over a big upholstered chair, but she just pushes it to the floor, sits down sideways with her feet over the arm, and gets me to tell her stories about the trip so far. I'm thankful she asked, because when I tell her a few, she seems to enjoy them, indicating maybe the book will be a big hit, and Newfoundlanders in exile all over the world will read it and decide to return to the place of their birth and never more roam.

She says she and Minny were snowshoeing near Windmill Bight last winter and found a couple experiencing intense pleasure on a picnic bench. Minny and April came up on them unawares and heard the couple's sighs of joy, and the couple heard Minny's gasp and April's groan. The lovers froze, as if someone had pressed the freeze-frame button on a skin flick. The well-bred ladies didn't gawk; they just turned and scurried in the opposite direction, embarrassed as all get-out. April noted that it was obviously a rendezvous, because there were two vehicles – a pickup truck and a car – parked at the side of the road. She said Minny's comment had been "I don't ever want to eat on a picnic bench again."

April helped me select the perfect top for today: an "I'm a Gravel Pit Camper" sweatshirt. It featured a picture of a guy with no shirt on, drinking a beer on the step of his camper, parked for the summer in a gravel pit. You want to get all the sun you can get when you live in Newfoundland, so what better place and time than a treeless gravel pit in the summer.

"Oh, you must wear this," said April. There was a nip in the air, so over the sweatshirt I wore my pearl-buttoned lumberjack shirt, an oversized one I bought at Riff's last week. It's already coming apart at the seams. Nobody's going to think I'm a tourist.

She doesn't want to talk about it, but it appears I'm forgiven, or at least we're having a truce. Maybe she feels a bit guilty for having been too critical of me, because after all I'm famous for my innocence. Maybe Sam on the phone from Toronto took my side on the issue and suggested she lighten up a bit. There was none of that awkwardness at all, just two old friends from the city finding themselves in the outports.

April and I had a rich day and we gabbed non-stop. It didn't even bother us when the friend she was taking me to meet wasn't at home – not even a note, though she knew we were coming. Yes, April can be a wonderful companion, and Sam's a lucky guy.

There are many architecturally interesting churches around the Eastport Peninsula, and we gawked at every one. Most were locked (forgiving trespassers can be tiresome), so we couldn't check out the interiors, which left us all the more time to contemplate the exteriors. April spoke convincingly and at great length of the "variations on a theme" aspect of church architecture on the Rock.

It was fun to become friends with Ben again, a smart dog, spectacular in his coat of snow-white fur. It's even pure white on his backside.

"How does he go to the bathroom without staining himself?"

"I have no idea," she said. "It's one of the great mysteries of the universe."

He loves to eat kelp, even though he can't digest it. It passes through his gastrointestinal valley of death without fearing evil, emerging unchanged. Eating kelp is the only time he gets stained around the back end. It's a pleasant green stain, and not disgusting at all, says April, but she doesn't like it anyway. That's why, when she takes him for a walk and he starts sniffing for kelp, she says, "No no, Ben. Don't eat any foreign objects." So now when you say "foreign objects," Ben's ears perk up and he starts sniffing around for kelp.

The ponds look so inviting, but nobody's swimming in them. April informs me that you can get the dreaded pond-itch from swimming in these beautiful, tempting ponds which sparkle like diamonds all over Newfoundland in the sunny summer months. "It's a duck-borne parasite, it gets under the skin, and it's a battle between you and your immune system. The local pronunciation is 'poundage,' or sometimes 'bondage,' and it can be horrible. So nobody swims in the ponds any more, except for some hardy souls who will swim if they don't see any ducks around."

But surely there would be "No Swimming" signs to warn innocent tourists. I'd often stopped at ponds to wash my hands and face; I was even wading once. What's the incubation period? She had no idea. Inoculation available? She didn't think so.

She said some of the most badly infected ponds have signs. I had seen signs posted at ponds, but I didn't get close enough to read them. In my innocence I thought the sign would be just giving the name of the pond.

"But the good news is," she said, "there are no ticks on this island."

THE SORROWS OF CHRISTIAN JOY

Traytown • Happy Adventure • St. Brendan's Ferry Dock • Traytown

Tuesday, June 12. April and I had arranged to rendezvous at the community of Happy Adventure. Almost as if by a fluke, we both arrive at exactly the right time, and she takes me to meet Gord and Flora at their tiny home/studio/giftshop/teashop called the Bosun's Whistle, a house not much bigger than a one-car garage, but perfectly organized. Two lovey-doveys don't need much room, especially when they have a big deck out front, sitting on stilts on the beach of an oddly-shaped and placid little cove all their own, with no neighbours as far as the eye can see, which isn't far, because their home is in a part of Happy Adventure that is surrounded by high ground.

There's little Gord, and his missus, Flora, who is twice his size, maybe three times, and who does the cooking and crafts, and provides two kinds of muffins with her excellent tea or coffee, which she serves at the card table and two chairs. She offers her crafts for sale, and miniature paintings depicting local scenes of natural beauty. Flora becomes flushed with pleasure as April raves about her paintings and her muffins.

Paintings were hanging from the walls, and her tiny dolls and painted boxes were revolving on strings tacked to the ceiling. You had to watch your head. Flora liked to get sea-polished pieces of driftwood and paint evocative little landscapes on them, with a few trees, the sea, an iceberg, and so on – basically what she sees from her window.

Gord spent years in Toronto, but now he's retired; he's fifty-three and he does "very little of anything." He came back home without any money, he latched up with this craft artist, and has a pretty good life it looks like. He has old lobster traps lying around for the tourists, but he doesn't fish for lobsters, because it costs ten thousand dollars to get a licence. He does have a sealing licence, but he hasn't caught a seal yet. He saw fifteen seals out on the beach one day. By God, he thought, I'm going to get me a sealing licence. So he did. But he hasn't seen a seal since, and he's been three years sitting here watching for them.

You don't need much money to live around here, said Gord, with the look of a fellow who, after all those lonely, hard-up years in Toronto, can't believe his luck in finding Flora and this perfect little house at this perfect little spot. Even Flora couldn't think of anything to complain about. They just love moose meat, in fact they don't much care for people who don't like it. As soon as one moose is gone, Gord goes out and shoots another. They're bright, and they keep close track of the big ugly world out there. What they may lack in urban sophistication, they make up for in outport sophistication, character, and honesty.

Gord's still glad Newfoundland joined Canada. Maybe he felt that's what we wanted to hear, so I asked him what would be different today if Newfoundland had joined, say, the United States – not that there was ever any important movement with that aim, as far as

I've heard. "There'd be amusement parks all over the place every-where you go, I suppose," he said. "We didn't want that at all."

April drove, with me in the passenger's seat, to the ferry dock going over to St. Brendan's Island, where there's an ancient stone quarry thought to have been used by the Beothuks five centuries ago. April had been under the impression it was five millennia old and had been a huge high-capacity stone quarry. When she found out it was just a little quarry for arrowheads around 1500 she lost interest. I'd read somewhere there was no evidence anywhere of stone construc-tion in Beothuk times. Later I was to hear differently. I also reminded her the Beothuk didn't arrive on the island, from parts unknown, till sometime after A.D. 1000.

Repairs were being carried out on a bridge up ahead, and a tem-porary stoplight had been installed at the roadside to control the flow of traffic along one lane. April came buzzing along, causing me to wonder if perhaps she didn't notice the light was red. I was just about to scream out "April! Red light!" but before I could, we bar-relled right through at full speed. And just as we did, the light turned green and we kept going right across the bridge.

"April, that was amazing the way the light turned green just as you got there. And you knew enough not to bother slowing down."

April scrunched up her face and said, "What light?"

We arrived just as the ferry was heading back to the island, and it wouldn't be returning till tomorrow. We let it go without regret. A lone fellow, an older guy, began chatting us up, and it began to dawn on us that, although he had a lovely name – he introduced himself as Christian Joy – he was a professional grouch, whose aim in life was to zero in on happy souls and infect them with his own misery. He was going on about all the murders in schools, and how it's spreading all over the place, even to Newfoundland, where they haven't had any murders yet, touch wood, but they've had threats of murders.

He could be described as having an insincere smile and a sincere frown, spiritless eyes, and a face that would have been handsome if it hadn't been so marked by his ugly soul. He took things personally. Anything that went wrong with the world was aimed at him. That's what Christian Joy has come to.

It was odd meeting such a dark soul on such a bright afternoon, and we talked for quite some time. I was okay, I could have chatted with him for hours, but April was emitting anguished sighs.

So I whispered, "Let's go," out of the side of my mouth, to the left, directing it at April, who was sitting in the car, while Mr. Joy was standing on my right. But he heard me. It came right in the middle of one of his morbid monologues. He immediately shut up.

So all that discussion didn't help him at all. He still retained his paralytic, simplistic view of the evil of the world. And with April and me taking off in the middle of a sentence, we left him hating the world just a little bit more. He was letting things get to him a little more than is sensible. He probably thought we wanted to go home and get naked, the filthy swine.

Now it was time for April to go home. She dropped me off at my car, which I'd left in Happy Adventure, and we said goodbye. I headed straight for what looked like an old whale-blubber warehouse or something along those lines. Maybe a former cod-liver-oil factory. It was huge. And it was grungy. We'd passed it earlier. It was called The Flea Market, with a big sign out front saying it offers Frequent Shopper Coupons.

In order to get in, you have to wend your way past a disorderly assortment of old bathtubs, bedsprings, bicycles, and baffed-out hot-water heaters. "Terrific store you have here," I said. They wanted me to know they were quite aware that it was the grungiest, greasiest, most disorganized elephant's graveyard imaginable. In their purse section they must have had ten thousand old purses: three large tables were stacked high with pyramids of old purses. Also under the tables were large boxes overflowing with old purses. There'd be more in the shed out back. Imagine coming in here shopping for a purse. "Yes, come this way, Madame."

There were piles of wrecked television sets, and even their book selection was lousy – Frank Yerby and Ayn Rand novels from the fifties, and a million old Harlequins, involving lonely but dedicated nurses who fall in love with guys recovering from burns suffered in rescuing all the nuns from a burning convent.

But who could resist buying a fake camera, slightly larger and more surrealistic than a normal single lens reflex would be, and with a neck strap studded with what looked like containers to store spare film, but inside each container was a shot glass. Instead of a film winder there was a cork stopper. A brandy lover could wear this hollow porcelain camera around his neck, secure in the knowledge that nobody – except possibly another drunk – would look closely enough to see it wasn't really a Nikon. He could go "Click," and take fake shots when people were looking, while taking real shots of hard liquor when the coast was clear.

"What kind of film does this take?" I said.

"Liquid film, but we're not allowed to sell that for some damn fool reason."

I gave them a dollar for it and told them I was taking it back to Toronto, where I knew I'd get at least two dollars for it.

The guy said, "Take my wife why don't you? You might get a dollar or two for her."

His wife stood there smiling sweetly, with hands clasped, as if she were about to start singing "What a Friend We Have in Jesus."

SPRING GARDENING

Traytown • Bonavista • Elliston • Trinity • Norman's Cove
Heart's Ease • South Dildo • Dildo • Dildo Harbour
Dildo Island • Dildo Beach • Dildo Arm
Heart's Content • Hant's Harbour • Daniel's Cove

Wednesday, June 13. I felt very rested and could have driven to Pluto and back today, so I drove pretty well non-stop from Traytown down through Terra Nova Park, then all the way up to Bonavista, drinking in the beauty of the powerful landscape, with green hills, villages, and soul-stirring views of Bonavista Bay and the Atlantic Ocean. Most of the way I was also listening to the spring gardening show on CBC radio from St. John's.

An old guy from Placentia wanted to know what was the best thing for dandelions. The guest gardener said, "Just cut your lawn more often." Could it be that simple? "Every dandelion that goes to seed means there's going to be a thousand more dandelions next year. So just cut your lawn more often before they go to seed, and then they won't go to seed."

The caller recovered from his embarrassment. "That's a good piece of advice you've given me," he said. "I knew the missus wasn't cutting the lawn often enough. I'll get after her." You could sense the entire island shaking with laughter, and Labrador too.

Thank God for public radio. If it had been a commercial station, the caller would have been advised to purchase expensive and dangerous chemicals.

Another fellow, from Deer Lake, wanted to know what he could do about steam medals. The guest gardener couldn't figure out what a steam medal was, but the charming hostess of the show said, precisely, "Caller, do you mean stinging nettles?"

"Yeah," said the caller. "Steam medals."

He says he eats them in the spring, before the steam comes in. But you can't eat them after the steam comes in. How can he have his steam medals in the spring, but get rid of them fast when the steam comes in?

"Have you considered clipping them off just before the sting comes in?" asked the gardener. Ah yes, the best ideas are always the simplest ones.

"Just like the last caller," said the caller, "I can get my wife to do that real easy. Thanks a million."

"But don't let her try clipping them after the sting comes in," said the gardener, but the caller had already hung up. This went on and on for hours.

In this area up near Bonavista, numerous baseball diamonds have been abandoned and are falling apart. It appears no serious ball has been played here in years. Yet these parks were really built for action, great little small-town baseball diamonds with big ads on the outfield fence, which was low enough to make final scores like 42–41 not uncommon. The bleachers with a canopy for sun and rain protection were falling apart, and old wrecked cars were scattered around, even in the infield. Maybe everybody was just too discouraged by the baseball strike a few years ago, which caused a lot of people to lose interest in the game.

Bonavista is a big, sprawling maze of a town, with a strange lack of services such as restaurants or filling stations. There are lots of old houses, badly in need of paint, but they don't seem to be in danger of being torn down by unscrupulous developers. Oh no, the people seem fully conscious of architecture being front and centre on the stage of history, but they know they're a bit behind in getting these old buildings freshened up, if only in order to ensure their preservation. . . .

Elliston, just east and south of Bonavista, and facing full out into the broad Atlantic, is the "Home of the Root Cellar." Root cellars dot the hilly countryside like the sudden appearance of a whole flock of birds thought long extinct. How to make a root cellar? Take a little hill, hollow it out from one side, put some stones around the entrance, and you have yourself a root cellar. They're called root cellars because you'll have roots dangling from the ceiling, and you can store anything you want in them, from crates of alphabet soup to your grandfather's old zither. Some may even store root vegetables in them. You never know when you're going to spot another root cellar. There's one, there's two – that makes fourteen so far. All shapes and sizes. Prehistoric Europeans would inter their dead in what we would call root cellars.

William F. Coaker (1871–1938) is the big name around this peninsula. Everything's named after him, and his statue stands taller than life by the famous Bonavista Lighthouse, currently under repair.

Coaker is suddenly such a big name that, as soon as I saw the statue, I sensed myself in the shadow of a greatness so profound that ordinary blokes like me should hang their heads in shame. Oh yes, it was Coaker, all right. He's the local hero, all right. They wouldn't go putting up any statues to anyone else but Mr. Coaker. He was a good guy – he formed a strong union of Protestant fishermen. But he had a dark side; he had zero tolerance for Catholicism. Today he's a Protestant icon on a Protestant peninsula. But such lack of tolerance, as far as I can tell, has gone the way of the great auk.

Trinity, where they have now finished filming *The Shipping News*, is an old-world town with narrow winding roads and beautifully maintained old houses, old churches and schools from the early nineteenth century, the site of an eighteenth-century British fort, old administrative buildings, and several museums and "learning centres" (including a railway museum).

But for me, Trinity was the site of a sad scene, rather yucky, and if you're squeamish please move on to the next paragraph. A man is driving along with his wife. They pull over and stop. As I slowly approach, the man has got out and is splattering vomit all over the trunk, and his wife's just sitting there in the passenger's seat, staring straight ahead, waiting for him to get back in the car and drive home, I guess. You would think she'd hop out and help him, but she's apparently accustomed to this. He drinks, he drives, he vomits all over the trunk of the car – and there's not much she can do about it.

For in almost every town there's a liquor store. In fact, there are a lot of liquor stores along the highway as well. But wherever there's a liquor store, there is, right next to it, like something out of a Dadaist poem, a yarn shop or a knitting-supplies store. Or sometimes, if it's a large liquor store, there'll be a whole crafts shop next to it. This probably has something to do with the hobbies pursued by Newfoundland couples: the man drinks, the woman knits or makes crafts, and that way they can each pick up the supplies for both at one stop.

This is of course a gross stereotype, but there is a grain of truth in it.

And quite possibly that fellow wasn't drunk at all. Maybe they'd just had breakfast at McDonald's.

Older Newfoundlanders bitterly remember how in the early fifties, shortly after Confederation, people from Quebec came to Newfoundland and made off with all the local antiques – mostly home furnishings such as lamps and tables. But I seem to remember hearing about Ontarians invading Quebec, in the late fifties and early sixties, and making off with all their antiques, not knowing they were Newfoundlandish in origin.

So probably a lot of Quebec antiques that grace the homes of many old Torontonians are really Newfoundland antiques.

But who's that knocking at my door?

"Howdy, ahm from Texas and I was jes' wonderin', do you folks have any antiques you might be willing to exchange for suitcases full of U.S. dollars?"

It would be nice if there could be rules about selling antiques, so that the people who got most badly ripped off in the food chain – the Newfoundlanders, for instance – might realize their share of some of the big profits the sale of the same antiques are getting today.

The Dark Zone, at Norman's Cove, is a long, low, one-room pub overlooking a rugged-but-serene saltwater inlet. The lady bartender was chatty, so I wanted to know, since she said she was born and raised in Newfoundland, how she came to be unencumbered of any Newfoundlandish intonations or syntactical oddities. She had no idea what it was that caused her to be a TFN (Twang-free Newfoundlander) – no special tutors or anything like that, and no strict instructress like Gina Hodge's mama, Bella. She does have family in small-town Ontario – Cambridge and Trenton – and she goes up to visit them on occasion. And she did work for a couple of months in Trenton, but she didn't like it.

She had an apartment all on her own in Trenton, and she was lonely. She would get to know a few people, but they would break dates all the time and stuff like that, and then she would be even lonelier. She said when she's up in Ontario, people always ask her where she's from. They never guess Newfoundland. But around home, where everyone has distinct Newfoundland accents, no one ever mentions it.

She said her father was a rolling stone, he was all over North America all the time she was growing up. But now he's back home, happily reunited with his family, and they have a camping van out by the old long-gone train tracks. People leave their trailers along the train line and just come up whenever they feel like it. They'll spend the entire summer there.

I'm a driving fool today. I've already reached Heart's Ease, which is at the base of the Baie de Verde Peninsula (a.k.a. Avalon West) that separates Trinity Bay from Conception Bay. The peninsula looks like a hitchhiker's thumb, and it has the feel of a distinctive island. In Heart's Ease, a Labatt's Blue truck goes by with the slogan "Manufactured Right Here." If I stopped the driver and asked for one Labatt's Blue please, I bet he'd say, "Just a minute, I'll manufacture it right here for you." But I don't feel like one just now.

In the South Dildo Ultramar, they had only granulated coffee whitener. Just reading the list of ingredients can make tumours you didn't know you had start throbbing. So I asked the chatty young woman behind the counter if she had any fresh milk. "I'm allergic to thermally extruded emulsifications," I stage-whispered, apologetically.

"What a coincidence! I am too!" she squealed. She grabbed the milk in a flash, bent over in such a way that allowed me to see, should I care to look, which I didn't, both mammary glands in full naked detail, and said, with the sexiest smile, "Say when!"

"I'm allergic to MSG too," I said.

"That hasn't bothered me since, since. . . ."

"When!" I said.

She stopped pouring and looked straight in my eye.

"Since about the time I stopped using it," she replied.

On the main street of South Dildo, there are only two houses. One had a sign saying Garage Sale, and the other had a sign saying House for Sale. The Garage Sale sign had under it in small letters the word "piano." That'd be interesting, to get a garage-sale piano. I could take a few lessons, get my chops back, invite a few friends over to hear my Thelonious Monk interpretations. They'd say, "Nice piano, where'd you get it?"

I'd say, "Exclusive Estate Sale in Newfoundland."

"Where in Newfoundland?"

"South Dildo."

"Where?"

"You heard me."

"How much was it?"

"A bargain considering it's a Stradivarius."

"A Stradivarius! It does have a warm sound to it," they'd say. "Keep playing. It certainly is an instrument of pleasure, but not like the one you normally think of in connection with that town."

While in Dildo I couldn't resist popping into the Salvation Army Thrift Shop to see if they had any valuable first editions wasting away on the three-for-a-loonie table. It's amazing how often I strike it rich this way, but not today. I was speed-reading Bertrand Russell's essay on Spinoza when a little lady who looked an awful lot like Nancy Reagan, except even shorter, and rather over-familiar with strangers, came up to me and barked out, "Is there anyone in the little girls' room?"

I turned my head and noticed that I was standing at the entrance to the washrooms.

"How should I know?" I said.

"I wasn't asking you, silly," she said. "I was asking a lady."

"You were looking right at me."

"Well, I'm sorry."

"And there's no one else around."

"I know that now. If there was anyone in the little girls' room they would have answered me."

"Oh, I get it."

"Good, but it took you long enough."

"We can't all be as smart as you, smarty-pants."

"Some are, some aren't."

Sudbury, Ontario, has a giant nickel out on the highway; Wawa, Ontario, has a giant goose; Toronto, Ontario, a giant hypodermic syringe; and Dildo, Newfoundland, has a giant whale. It's standing on its tail, with its nose pointing at the skies above. It's larger than life by a long shot and seems to be made out of a great piece of driftwood of enormous girth. It's standing there next to the Blue Whale Lounge and Mudder's Take Out.

But it's not driftwood; it's made of unpainted, dressed wood, all cunningly interwoven to follow the beautiful lines of a whale on the move, leaping out of the sea, the tip of its tail just brushing the surface. One of the flippers is falling off, hanging in an awkward manner, as if a tourist had sat his kids on it for a photograph, but it snapped, causing them to fall to the ground while he was still trying to get the film in the camera. As soon as the artist returns from the whale sculptors' convention in Reykjavik, he's going to fix it up.

Many little round stones pasted to its face represent barnacles.

It's just my imagination, but it seems real to me that the streets and shops of Dildo and South Dildo are full of beautiful women. An old beat-up Oldsmobile goes by with a bumper sticker saying Battery Operated, perhaps a sly reference to the name of the town. Dildo is a large and livable town, with lots of big old houses, well maintained, an aura laden with history, and an extremely pleasant atmosphere. A quasi-obscene thought will tend to pop up in the mind of a short-term visitor, but the residents never think about it.

Dildo Harbour is full of brightly painted boats bobbing up and down and in and out in the waves, and some not-so-pretty ones inverted and rotting on the beach. A lady is taking quick puffs on a cigarette outside the Dildo Quick-Mart, where the latest red-hot videos are *Vertical Limit* (about mountain climbing) and *Traffic* (about another way of getting high).

Local author Joe Lafitte makes the inarguable but interesting claim on his Web site that Dildo is not a town of perverts. Its name either derives from a town in Portugal or is an allusion to the shape of the headland that forms Dildo Harbour. Or maybe both!

But I prefer to think that it was named after a crusty old sea captain named Dildo Joe.

And supposing, for the sake of argument, that Dildo was a town of perverts? What would that make the town of Heart's Content?

My Webster's Ninth says the earliest known use of the word "dildo" (defined as "artificial penis") was in 1598. That's interesting, because I'll soon be told, at the Dildo Museum, that there is a historical document claiming that, just fifteen years later, Henry Crout and four other sailor/whalers landed on Dildo Island, a sliver of land of much historical interest visible on the horizon from Dildo Beach, and moved into one of the "deserted" Beothuk stone houses there.

I doubt if Crout and the boys would have known of Shakespeare and Jonson, both of whom employed the word. My hunch is that, in Elizabethan times, the word "dildo" had the dual meaning of both an artificial penis and a real one. Elizabethans didn't make the fine distinctions between real and artificial that we tend to, but I bet the word would have been part of Crout's vocabulary. In fact, one could easily imagine him and the boys sitting in their ripped-off Beothuk house exchanging dildo jokes.

There was even a reference to a "Doctor Dilldoes Dauncinge Schoole" in a bawdy Elizabethan ballad.

Yes, said the lady at the Dildo Museum. The ancient Beothuk houses on Dildo Island are being excavated right now. They had stone houses with fireplaces.

She'd been told that the Beothuks didn't have boats and didn't have dogs to pull their sleds. But they used seal oil to heat and light their little stone houses.

I told her I had seen pictures of a very handsome and unusual canoe, said to have been of traditional Beothuk style and manufacture. As I was soon to find out, the boat is actually on display in the

Newfoundland Museum in St. John's. It's very graceful, ornate, and of an unusual but characteristic shape, with the gunwales curved to a high point midway along the length of the canoe, as if they were designed to resemble waves. If there were functional aspects to this unusual and intricate design, no one has been able to figure out what they were. There are pictures of these canoes in Howley's book. People will often make the claim that the Beothuk were drooling knuckledraggers, and therefore their demise is not worth wasting tears over, but such people are either lying or grossly uninformed.

The famous German airplane, the twelve-engined *Dornier Do.X*, which resembled a flying *Titanic* and could accommodate a hundred passengers in great luxury, made a surprise landing for fuel off Dildo Arm in 1932. It was the largest heavier-than-air flying machine in the world, and you can imagine the astonishment of the locals. They had no warning whatsoever this was coming.

The plane had been built in 1929, but the stock-market crash had rendered it an unprofitable and superfluous oddity. It was decommissioned shortly after its brief visit to Dildo.

Silently, out of fuel, the magnificent plane descended out of the sky and splashed down a hundred feet offshore. It took off as soon as its tanks were topped up, and immediately everybody in town started carving a replica of the plane, to see who remembered it best. Many of these replicas are excellent, and they are on display in the local museum. But the *Do.X* is not on display, unfortunately. It was on display for years in the German Aviation Museum near Berlin, but the museum was firebombed in 1945.

As if that weren't enough excitement for one town, Dildo was electrified a few years later when a giant squid was found dead on a chunk of ice that came in off Dildo Arm into nearby Patterson's Cove.

Gladys Jackson is my intelligent and informative guide around the museum. Gladys is a cute, energetic, youthful-looking little grandmother, about five feet tall and wearing a Mighty Ducks ball cap, a sweatshirt, a pair of blue jeans, and white running shoes, with beautiful blond hair to her shoulders. She's not an archaeologist, she's an archaeological interpreter, she says. Her job today, though, was to paint the windows and get the museum ready for the new season. But she generously took time out to show me around.

Gladys gave me a shot of inspiration when she said the defining moment in her life came at age ten, when her Sunday-school teacher told her: "We call this moment the present, because it's like a birthday present from the past to the future." She said she thinks of herself and her archaeological colleagues as gift-wrappers, preserving the past and making sure it's available for interested souls in centuries to come. At times, in a way, I like to feel that I'm doing the same, in books such as this.

Perhaps because of its name, Heart's Content seems on its way to becoming the Gretna Green of North America. They have couples from as far away as Virginia Beach, Virginia, coming up here to get hitched the old-fashioned way, so I'm told – in the cable station. Marriage is a bit like hooking up a transatlantic cable, I guess.

The people lucky enough to live in the town of Heart's Content should be content, if they're not, because it's such a pretty town, with such a pretty river running into the bay like that, with such a pretty name, and with such a pretty piece of history. Heart's Content Cable Station is an official provincial historical site, a charming red-brick building, from around 1875, eighteen years after the first transatlantic cable was laid, running from Heart's Content to Valentia Island, Ireland. When you are on Valentia Island, says the *Rough Guide to Ireland*, "there's nothing but ocean between you and Newfoundland, 1,900 miles away."

So the building is now a museum, and apparently it's devoted to the laying of the cable, but the museum is closed. Satellite communications have got underwater cable on the ropes, and there's not a foot of train track left in all of Newfoundland, once world-famous for its thundering low-speed narrow-gauge "Newfie Bullet." The Trans-Canada Highway, though a wonderful engineering feat, doesn't have the same aura of romance.

In one window of the museum it says Open, the other says Closed. But the front door is locked, and just as I get into the car to leave, up comes a plump young red-faced fellow who would rather hitch than hike.

He hops in and tells me he's been lucky today, he got a ride to Heart's Content all the way from St. John's, and now it looks as if he'll be home in an hour. He seemed happy to be getting home. He still lives with his parents.

"Nothing doing in St. John's?" I said.

"Nope, nothin'. No better than nothin', for sure."

Then something he said, I misheard, because I thought he was saying that he was doing a lot of "boozin'" down in St. John's.

"Booze can really get ahold of you," I offered, just to keep the chit-chat afloat.

"Not boozin'," he said. "Music." He goes down to St. John's and visits the pubs that have interesting traditional Newfoundland and Irish music until his money runs out, then he hitchhikes home. But it appears it's a way of life he's getting tired of.

"I don't drink the beer like I used to. I used to drink a few bottles now and then just to be a good . . . companion, y'know? But I don't drink no more. I just like to have fun. Heaven knows, you don't need to be always drinking to have any fun at all. You drink a beer and right away you want to start smoking. And I haven't smoked in a year now. It's the smoking that gives you the hangover more than the beer."

"Yes, it's a big problem all over the world."

"I give it up though. I give up the beer and I give up the smoking."

At first, when I asked what he did, I thought he said he fished for crabs, but it later appeared that he hadn't been out on the high seas more than once or twice. It's not that he finds it overly dangerous or anything like that, it's just that "I gets seasick all the time. I always vow I'll never go back out. But when I get back to land, I feel better right away."

"If you persevere maybe you'll get your sea legs."

"Maybe."

"But maybe you'd be better off not persevering."

He seemed torn between persevering and not persevering. He seemed to think he could talk himself into not getting sick. And it would always work for a while. And then . . . living death. Only those prone to seasickness will understand.

What did he do in the winter? Hunt?

"No, I don't like hunting. I did it once but didn't like it."

"What didn't you like about it?"

"Don't like guns, don't like blood."

"You seem like a tender-hearted guy."

"You could say that."

He said he knew lots of guys, if they see something on the road they'll go out of their way to run it over – so long as it's not so big it would cause damage to the vehicle. "Even a bear, if it's not too big-looking."

"Welcome to Planet Earth. Not a nice place at times."

"Sometimes they'll go right over to the other side of the road to kill it. They just laughs at the likes of me."

His name is Jason Butt, and with an ironic smile he admitted he doesn't mind eating things other people have caught or shot. He lives with Mom and Dad, has a girlfriend, doesn't read books, doesn't watch television.

"I likes the radio," he confesses. You could tell in his voice he was dying to get home and listen. His brother bought the radio originally – a "really good setup" costing sixty-five bucks. Now Jason loves to listen to short-wave every chance he gets.

And he's fascinated with stringed instruments. He has a guitar, a bass guitar, a mandolin, a banjo, and of course his radio.

He's a pleasant-looking young fellow, twenty-two but looks a bit older. He has modest sideburns and a thin moustache. I dropped him off in front of his home at Hant's Harbour. I didn't ask if he knew about the massacre of four hundred Beothuk alleged to have occurred on the beach there, in the mid-eighteenth century. According to Bernard Assiniwi, in his *Beothuk Saga*, fur trappers with rifles cornered several families of Beothuks, males and females, ranging from infancy to old age, all of whom had travelled to Hant's Harbour to dig for clams and mussels. The trappers fired till all the Beothuks were dead. Similar slaughters are known to have occurred in early Tasmanian history, before the ghastly systematic elimination of the aboriginals was implemented.

On the shores of Daniel's Cove there are colonies of tiny, tender white wildflowers, each with five long graceful petals, remarkably like the morning star. The closest thing to it in my guidebook would be the mountain sandwort (*Arenaria groenlandica*). They're ephemeral but they eternally return.

Very long, low, sweeping waves are crashing along the cove, and the sound of them hitting the beach is much greater because of their length, and also because the beach is steep and shingled. There's even a ruined old wooden breakwater of some sort. The waves are like swells, at first almost indiscernible, and as they come in they transform themselves into gentle, graceful waves . . . until the waves are about three feet high, then they spill over, like joy, and crash into the shingle shore. A wave a half mile long can hit the shore all at the same moment, causing the five long petals of all the mountain sandworts above the beach to tremble with sympathetic pleasure.

What a lovely world to live in. It's a five-star planet, covered in spring with tiny flowers that are the microcosmic twins of our planetary neighbour, Venus, the goddess of love, as it hovers low in the eastern sky before dawn, watching over these little flowers, while immensely long low waves mate symphonically with the sand.

In a search for batteries for my Walkman, I went into a convenience store farther north. "You've got every kind except the kind I want," I said. The woman behind the counter looked sympathetic, but the customer, who on her way in earlier had given me a rather suspicious and haughty look when I was sitting in my car taking down a note or two, started laughing.

"Are you sure?" said the kind woman. "I thought we had all of them there." She seemed a bit annoyed at the other woman for laughing in such a supercilious manner.

"I better look at my Walkman again." Sure enough, it took AA size rather than single A, as I had thought. I often get confused when it comes to battery sizes, but I never forget my shoe size.

"My mistake!" I admitted.

The mocking lady shot one more laugh my way and left. The sympathetic lady wanted to know who I was and what I was doing in this neck of the woods. She was so nice, we chatted for an hour. She seemed to have no ambition to be anywhere but where she was, but she wanted to know my life story right away. She'd never been to Toronto, but had a lot of friends there and didn't think she'd like it.

She had seductively hooded eyes like Susan Sarandon, and her face was full of accumulated wisdom and amusement. She was also fast and funny. She had a thick, juicy, well-barbecued Newfoundland accent when she was talking to the locals, but she could turn it off and speak with a tourist accent, as she did with me. I understood every word – almost before she said it.

"Is that your motorcycle out there?" I asked.

"It's my son's."

I didn't ask how old he was, or even how old the motorcycle was. "There seems to be a lot of young mothers in Newfoundland," I offered. "Newphilanderers – er, I mean you Newfoundland girls seem to get started early on in life."

"I only want the one," she said. "That's enough for me."

As we spoke, a man came in, then another, until there was a group of about eight, just standing there – not buying anything, but just staring at her like a congregation of wretched suitors out of a Thomas Hardy novel, giggling among themselves, elbowing each other in the ribs, and hoping against hope to be selected to deliver a message or whatever. I asked if this was the intellectual centre for the Bay de Verde Peninsula. She looked at me, shook her head, and mouthed the word "Nooooo!" I had the strangest feeling they kept the store under surveillance and had noticed that I'd been in beyond my allotted time.

She grabbed her map and started pretending to be giving directions. "Yer goes up here to Perlican Bay," and stuff like that. It was embarrassing, and I felt badly for her. It was time to leave. I doffed my cap and said, "It was a great pleasure to meet you, madame," and she held out her hand and said, "It was a great pleasure to meet you too, sir."

VANISHING IDENTITY CRISIS

Daniel's Cove • New Perlican

Thursday, June 14. One of the giant foreign fishing trawlers is sitting on the horizon on Trinity Bay, with twelve fishing boats closer to shore. On a grassy hill, a cow stands staring out at the boats, and a dog is lying between the cow's front legs and looking sad, with his paws crossed in front of him and his chin resting on his crossed paws. The cow appears to be condemning the boats for overfishing, while the dog seems to be looking down at a cemetery in the hollow below the hill, gazing at his master's grave. Even though his master has been dead for a year, the dog still hears his voice from the other world.

In Daniel's Cove a young fellow is wearing a Toronto Maple Leafs sweater – a white one – but he looks blue. It's not the sort of sweater you wear every day; you save it for special occasions such as the Stanley Cup playoffs (should Toronto be playing), or Christmas time. I think he put it on this morning to cheer himself up. The fact that it's not working is making him feel even worse. After all, it was only a few weeks since the Colorado Avalanche won the Stanley Cup. And Toronto never was a serious contender. He was a pudgy fellow in his late teens, with a blond brush cut, and he was wearing black leather gloves, for no apparent reason.

You see a lot of Toronto Maple Leafs bumper stickers here – and all around Newfoundland. The Leafs are Newfoundland's parent team, and they are scheduled to fly up to play an exhibition game on September 16 with the St. John's Maple Leafs, and to baptize the beautiful new hockey arena, known as Mile One Stadium.

The surrounding region is one of homemade rather than store-bought Lawn Art. One fellow has created a set of brightly painted mushrooms and fairies, in primary colours. It's set on the side of the main road, apparently as a contribution to civic beauty. And he's propped up a large sign over it saying, "Compliments of VIC." At first I thought this stood for some social organization, such as Virgins in Christ, or some kind of psychological problem, such as Vanishing Identity Crisis.

But apparently it was just some guy named Vic who liked to write his name in full caps. Vic wanted everybody to see these fairies and mushrooms as his work. But there did turn out to be a commercial enterprise – Vic's Gift Shop or something like that – in the next community. And maybe the work he had on display is merely part of a consignment of Lawn Art he's accepted for his store, and not a product of his own genius at all. If that's true, and the real craftsman finds out that Vic is passing the work off as his own, there could be trouble. But let's hope not.

After yesterday's big burst of driving mania, today, predictably, I'm just sitting on the end of the dock on Trinity Bay, somewhere around New Perlican. For the reader's information, I don't always drive around like mad, I'm not used to it, and I'm getting weary of it. In my ordinary life, I haven't owned a car in twenty years, and this is the first big bout of driving I've done since Scotland five years ago. In other words the automobile, as far as I'm concerned, is merely an artistic device, rather than an everyday necessity.

It's the hottest day of the year so far, yet there are swarms of people wearing parkas. Being overly warm and profusely perspiring doesn't seem to torment the rugged Newfoundland spirit. Some even have their hoods up.

EXCAVATING CUPIDS

Cupids • Brigus

Friday, June 15. In 1910, the three-hundredth anniversary of the settlement of Cupids was being celebrated. It was the first English settlement in Newfoundland. A flagpole was specially erected to fly the largest Union Jack in the British Empire. The flag measured twenty-six by thirty-six feet, but has since been retired. An even larger one is now on hand for "special occasions" – of which I expect there would be many. But today is not one.

Traces of the original Cupids were discovered in 1995, and excavations are ongoing. Hints of the exact location of the earliest settlement were derived from entries in colonial entrepreneur John Guy's diary jottings of 1611. He seemed to have had an instinct for writing for people far into the future, because he stated that the settlement was twelve score paces from Cupids Pond, and that "every morning I went to the brook which runneth by our house to wash." He gives many other broad hints to the precise location, including the innocent comment that Garland Baker tried to grow potatoes on his land, but found it too rocky. Could John Guy have sensed that, three centuries hence, his happy little diary would be put to such a use? Maybe, for he was known to be a pretty swift fellow.

In the Cupids Museum, there is a painting showing John Guy meeting with a group of Beothuks the following year, 1612. They're standing on the beach. John Guy is holding a knife in a manner that seems somewhat threatening. The museum's note states that he is offering it for trade, but it's not clear what the Beothuks may be offering in exchange. In the background, three generic English ships and twenty idiosyncratic Beothuk canoes bob in the waves. It seems like a fairly ordinary scene for the time, but it must have represented something important, because the painting is dated 1627 – fifteen years after the event.

And indeed it was important, because the scene represents the first meeting between Newfoundland natives and newcomers at Cupids. The notes declare that Guy was eager to establish friendly relations with the Beothuk, and who could possibly doubt that? The first meeting, as pictured, was a happy occasion, and subsequent meetings would also be mutually satisfying. But the meetings didn't lead to continuing friendship. Things went wrong, and they kept going wrong. The Beothuk found themselves being treated in a way reminiscent of the tales Newfoundlanders relate about their experiences in Toronto. Things never go well for long in our uncharitable world. Two centuries after this painting, the Beothuks were toast.

Earlier, Guy and thirty-nine settlers founded a colony known as Cooper's Cove, in Virginia. Cupids was the second colony he founded, and it was here that the first European child was born in Newfoundland, the first livestock was raised, the first grain sown, and the first effort made to establish the European version of the rule of law.

The Cupids town hall bears a plaque saying that, in a house on this site, was born the first "Anglo-Saxon" baby in Newfoundland. In the museum, that same baby is referred to as the first "European." I bet there were some interesting arguments about which term to use.

Given that there is no evidence of there being a human birth at the short-lived L'Anse aux Meadows colony a thousand years ago, I'd prefer to use the term "European." But the whole thing is rather meaningless when one considers that there must have been a vast number of earlier unrecorded births of babies who were at least half European.

Nobody could deny that Brigus is a beautiful old burg, with tons of old houses going back to the earliest days of British imperialism, blending nicely with the newer ones, which are often built with taste and a fine feel for the surroundings. With its gridless hills, winding roads, and no two buildings facing in the same direction, Brigus has an extraordinarily charming New World/Old World feel to it. This is the way it could have been all over North America, but lesser minds ultimately prevailed.

My stay in Brigus was brief, but I loved the many miles of wonderful winding stone fences, some built without mortar but in no danger of collapsing. Maybe the walls aren't as grand and permanent as the ancient Pictish walls of Scotland, the Etruscan walls of Italy, or those in parts of Mexico or Peru, but they're more beautiful and more skilfully built than anything you'll find anywhere else in North America. And I'd hate to be here in the high season of tourism, with thousands of little McFaddens coming through, quacking like ducks, barking like dogs, and generally making asses of themselves.

An old philosopher was sitting on a rock overlooking Brigus Harbour. He had a blank look on his face, as if in contemplation of great profundities. I caught his eye and said to him, "Is this your day off?" It was intended as a joke, because he looked far past the normal age of retirement.

"Ngk," he said, without expression.

Apparently this old-timer has been the Brigus mascot since before the Jazz Age. He couldn't talk, but he seemed to have plenty of intuitive understanding. In spite of his advanced years, he hadn't picked up certain elemental aspects of knowledge, such as left from right. But he could smoke cigarettes, and he certainly looked as intelligent as your average head of state. Nobody would guess there was anything unusual about him until he began to "speak."

"Where's this tunnel I've been hearing about?" I ventured.

"Ngk!" he said.

He stood up and motioned me to come with him. He led me to the tunnel, with a look on his face that could only be described as empty, but a little on the serious side. He definitely was no joker.

"Is it natural?" I said, meaning the tunnel.

"Ngk," he said.

"Man-made?"

"Ngk."

We walked through to the end.

"It opens into the sea. But it doesn't look as if it was caused by wave action."

"Ngk."

It was a curiously blasted-out tunnel, and the walls were covered with the names of ordinary people, lovers long dead, lovers bereft of aught but memories.

I hadn't visited Bernice Hopcraft's convent yet, so I asked him where it was. "Ngk," he said, and pointed to the car, indicating he'd direct me if I let him ride with me.

I proceeded to get all my stuff out of the passenger seat and into the back seat to make room for him – electronic gadgetry, tapes, field glasses, maps, books, notebooks, pencils, a battery-operated pencil sharpener – the kind of stuff not easily organized in a small car.

But all the time I was trying to move things to the back seat, he was overenthusiastically squeezing his gargantuan egoless bulk into the passenger seat. He really wanted a ride in the car, and he didn't want to wait. Somehow, the wildflower book had fallen to the floor, and before I could pick it up, he had managed to cram himself in and stretched his legs as far as they could go, jamming the book up against the firewall. The book sprang open, a couple of pages tore, and photos of family and flowers became even further smudged than they had been. Perhaps he had no reason to think books were of any value.

But he was good at pointing directions to the convent. I was beginning to admire the old boy. He reminded me of old Satchmo; when some interviewer asked him how he got along when he travelled to foreign countries to give concerts, given that he couldn't speak any foreign languages, "I is the pointingest cat you ever did see," he said.

I have some sad news for Bernice Hopcraft. She forgot to seize the day. The Mercy Convent in Brigus that she has had her eye on has been sold and is being gutted. According to one person, it's going to be turned into a B&B. But they don't actually say B&B in Newfoundland generally – except with a pinch of sarcasm. The Newfoundlanders see the term as a vulgar Americanism (even if it does originate in Britain). "Guest home" is much nicer, and less presumptuous. To most Newfoundlanders B&B is a sophisticated liqueur.

The owner was inside directing the workmen, who were busy tearing out all signs of devotion. The idea of having a chat with him didn't appeal to me any more than watching a splendid ancient convent being perverted into some sluttish commercial enterprise. A workman on break said it would become a tourist home, someone else said a restaurant, another said an Irish pub. They all had it on good authority. But the cross will be staying on top, it seems. The place was built as a convent in 1860, and nuns of the Irish order of Sisters of Mercy lived here for many years.

One workman told me he had instructions to tear out anything that looked religious. He and his friends laughed a bit too loudly when I jokingly told them that, after a stunt like this, they'd for sure go to hell when they died.

When we first got there, we beheld one woman and a whole bunch of men sitting around having a great old time doing nothing. We chatted about the convent, the sale, the purchase, the history, the future.

The workmen informed me that the Brigus tunnel had been built around 1860 – six years before Alfred Nobel invented dynamite – by a Cornish miner named John Hoskins, who wished to provide easier access to a wharf. It's not all that hard to blast a tunnel through solid rock. If you ever wish to do it yourself, it's best to start off by using the traditional method of hammering spikes into the rock, then yanking them out (that's the hard part), then filling the holes with gun-powder and a long fuse, which of course you must not forget to light.

Should you survive the blast, you do it all over again, until you break through into the light. If Hoskins had waited only six years, the tunnel could have been blasted in one-fifth the time, given that dynamite is said to be five times as powerful as gunpowder. Dynamite is that much safer as well, or so I'm told. I think I'd stick with gun-powder if it ever comes to that.

The tunnel does resemble a birth canal connecting the wet womb of Conception Bay with the dry rolling hills of the outside world. It's a hundred feet long, and even the tallest basketball players could walk through it without bending. Hoskins, with the shrewd frugal-ity of the age, apparently used only two spikes, although of course the number of blasts would have been much more than that. The spikes, twisted and bent, are on display in the museum, but I'd over-looked them when I was there.

I bet that Cornishman was the man of the hour after he finished that tunnel. Everybody in town would have wanted to buy him a drink or maybe even two. God knows he deserved it.

And now it was time to leave. My old friend was smoking a ciga-rette. I asked if he wanted to go back. He indicated wordlessly but eloquently that he'd be happy to stay here for now. After all, the people here had cigarettes – and I didn't seem to have anything to give him.

A bit farther south, two painted plaster Afro-Newfoundlanders with beautiful big bright red lips to die for were sitting fishing on the lawn. I asked if they'd caught anything, but there was no answer. The Lawn Art in parts of Newfoundland is out of control. Many houses have their lawns so loaded with Lawn Art it appears to be for sale – except there are no price tags. But then again, what isn't for sale in this soulless world. Some lawns appear to be aspiring to the state of Lawn Art museumhood.

But with all that Lawn Art on their lawn it ruins the effect of each individual piece. One Picasso is all you really need on any given wall. One plaster donkey pulling a cart of flowers is sufficient for even a large front lawn. Too much Lawn Art makes lawncutting more of an ordeal. It'd take about an hour to cut the lawn and the entire rest of the day would be spent removing the Lawn Art then putting it back. And some of that Lawn Art looks heavy. But, of course, as we have seen, time is seldom in short supply in Newfoundland. If time is money, Newfoundlanders are rich beyond belief.

For Lawn Art, it's hard to imagine anything more glorious than the giant silver cod-jigger, the painted plaster and plywood iceberg, or the vanilla-cherry cakes on the Port au Port Peninsula, but on lawns in this area there are some interesting wooden models of beautiful old houses from the past, with special emphasis on ones that are no longer with us, examples in miniature of the special Brigus architecture from the earliest days.

Also spotted were several pieces depicting horse-and-buggy scenes from the nineteenth century.

The Conception Bay highway forms a horseshoe around the vast hoofprint of Conception Bay, and I can see myself in St. John's tomorrow, by golly. Maybe even later today. Next door to the Chicken Delight, in the town of Conception Bay, is a big old lawn with trees, and men with no shirts on seem to be spending the day doing repairs, wheeling around lawn mowers and wheelbarrows, and smoking cigarettes. But I needed a coffee, and so went into a convenience store looking for one. There was a lineup of twelve people paying their phone bills and buying lottery tickets. It would take me till closing time to get a coffee to go.

But then a man about forty, with a devilish little John Waters moustache, came in, just as I was leaving, and the girl on cash yelled out to him at top volume, "Yer ma phoned and asked yer ta bring back ten pounds of potatoes."

The man nodded an unsmiling and irritated acknowledgement. Nobody in the lineup was actually laughing out loud or turning to see how he was reacting to the news. But all twelve of them were busy hiding the little smile of amusement on their face. The fellow wasn't happy about it. I almost expected him to start whining, as in "Aw, do I have to?"

This story shows the two sides of Newfoundland. He may have been a hopeless middle-aged man tied to his mother's apron strings, but he represented the new Newfoundland, where one aspires to become an individual, on a path of one's own. The cashier represented the old Newfoundland of the fishing communities, where nothing is embarrassing, and where individual identity is almost seamlessly fused with the larger identity of one's extended family.

To try to spare him embarrassment would have never occurred to that cashier. To have prepared the spuds for him in advance, and to tell him quietly that his mama had phoned – this would have been outside her frames of reference. She would have seen no need for it.

But whether of the old or the new Newfoundland, and whether they be local or from away, all twelve people in that lineup now knew that (1) he still lived with his mother, (2) he didn't have the brains to know when they were getting low on potatoes, and (3) that pencil moustache didn't suit him.

CITY OF FOGHORNS
AND SNAILS

St. John's

Saturday, June 16. The capital city of Newfoundland has an attractive, intriguing new official nickname: the "City of Legends." Let's give it top marks in every category except originality. Imagination seems in such limited supply this year.

Here are some of the cities of the world sporting the same soubriquet as St. John's: Timbuktu, Nottingham, Samarkand, Rome, St. Malo, Rijeka, Istanbul, Krakow, San Francisco, Los Angeles, Santiago, Gordion, Copenhagen, Guilin, Memphis (U.S.), Eleousa, Langkawi, Santa María del Puerto del Príncipe, Bikaner, Ioannina, Nuremberg, Tangiers, Vienna, Albuquerque, Prague, Hanoi, Thessalonika, Vladivostok, Gauhati, Washington, Manchester, Tarifa, and Edinburgh.

There are high-school poetry projects called "City of Legends," and poetry publishing companies of that name.

City of Legends is a golf-course management company run by Arizona Diamondbacks pitcher Todd Stottlemyre.

Who knows what'll be next? City of Legends Root Beer? City of Legends Cockroach Spray?

Bartlesville, Oklahoma, calls itself the "City of Legends," because it's a "unique blend of Native American and Western heritage, sky-scrapers, technology, and international influence."

Would it be possible to find, for the proud, long-suffering colonial city of St. John's, a slogan that is every bit as seductive as the "City of Legends" – but original, as unique as the city it refers to? How about a contest? A prize of a thousand dollars would get smart minds thinking.

What's the matter with stealing other people's nicknames for your own town? It causes bad feelings. It wouldn't be nice to have Bartlesville, Oklahoma, mad at you.

According to the weather channel, St. John's just happens to be the least likely place in the world to be hit by a tornado. Just to get things started, see what you think about this:

> St. John's, Newfoundland
> That Totally Twisterless Town

I booked into the big old Captain's Quarters, at 19 Merry Meeting Road, and returned the car to the rental agency in the big suburb of Mount Pearl. The fellow who drove me back to town said he had worked on the railroad all his life, but took an early retirement in 1988 after the railroad closed down. Now he spends his time hanging out at the car-rental place, reading novels, and jockeying cars and people around as required.

He was a telegraph operator for quite a stretch and still hasn't forgotten a dot or a dash of it. He also had to memorize the different codes for different towns. Three dashes for one town, four for another, and so on. Dash dot dash for Carbonear, etc. It wouldn't do for two towns to have the same code – or the same slogan.

This fellow told me a few brief stories that pushed me into a more vivid sense of what the island was like in the years before the highway was laid down and the railroad ripped up. It was different. For instance it was quite the adventure motoring across the entire island before the Trans-Canada Highway was built. It could take a lot more than a few days. Now and then there'd be a short stretch of paved road. Now and then there'd be a bridge. But mostly the roads were mud, with vast distances between filling stations. The ferries would be stubby little barges, barely able to handle taking two cars at a time across a raging river. Fishermen kept strong horses just to pull cars out of the mud.

"I was born in 1947, and that was pre-Confederation," he said. "By one year anyway. So I can't honestly say I have strong memories of what it was like before we became part of Canada."

But in a way he had experienced pre-Confederation days: the days before the Trans-Canada Highway, the days when the world-famous Newfoundland Bullet was still going strong. He confessed he often wishes the train was still running, and the highway hadn't been built.

"It's a good highway, but maybe a bit too good," I offered.

"I know what you mean."

"No challenge."

"That's right," he said. "You can drive all the way from St. John's to Corner Brook now the way you used to go around the block. You don't pat yourself on the back for having made it in one piece."

"The only challenge is to drive slowly enough to avoid hitting large mammals."

"Yes, and before the Trans-Canada Highway was built, the roads were so bad you couldn't get up enough speed to put a moose's nose out of joint."

"Ah, them were the days." It was as if I'd been there too, and was grieving the loss of the railroad right along with him.

He'd become a big reader in his retirement years. He was reading all of Dickens chronologically. He was all the way up to *Bleak House*, but he was fading fast. His favourite Dickens is still the first one,

Pickwick Papers. So he was thinking he might put Dickens aside for a while and try another author. Any suggestions?

I mentioned several Newfoundland novelists, but he seemed to have read them all. So, given that my friend was born in 1947, I suggested *Midnight's Children* by Salman Rushdie. It's a big, fat novel that follows the semi-fictional lives of all the Indians who were born on January 1 of that year, the day of India's official independence from Britain, and it's a hard one to put down.

I must have said the right thing, because his eyes lit up. He thought that was a terrific idea and had me write down the title and author for him.

He gave me an interesting tour of St. John's. It was more relaxed than the cabby's tour I got upon arriving weeks ago, but I neglected to write about that for reasons of time and space. He took me along leafy, mansion-lined streets stinking of money from the good old days and gave me thumbnail histories of the families who built the homes and of their descendants who still maintain them. He pointed to the house Brian Tobin grew up in. Pretty handsome digs for a young fellow. Then he dropped me off at the Newfoundland Museum on Duckworth.

A Newfoundland black bear is standing on its hind legs, with one front paw on the branch of a tree, and the other front paw just dangling. An owl sits on the branch, but the bear's chances of grabbing it are slim. The bear's expression says, "I know you're cute, Mr. Owl, and I don't want to kill you, but a fellow's got to eat." The owl's expression says, "Oh, not this idiot bear again. Doesn't he know when to quit?"

This is at the entrance to the Newfoundland Museum. Both the bear, the tree, and the owl are long dead, but only the bear and the owl appear to be stuffed.

I ask a smart-looking museum employee about the "City of Legends" soubriquet. Where does that come from? She says, "Oh, it's just something they dreamed up." She knew that, if she gave me a better answer, it would just lead to more difficult questions. You know what guys are like.

The museum has a large display on Beaumont–Hamel, and it's sad beyond words – machine guns, magazines, bayonets, and so on, retrieved from the site, and photos of the soldiers, both dead and alive. Words can't express the horror and disgust. Eight thousand poorly educated men, who just wanted to see Europe for free, were ordered to march into overwhelmingly superior firepower because they came from a poor island with no real government.

The extra-large, extra-merry bartender at the Captain's Quarters is telling me that I should go to the Longshoreman's Protective Union Hall on Victoria Street tonight. There's going to be a Festival of Nude Aunts. She laughs.

"Nude aunts?"

She said, "Oh yeah, it's going to be great, believe me." She said there'd be a series of short but highly political – some might even say radical – films by Newfoundlanders, and a dance performance called "They Cut Down Trees So You Can Wipe Your Ass and Blow Your Nose with the Softest Tissue Ever."

"You mean the dancers will be aunts with no clothes on?"

"Er, no! Aunts? With no clothes on? Whatever gave you that idea?"

I'd misunderstood. Turns out she was talking about the Festival of New Dance.

A woman with her eyes focused on me came up to the bar. She had a big hairy wart on the side of her upper lip, but it did nothing to take away from her attractiveness. She wasn't dressed fashionably, but she was an attractive woman, with a ton of character, and I bought her a drink. She said let's go sit down. So we did. We talked. She's on welfare. All her friends are on welfare. They don't work.

They live in cheap apartments. They get enough pogey to pay the rent. And I think they hustle a little bit. I'm not exactly sure which way they hustle, but they need to hustle I suppose, like everyone else, to get enough money to live.

Then another woman came in, about the same age, equally attractive, short hair, a mischievous and intelligent smile, and a fastidious, almost intellectual, look about her.

"Oh no," said my friend. "I hope she doesn't come over here. She's really crazy. She's really fried her brains with the cocaine."

So woman number two came over and sat down, with no further protest from woman number one. I bought her a drink too. The only problem was, we didn't have anything to say to each other. All three of us were suddenly devoid of any curiosity about each other. We just sat there looking bored. It was time to go.

The next night there was a party at Word Play – upstairs in the spacious gallery over the bookstore – for someone retiring from the Newfoundland Art Gallery, but I didn't get around to giving the retiree my best wishes or even learning his name. I was too busy admiring the paintings and chatting with the painters.

Gabrielle Kemp, an enthusiastic hi-vibe curator at the gallery, wanted me to know she was descended from an old and distinguished shipbuilding family.

I knew there was something special about you, I said.

She and her roommate had just bought a house, and she wanted to tell everybody all about it, except that everybody already knew. So she told me.

Was she enthused?

She said she was percolating with pleasure over this palatial purchase. Or words to that effect.

She said she was "a real night owl" (unlike the fake one in the museum) and she was going to be up all night painting a room. She showed me the colour. It was called Tiger Lily. I told her that and Hollyhocks were my two favourite flowers from childhood.

She told me I must have had a good eye in my childhood.

I looked at her admiringly and said I still do.

She blushed. Not a big blush. Just a small one.

On the way home from the bash, I'm in a terribly quirky mood. There's a lady leaning against the wall, smoking a cigarette. She looks as if she's soliciting, but I, the innocent one, assume the best and think she's not. I think she's just standing outside smoking a cigarette. Having a breather, shall we say.

But I couldn't resist saying as I went by, "Sorry, not tonight." She smiled pleasantly.

A block farther on appeared an anguished-looking lady, who gave me the impression she was a tourist who had lost her party. She was all by herself, had a terribly out-of-place look about her, and was biting her lip impatiently as she waited for the light to turn red, even though there were no cars on the road. She was having some terrible problem that was beyond me, but boy, was she stressed out, as if her husband and children were waiting for her but she had forgotten the name of the hotel or even what part of town it was in.

As I passed, I pleasantly wished her a good evening.

She rolled her eyes and turned away.

Beautiful buildings abound in this well-weathered town, all frame and wood and gingerbread and sometimes with the lower floor turned into retail stores and the upper floor into offices. Everything looks firmly rooted, as if even the fiercest winter storm would leave the town fundamentally unchanged, although some of the cars in the parking lot may become rearranged.

Along Duckworth, there's the India Gate Restaurant, with its ersatz Indian love-palace façade. A few doors along, there's the tiny Adopt-a-Spot park, with a fat guy stretched out and snoring on the single park bench. Then there's W.D. Ryan Plumbing Supplies (with "Glass" and "Screens" crossed out). Then we have International Flavours (ORS) Home-Style Curry Grocery (it's closed). Then we have Accent on Duckworth: Fine Gift Ware and Home Accents (it's open). Then there's Arthur Arthur ("Whole-Grain * Bakery * Desserts"), where one can get a gourmet sandwich while being briefly amused by the allusion to opening night. Rendell's Wholesale Beer and Wine Supplies is closing up for the night, and by the look on the owner's face business has not been bubbly.

At the Captain's Quarters, people come up to you at the bar and tell you jokes. You think they're on the wagon, because they don't have a drink and they're not ordering anything. The bartender is keeping her distance. And then it dawns on you: the joker at your elbow is angling for his sixth free drink of the day. This would appear to be a town where it's not unusual to see the same few fellows coming in every day at opening time with no money for a drink. It's great that the bartenders sympathize.

So this fellow is telling me joke after joke, but he's beginning to weaken – he's phasing out, afraid I'll never get the hint. So finally I wake up and buy him a Black Horse, and he takes the beer and – mission accomplished – goes and sits with his friends, who say to him, "What the hell took you so long?" And everybody laughs.

Then a guy comes up with a peg leg and starts tap dancing. He'll just keep on tap dancing till your head hurts so much you buy him a drink. Then he too joins his friends – one of whom says, "Where's mine?"

Another guy keeps asking you to give him hard words to spell. This guy could spell like a wizard, and in case of dispute there was a

Funk and Wagnall's on a shelf among the bottles of Screech and
Canadian Club.

It's the oldest tourist trick in the world: act like a bit of local
colour, so that the tourist gets interested, then start becoming
shriller and more insistent and irritating until he buys you a drink.
But it can be more a sign of tolerance than a sign of poverty. There
are no panhandlers in a fascist state.

So they get their drink and they're so happy they don't need to
tell any more jokes. Until the drink's all gone.

There's an old greybeard, dressed in an old black suit, with cardigan
and grey shirt, sitting in the bar of my hotel, with a suitcase and a big
bag sitting next to him. But he's a lonely one, for sure. He's been
sitting there all day, since opening time, on a hardbacked, armless
chair pushed against the east wall of the smaller of the two pool
rooms, not even at a table. He's drinking beer, after beer, after beer,
slowly, with his ghost-like eyes continually circling the room and
settling on nothing.

All his belongings are in those two bags. Other things he once
owned have now disappeared. He can hardly remember them.
Should he collapse and be taken to the hospital or the drunk tank,
at least he'll have his bags all packed.

Despair is in the air.

When I came down first thing for my morning coffee, there he
was, slowly drinking a beer and paying no mind to the slot-machine
addicts. When I came down at lunchtime there he was again, in the
same chair, in a long row of identical vacant chairs, all against
the same wall on the other side of an empty pool table.

And now I've just come down again, it's 8:17 p.m., and he's
still drinking a beer, though he seems to have picked up speed. He
knew when to slow down and when to pick up the pace. If you just
looked at him for the first time, nothing would be amiss. But it's

strange to see him sitting there like an old grey lizard, scanning the room mindlessly.

If he senses that someone is looking at him, he lowers his eyes, and adopts a woebegone look on his face, but when he thinks no one is looking at him, the little ripples of angst subside, and he reverts to his rather relaxed and unworried manner.

He's had nothing to read all day long. He doesn't smoke, he doesn't eat. He just sits there, occasionally remembering something – but who knows what?

There's a sense of terrible waste in this man's face. Twenty years ago, he might have looked a bit like that old photo of Vernon Reed.

What's bothersome in Newfoundland, though somewhat less so in St. John's, is the scarcity of newspapers, magazines, bookstores. Even local news seems under-reported and unreliable. Of the two so-called national newspapers, the *Globe and Mail* shows up, but disappears fast. The somewhat over-ideological, neo-conservative *National Post*, meanwhile, is being dumped in St. John's, given away free – but its Yankee Doodle Dandy slant on just about every story imaginable fools nobody around here.

The first welfare woman sits in the pub drinking water and reading the *National Post* every morning, because it's free, even though she tends to distrust its ideology. She says, "Even the simplest news stories seem chosen to prove a point."

But she really likes one columnist. "She's the only warm body in that morgue of rightwingicity," she says. And in fact she e-mailed her to tell her that very thing, to compliment her on some story or other, or to correct some factual error about public welfare in Newfoundland. She added a postscript: how could a good writer like you want to write for such a lousy newspaper?

The columnist e-mailed back immediately and said she could never write politics for the *Post*, but she thought there were some good writers on the paper, and all in all it wasn't that bad as papers go.

On late-night cable TV, Ray Guy, Newfoundland's smarter, funnier, more serious Stephen Leacock, has just been given an honorary degree from Memorial University and is delivering a long speech, speckled with bon mots and witticisms.

When he first went to Toronto, his mother told him: "Always say please and thank you, always says yes sir or no sir, or yes ma'm or no ma'm – and always go to the bathroom when you can find one."

Maybe that's what the Newfoundlanders dislike about Toronto. In Newfoundland you can always find a bush to hide behind when your top teeth are floating. But nobody told you there'd be no public toilets in Toronto.

"I've got youngsters older than me," says the lady bartender at the Captain's Quarters, to anyone who cares to listen.

"How do you get along with them?"

"Aha! A man who understands!" Then she shrugs and says, "So-so."

The St. John's Cenotaph, erected in 1924 by a solemn Field Marshal Earl Haig, looms above the rather limp-wristed Bible passage from Isaiah, obviously chosen because of the word "islands": "Let them give glory unto the Lord, and declare his praise in the islands." The stonecutter lists 1,300 as the official number of First World War dead from the Royal Newfoundland Regiment, with another 192 from the Newfoundland and Royal Naval Reserve, and 117 from the Newfoundland Mercantile Marine. Newfoundland has suffered many great tragedies, but this slaughter has to be right up there with the worst of them.

I sobbed, sure I did, standing there, with hat in hand, in the fog and rain.

Who wouldn't?

This interesting little cenotaph in damp and leafy Harbourside Park has four figures representing the cream of Newfoundland manhood – a fisherman (in raincoat and hat), a logger (with an axe over his shoulder), a soldier (with helmet, rifle, and ammo), a sailor (with telescope in hand) – and is dominated by the huge figure of Liberty, with the sword of death to infidels in her right hand, and the flame of civilization in her left.

Imagination is a public thing, and we're free to imagine the world in any way we wish. The powerful interests behind the major wars of the past two or three millennia certainly felt free to do so.

But as for ordinary folk, we try to imagine things that wouldn't offend anyone. The world we imagine is pretty well always an optimistic world, one lying within the bounds of public decency, kindness, and morality.

In the immortal words of silly old Quince:

> *If we offend, it is with our good will.*
> *That you should think, we come not to offend,*
> *But with good will. To show our simple skill,*
> *That is the true beginning of our end.*

HEADING HOME

Newfoundland • North Sydney • Fredericton • Montreal • Toronto

Wednesday, June 20. The ferry rips through the oceanic night. I'm slouched in a chair watching a fly on the wall and wondering if it's from the Mainland or from Newfoundland.

Somebody is arguing with the captain about the no-smoking rules. You can hear him all over the boat. He demands to know immediately how much it is costing the federal government to make sure nobody on the ferry is smoking. He can't abide this no-smoking rule. He's just going nuts.

All yesterday I sat in a bus zooming all the way from St. John's back to Port aux Basques, with a little nod now and then to familiar spots along the Trans-Canada Highway, and certain memorable roads that lead off it into interesting areas where interesting people live and work. The Burnt Berry looked small and insignificant from the window of a bus steaming off to Toronto.

The Mainland brings a big change. Everything is different – blossoms and wildflowers everywhere, more lush greenery, less grey rock, an aura of respectable prosperity, comfortable conventionality.

Everybody seems to be eating a chocolate bar as they get off the ferry and board the bus. If anyone's excited about being on the Mainland (some maybe even for the first time) they're not showing it at all.

It was meanwhile my good luck to be sitting next to a thoughtful young married woman from Corner Brook. She was en route to Ottawa, to spend some time with her husband, who had recently joined the army. Today was his last day of basic training. He was thirty-five years old.

She said the army has had an "attitude shift": because of a series of recent military scandals, they are encouraging older, more mature, men to enlist. I told her it's never too late for basic training. Let's hope not, she said. Twenty years and out. Her husband will have a good pension by the time he's fifty-five.

At a stop in Moncton, she had overheard a heated little exchange I'd had with the driver. I thought he'd been very rude and condescending to some of his passengers from Newfoundland, and he didn't like it when I told him what I thought of that. So I told him off a bit more. Then he finally apologized.

When the bus got going again, I confessed to my seatmate that I hate myself for hours after I've given someone a piece of my mind. It's a terrible habit to get into. But she cheered me up considerably with some good old Newfoundland wisdom.

"What you're doing is attitude adjustment," she said. "Look at how the driver had a change of heart and apologized. He wouldn't have apologized if you hadn't adjusted his attitude by calling him that nasty name."

"I didn't mean him specifically; I meant all people who boss people around like little Mussolinis."

She laughed.

I said, "Does this mean you think it was a good thing what I did?"

She said, "Definitely."

"I don't like hurting people."

"Everybody needs a little wake-up now and then."

I felt as if she had touched me with a magic wand and given me carte blanche to go around adjusting people's attitudes whenever I want and without any pangs of guilt. But it's not my job to adjust anyone's attitude. Let them have their own attitude. I should worry about my own attitude.

There was a change of drivers at Fredericton. I kept trying to figure out where I'd seen the nice new driver before. Yes, it was a month ago, on the road to the Newfoundland ferry, in a little restaurant about twenty miles southeast of Fredericton. Same guy. He drives the bus and his wife takes care of the restaurant. My seatmate said I should go up and say hello to him. But I demurred, even when she threatened to go up and tell him.

Her Newfoundland sensibility thought I was crazy.

My Toronto sensibility cringed at the idea.

All through the night, when we stopped here and there for coffee or a sandwich, I'd chat with a young fellow who couldn't stop burping. He was from St. John's and was going all the way to Toronto, but he had no luggage, not even a plastic bag. My impression was that he had been given a one-way ticket to Toronto by the social-services people in St. John's. They thought he may have better luck in Toronto, and it was a way of getting him off their strained welfare budget. Friends in the know later told me this happens a lot.

He said he likes to travel light. As for the burping, which was very loud and very annoying to everyone on the bus, he thought it could have something to do with the contents of an entire bottle of Tylenol 3 he stupidly wolfed down before boarding the bus. He was expecting them to put him into a pleasantly comfortable sleep state for the entire long trip, but they caused his esophagus to go into convulsions. How could he sleep when he was burping constantly? I started worrying about the poor fellow. . . .

In the morning we pulled into the Montreal terminal. I spotted a likely person. "Excuse me, you're not a nurse by any chance?"

"I speak French," she said. "I speak French."

"Oh, I am sorry."

"But . . . yes, I'm a nurse."

This was Maryse Lamour, RN. When anyone went to speak to her, it was always in English, because she was black, and *les Québécois* tend to think all black people speak English only. And she would say, irritably, "I speak French. I speak French." However, she had been working hard on her English. It was slow, but it was much better than my French.

She said I was perfectly right to be worried about our friend the Burper. Tylenol 3 is codeine, an overdose can be a dangerous thing, and he had to be given plenty of fluids. He should have been drinking water all through the trip. That was the main thing, a lot of fluids. She said he had to "dilute it or he'll get poisoned."

So I got him a half litre of orange juice and a half litre of water. He seemed thankful, and I told him he had to drink it all to dilute the poison. The more he drank the less he'd burp.

For the last leg of the trip, the six hours from Montreal to Toronto, the Burper didn't burp once. All those fluids worked. Thanks, Maryse. You may have saved another life. You could be a Newfoundlander.

INDEX